McDougal Littell

WORLD HISTORY

PATTERNS OF INTERACTION

Chapters in Brief

McDougal Littell

A DIVISION OF HOUGHTON MIFFLIN COMPANY

ISBN - 13: 978-0-618-40935-8   ISBN - 10: 0-618-40935-1

Printed in the United States of America.

7 8 9 - DOM - 09 08 07

Answer Key at the end of each chapter

To the Teacher

Chapters in Brief consists of summaries of each chapter in *World History: Patterns of Interaction* to give you support and flexibility in teaching U.S. history to your students. Spanish translations of these summaries can be found in the booklet, **In-Depth Resources in Spanish** Also available are audio tapes of these chapter summaries in both English and Spanish.

ORGANIZATION

Each three-page chapter summary is organized in the same way: A brief overview, which states the central idea of the chapter, is followed by a summary of each section of the textbook. Each section summary, in turn, begins with a statement of a key idea to focus students' reading and to help them comprehend the large issues of the chapter. Review questions at the end reinforce key ideas in the chapter, and an Answer Key follows immediately.

USES

There are a variety of ways to use these summaries. Here are a few suggestions:

- **To preview a chapter.** Having students read the summary before they begin studying a chapter will give them a context for understanding the details provided in the chapter itself. Slow readers gain special help by such a previewing strategy.

- **To reinforce and summarize main ideas.** Because the chapter summaries distill information into large issues and major trends, they are a perfect medium for teaching students how to identify main ideas in their reading.

- **To accommodate time constraints.** If it is not possible to cover every chapter in detail in the course of a semester or a school year, these chapter summaries offer a way to highlight chapters that may otherwise get skipped. Teachers using block schedules are especially grateful for these time-saving measures.

- **To review a chapter.** After students have read a chapter, they can use the summary to review key ideas, events, and people before taking the chapter test.

CHAPTER 1

Summary

CHAPTERS IN BRIEF *The Peopling of the World, Prehistory–2500 B.C.*

CHAPTER OVERVIEW *Scientists study stones and bones to learn about the life of the earliest humans. Humans developed first in Africa and spread to other parts of the world. After hundreds of thousands of years of a wandering existence, people started settling in one place. They got food by farming and by raising animals. This success and their new technologies soon led to the first civilizations.*

❶ Human Origins in Africa

KEY IDEA *Fossil evidence shows that the earliest humans first appeared in Africa.*

People can learn about the past by using written records. However, these records cover only the last 5,000 years or so of human life on Earth. To learn about the more distant time before the first written records, scientists need to use special skills and tools. They are like detectives trying to solve a mystery. That mystery is the puzzle of the prehistoric human past—the story of humans before history.

The scientists concerned with this mystery are called archaeologists. They work at places called digs, pits dug into the ground to find objects buried for thousands of years. They uncover tools, jewelry, or other things made by people. Such objects are called artifacts. Archaeologists also dig up bones—the bones of ancient humans and of the animals that lived with them. Some of these bones have become fossils, meaning they have survived over time because they were preserved in stone. By studying bones and artifacts, they can find clues about how the earliest humans lived.

In the early 1970s, archaeologists made some important finds in Africa. In East Africa they found the footprints of humanlike beings, called humanoids, who had lived about 3.5 million years ago. In Ethiopia another team uncovered a rare, complete skeleton of one of these humanlike beings—a female that they nicknamed Lucy.

Because these early beings walked upright, they could travel long distances more easily than four-footed ones. They could also use their free arms to carry food, tools, and children. These creatures also developed one other major human trait. They could move their thumbs across the palms of their hands and touch their other fingers. Because of this opposable thumb, they could pick up and hold objects.

Humans made important advances during a period called the Stone Age, when people used tools made of stone. In this time, they also began to use fire and developed speech. Scientists divide the Stone Age into two parts. The Paleolithic Age, or Old Stone Age, began about 2.5 million years ago and lasted until about 8000 B.C. The Neolithic, or New Stone, Age went from about 8000 B.C. to around 3000 B.C.

Much of the Old Stone Age overlapped the Ice Age, when the earth was colder than it is now. Vast sheets of ice—glaciers—covered much of the land. About 10,000 years ago, the temperature warmed and the ice melted. The ice sheets grew smaller and people began to roam wider stretches of land.

In East Africa, archaeologists have found a humanoid fossil that they named *Homo habilis*. The name means "man of skill." It was given because the site also held tools made of lava rock by these humanoids. *Homo habilis* lived about 2.5 million years ago. About 1.6 million years ago, another kind of humanoid lived. This one, called *Homo erectus,* began to use tools for special purposes. They dug for food in the ground, cut meat from animal bones, and scraped animal skins. *Homo erectus* also began using fire and may have had the first spoken language. Many scientists believe that *Homo erectus* developed into humans or *Homo sapiens*.

Scientists once thought Neanderthals were ancestors of modern humans but no longer do. These hominids appeared 200,000 years ago. They lived in caves or built shelters of wood or animal skins. At one time, they were thought to be rough and wild people. Now scientists think that they may have held religious beliefs. These people found ways to survive the freezing cold of the Ice Age. About 30,000 years ago, though, the Neanderthals strangely disappeared.

About 10,000 years before these people vanished, a new group of prehistoric people appeared. They are called the Cro-Magnons. Their bodies were just like those of modern people. Scientists think that these people worked with one another in planning large-scale hunts of animals. They may have also had more skill at speaking than did the Neanderthals. Because they had these skills, the Cro-Magnons were better at finding food. That may explain why Cro-Magnons survived and Neanderthals did not.

Scientists have only a vague picture of the origin of humans. The fossil record is sketchy. However, more discoveries may lead to new ideas about early humans. What is clear now is that humans had skills that helped them adapt and survive in different lands and climates.

❷ Humans Try to Control Nature

KEY IDEA *Humans began to grow food and raise animals. Their population increased, and they began to live in settled communities.*

The first humans had faced a struggle for survival. For thousands and thousands of years, they were concerned first with finding food and protecting themselves from the dangers of life in the wild. They used fire, built shelters, made clothes, and developed spoken language. These areas of life are all part of culture, the special way of life followed by a group of people. Human culture changed over time as new tools replaced old and people tested new ideas. Later some modern humans increased the pace of change.

The people who had lived in the early part of the Old Stone Age were nomads. They moved from place to place, never staying in one spot for long. They were always looking for new sources of food. They found that food by hunting and gathering nuts, berries, leaves, and roots. The Cro-Magnon people, who came later, made tools to help them in their search. With spears, hunters could kill animals at greater distances. With sticks, those who gathered plant food could dig plants out of the earth.

These modern humans had a large kit of tools—more than 100 different ones. They used stone, bone, and wood. They made knives to cut meat, hooks to catch fish, and even a tool to make other tools. With bone needles, they sewed animal hides into clothes.

Cro-Magnon people also created works of art. This art gives us a fascinating glimpse into their world. These early humans made necklaces out of seashells, the teeth of lions, or the claws of bears.

They took the tusks of mammoths—hairy elephant-like animals—and ground them down to make beads. The most remarkable art from the Stone Age, though, is paintings. Thousands of years ago, artists mixed charcoal, mud, and animal blood to make paint. They used this paint to draw pictures of animals on the walls of caves or on rocks.

Humans lived by hunting animals and gathering plants for thousands of years. They lived in small groups of only 25 to 70 people. They often returned to a certain area in the same season each year because they knew it would be rich in food at that time. Over the years, some humans realized that they could leave plant seeds in an area one year and find plants growing there the next year. This was the beginning of a new part of human life: farming.

Scientists think the climate became warmer all around the world at about the same time. Humans' new knowledge about planting seeds combined with this warmer climate to create what is called the Neolithic Revolution. This was the agricultural revolution that took place during the Neolithic period.

Instead of relying on gathering food, people began to produce food. Along with growing food, they also began to raise animals. They raised horses, dogs, goats, and pigs. Archaeologists have studied a site in the northeastern part of the modern country of Iraq. It is called Jarmo. The people who lived in this region began farming and raising animals about 7000 B.C. People were entering a new age.

People began to farm in many spots all over the world. Each group developed farming on its own. Many of the places where farming worked best were in the valleys of major rivers. In Africa, people began growing wheat, barley, and other crops along the Nile River. In China, farmers began to grow rice and a grain called millet. In Mexico and Central America, people grew corn, beans, and squash. In the high Andes Mountains of South America, they grew tomatoes, sweet potatoes, and white potatoes.

The study of one village in what is now Turkey reveals what early farming communities were like. The village, called Catal Huyuk, grew on the good land near a river. Some workers grew wheat, barley, and peas. Others raised sheep and cattle. Because these workers produced enough food for all the people, others could begin developing other kinds of skills. Some made pots out of clay that they baked—the first pottery—while others worked as weavers.

Some artists decorated the village.

Archaeologists have found wall paintings that show animals and hunting scenes. They have found evidence that the people had a religion, too.

Some people in the village worked as traders. Near the village was a rich source of obsidian, a stone made from volcanic rock. Pieces of this rock could be made into a very sharp cutting tool or polished to be used as mirrors. People in the village traded the rock to those who lived far away.

Life in the early farming villages had problems, too. If the farm crop failed or the lack of rain caused a drought, people would starve. Floods and fires could damage the village and kill its people. With more people living near each other than before, diseases spread easily. Still, some of these early villages grew into great cities.

❸ Civilization
Case Study: Ur in Sumer

KEY IDEA *Farming villages produced extra food and developed new technologies. The result is the rise of civilizations.*

Over time, farmers developed new tools—hoes, sickles, and plow sticks—that helped them grow even more food. They decided to plant larger areas of land. The people in some villages began to irrigate the land, bringing water to new areas. People invented the wheel for carts and the sail for boats. These new inventions made it easier to travel between distant villages and to trade.

Life became more complex as the villages began to grow. People were divided into social classes, some with more wealth and power than others. People began to worship gods and goddesses that they felt would make their crops safe and their harvests large.

One of the first civilizations arose in Sumer. It was in a region of Southwest Asia known as Mesopotamia—between the Tigris and Euphrates rivers of modern Iraq. Historians consider a civilization to have these five features:

1. advanced cities, which can hold many people and served as centers of trade;
2. specialized workers, who can focus on different kinds of work;
3. complex institutions, which can give the people a government, an organized religion, and an economy;
4. record-keeping, which can lead to other purposes for writing; and
5. advanced technology, which can produce new tools and techniques for solving problems.

Sumer had all the features of a civilization. One of the new technologies that the people of Sumer created was the ability to make a metal called bronze. Workers used it to make points for spears.

One of the early cities of Sumer was named Ur. It was surrounded by walls built of mud dried into bricks. It held about 30,000 people, divided into such social classes as rulers and priests, traders, craft workers, and artists. They were all supported by the food raised by farmers outside the city walls, where they watched the animals and tended the fields. Some workers dug ditches to carry water to the fields. Officials of the city government planned all of this activity.

Inside the city, people hurried about their busy lives. Metal workers made bronze points for spears, while potters made clay pots. Traders met people from other areas. They traded the spear points and pots for goods that Ur could not produce. Sometimes their deals were written down by people called scribes. They were educated in the new form of writing that Sumer had developed. Ur's most important building was the temple. There the priests led the city's religious life. Temples also served as storage for grains, fabrics, and gems as offerings to the city's gods.

Review

1. **Determining Main Ideas** What evidence do scientists use to study the life of humans before written history?
2. **Comparing** How did the Cro-Magnon people differ from *Homo erectus*?
3. **Drawing Conclusions** What great change came in the Neolithic period? Explain why it was so important.

Summarizing
4. What are the five features of a civilization?
5. What different kinds of activity went on in Sumer?

Answer Key
Chapter 1
SUMMARY

The Peopling of the World, Prehistory–2500 B.C.

Responses will vary but should include points similar to the following:

1. Scientists study the life of ancient people by examining the evidence left behind—tools and other objects, artwork, and bones of humans and animals.

2. *Homo erectus* had tools, used fire, and may have developed the first language. The Cro-Magnon people were more advanced. They had large tool kits with items that could be used for many different purposes. They planned their hunting trips, which required advanced language skills and close cooperation.

3. The great change of the Neolithic Age was the adoption of farming by many people around the world. It led to rapid advances in human culture.

4. These are the five features of civilization: advanced cities, specialized workers, complex institutions, record-keeping, and advanced technology.

5. Sumer had farmers who raised food, craft workers who made goods, traders who traded those goods with other people, government officials who planned the trading and production in Sumer, scribes who made written records, and priests who led the city's religious life.

CHAPTER
2
Summary

CHAPTERS IN BRIEF *Early River Valley Civilizations,*
3500 B.C.–450 B.C.

CHAPTER OVERVIEW *The world's first civilizations developed along rivers in four different regions. Each culture met problems caused by the geography of its particular area. While the cultures shared many traits with each other, each had a special characteristic that made it unique.*

❶ City-States in Mesopotamia

KEY IDEA *The first civilization in the world arose in Mesopotamia. It took the form of city-states.*

There is an arc of rich land in Southwest Asia that is called the Fertile Crescent. Two of its rivers, the Tigris and the Euphrates, flow southeastward toward the Persian Gulf. Each spring the snow in nearby Turkish mountains melts, swelling the rivers. This flooding leaves rich mud in the plain between the rivers. Because of this, many thousands of years ago humans began to settle in that plain, known as Mesopotamia. They grew wheat and barley. It was here that the first civilization began.

About 3500 B.C., the Sumerians moved into this region and settled. They faced three problems. First, the floods were not regular. One year they would come in April, and the next year they might come in June. Once the flood passed, the hot sun quickly baked the land into clay. Second, the small farming villages had no protection against enemies. Third, the area lacked stone, wood, and metal to use for tools.

The Sumerians solved these problems. They dug ditches from the river to their fields so they could bring water to their crops. They built walls of baked mud around their villages for defense. Because they could grow more food than they needed, they traded the extra for stone, wood, and metal from other lands.

Several large city-states were at the center of the Sumerian world. These cities had control over a surrounding area and could act independently much like a country does today. Slowly some people rose to power in many of the city-states. They became rulers, as did their children after them. Rule of an area by the same family is called a dynasty.

The Sumerians believed in many gods, each of whom had power over different forces of nature or parts of their lives. People, they thought, were just the servants of the gods. They believed that the souls of the dead went to a joyless place under the earth's crust. These views spread to other areas and shaped the ideas of other peoples.

Society was divided into social classes. At the top were the priests and kings, after whom came wealthy merchants. Next were ordinary Sumerian workers in fields and workshops. Slaves made up the lowest level. Women could enter most careers and could own property, but there were some limits on them.

The people of Sumer invented the sail, the wheel, and the plow. They were the first to use bronze. They also developed the first writing system—on clay tablets. They invented arithmetic and geometry, which they used to help them build large structures.

Centuries of fighting between the city-states made the Sumerians weak. In 2350 B.C., the conqueror Sargon defeated Sumer and captured other cities to the north. By bringing together many different groups, he made the world's first empire. It spread the culture of Sumer to a wider area. A few hundred years later, a different group of people conquered the Sumerian region. These people were led by a king named Hammurabi, who is famous for his code of laws. It was a harsh code that punished people for wrongdoing. However, it also made it clear that the government had some responsibility for taking care of its people.

❷ Pyramids on the Nile

KEY IDEA *The earliest civilization in Africa arose along the Nile River. A ruler called the pharaoh brought people together in a united kingdom.*

Another civilization arose along the banks of the Nile River of East Africa. The Nile flows to the north, toward the Mediterranean Sea. It, too, floods each year, and the waters leave rich soil on the river banks. There the people of ancient Egypt grew food and began to build their own culture. They worshiped the Nile as a life-giving god.

For many centuries, the people of Egypt lived in two kingdoms, Lower Egypt and Upper Egypt.

The former extended from the Nile's marshy delta region north to the Mediterranean, just 100 miles away. Upper Egypt began at the Nile delta and extended south to the Nile's first area of churning rapids. About 3100 B.C., the king of Upper Egypt united the two kingdoms.

In the years between 2660 and 2180 B.C., the basic marks of the culture of Egypt arose. Ruling over the land was the pharaoh, who was not only a king but also seen as a god. Pharaohs believed that they had an eternal spirit that allowed them to rule the land after their death. So these kings built themselves magnificent tombs. The tombs were huge pyramids made out of massive limestone blocks.

Egyptians believed in many gods and in an afterlife. One god, they thought, weighed the hearts of each dead person. Hearts judged heavy with sin were eaten by a beast. Good people, with feather-weight hearts, would live forever in a beautiful Other World.

The pharaoh and his family were at the top of Egyptian society. Below them were people of wealth who owned large amounts of land, the priests, and members of the government and army. Then came the middle class—merchants and people who worked in crafts. At the base were the peasants. In later times, the Egyptians had slaves. People could move from one rank of society to another. Those who could read and write held important positions.

The Egyptians, like the Sumerians, developed a way of writing. They used pictures to stand for sounds. The pictures could be put together to make words and sentences. At first they wrote on stone, but later they began to make a kind of paper out of a water plant. The Egyptians invented many new things such as a system of written numbers and a calendar. Their calendar had 12 months, each of which had 30 days. They were famous in the ancient world for their ideas in medicine.

After 2180 B.C., the pharaohs lost power. Egypt went through a time of troubles until strong rulers once again took control. They ruled for four centuries until the land fell prey to invaders in 1640 B.C.

❸ Planned Cities on the Indus

KEY IDEA *People of the first civilization in India built cities on the banks of the Indus River.*

South Asia—modern India, Pakistan, and Bangladesh—lies separated from the rest of Asia by tall mountains. Just below the mountains are two large plains that hold the Ganges and Indus rivers. The high mountains gave the people safety from invaders. Because they lived close to the sea, the people could travel over the water to trade with other peoples.

The people along the Indus River had many of the same challenges that the people in Mesopotamia had. Their river flooded each year and left soil good for farming, but the floods did not occur at the same time each year. In addition, the river sometimes changed course. The region's weather caused problems also. Each winter, strong winds blew dry air across the area. Each spring, the winds brought heavy rains.

Historians have not learned much about the people who settled in the Indus Valley because they cannot understand their way of writing. They know that people were farming along the river by about 3200 B.C. They also know that the culture of these people covered an area larger than either Mesopotamia or Egypt.

About 2500 B.C., these people began building their first cities. The cities showed careful planning. In Mesopotamia, cities were a jumble of streets laid down without planning. In the Indus Valley, however, the builders of cities created a grid of streets. They built a strong area called a citadel that was easy to defend and held all the important buildings. They also had systems for carrying water and sewage. These features suggest people had developed a strong central government.

The civilization of the Indus was peaceful. Because the houses were mostly like one another, scholars think that the Indus culture did not have sharp differences between social classes.

These early people left an important mark on the region. Some religious objects include symbols that became part of the culture that developed later in India. Historians have discovered that the people of the area traded with the people of Mesopotamia.

Around 1750 B.C., though, the cities began to show signs of trouble. The Indus Valley civilization collapsed around 1500 B.C. No one knows the reason, but there are several possibilities. Satellite images show there were earthquakes in the region. Because of the quakes, the Indus River may have changed its course. This ended the good effects of the yearly floods. The people may have overworked the land and left the soil too poor to produce crops any longer.

❹ River Dynasties in China

KEY IDEA *The first rulers of China introduced ideas about government and society. These ideas had a lasting effect on Chinese civilization.*

The last of the great early civilizations arose in China—and continues to this day. China's geography insured that it would develop apart from other cultures. It was isolated from other areas. The land lies protected by a great ocean, huge deserts, and high mountains. Within China, though, are two rich rivers, the Huang He and the Chang Jiang. Almost all the good farmland in China lies between these two rivers. The Chinese people also made use of the flood waters of these rivers. They had to be careful, though, for the Huang He could cause terrible floods that could kill whole villages of people. The mountains did not protect China totally. Many times during Chinese history, people living to the north and west of China invaded the land.

Just a few thousand years ago, some people began to farm along the rivers. About 2000 B.C., the first dynasty of rulers brought government to China. A Chinese legend tells of a clever engineer who told the people how to build walls to control the flooding river and bring water to the farm fields. It is not certain that such a person lived, but it is known that about this time the Chinese began to build cities.

Around 1500 B.C., a new dynasty began to rule. They are called the Shang, and they began to leave the first written records in China. Objects found in their palaces and tombs also tell us much about their society. Chinese people built their buildings of wood, not mud-dried brick as the other early cultures did. Huge walls made of earth surrounded these buildings to protect them. The walls were needed because it was a time of constant war.

At the top of Shang society were the king and the nobles who helped him fight these wars. At the bottom was the mass of peasants who lived in huts outside the city walls. They worked hard on the farms, using wooden tools because the Shang believed that bronze was too good to be used for farming.

Shang society was held together by a strong belief in the importance of the group—all the people—and not any single person. The most important part of society was the family, and children grew up learning to respect their parents. The family played a central role in Chinese religion, too. The Chinese thought that family members who had died could still influence the lives of family members still alive. They gave respect to dead members of the family, hoping to keep them happy.

The Chinese system of writing differed from those of other groups. Symbols stood for ideas, not sounds. As a result, the many different groups in China, who all had a separate spoken language, could still understand the same writing. The written language had thousands of symbols, however, which made it very hard to learn. Only specially trained people learned to read and write.

About 1027 B.C., a new group, the Zhou, took control of China. They adopted Shang culture, but started an idea of royalty that was new to China. Good rulers, they said, got authority to rule from heaven. They claimed the Shang rulers were not just and had lost the favor of the gods. That is why they had to be replaced. From then on, the Chinese believed in divine rule. However, it also meant that disasters such as floods or war pointed to a ruler that had lost the support of the gods and needed to be replaced.

The Zhou gave the rights to large areas of land to members of the royal family and other nobles. The nobles promised to fight for the rulers and to protect the peasants who lived on the land. Later the power of these nobles grew great. Eventually the Zhou rulers lost all power. The nobles fought each other for control of China in a period called the "time of the warring states." It lasted many hundred years, and the Chinese people suffered during this time.

Review

1. *Determining Main Ideas* What challenges did the Sumerians face, and how did they solve them?
2. *Comparing and Contrasting* How was the religion of Egypt different from the religion of Mesopotamia?
3. *Analyzing Causes and Recognizing Effects* Why did the pharaohs of Egypt build large tombs?
4. *Clarifying* What was special about the cities built by the people of the Indus Valley?
5. *Determining Main Ideas* What new idea of kingship did the Zhou rulers bring to China?

Answer Key

Chapter 2

SUMMARY

Early River Valley Civilizations, 3500 B.C.–450 B.C.

Responses will vary but should include points similar to the following:

1. The floods were not regular, and, after the flood passed, the land was baked dry. The Sumerians built irrigation works to bring water year-round. Because the small farming villages had no protection against enemies, they built high walls. Since the area lacked stone, wood, and metal to use for tools, they traded extra food they grew to other peoples for these goods.

2. In Egypt, people believed in life after death and thought that the king, or pharaoh, was a god. In Mesopotamia, people believed the soul went to a joyless place after death, and the king was human.

3. The pharaohs built huge tombs because they believed that kings would help rule the kingdom even after death. Therefore, kings should have magnificent tombs.

4. The people of the Indus Valley planned their cities carefully, unlike the other ancient peoples.

5. The Zhou people brought to China the idea that a just ruler had the support of the gods. When disasters occurred, this was a sign that the ruler no longer had divine approval and should be replaced.

CHAPTER

3

Summary

CHAPTERS IN BRIEF *People and Ideas on the Move, 2000 B.C.–250 B.C.*

CHAPTER OVERVIEW *People of the plains of western Asia moved into the settled areas of early civilizations. Hittites created one empire. Aryans brought new ideas into India. Partly in response to Aryan rule, the Hindu and Buddhist religions took shape. Around the Mediterranean Sea, others spread their culture through trade. Hebrews struggled as they followed their religion based on belief in one god.*

❶ The Indo-Europeans

KEY IDEA *Indo-European peoples moved into areas new to them, including Europe, India, and Southwest Asia. They met people already living there.*

While some peoples built civilizations in the great river valleys, others lived on the huge plains of western Asia. They rode horses and tended cattle, sheep, and goats. They spoke many different languages, but all of them came from the same original language. These people are called the Indo-Europeans. Then, for some reason, starting about 1700 B.C., they began to leave their homes. They moved into some of the settled areas and began to conquer them.

One of these Indo-European peoples was the Hittites. They rode two-wheeled chariots and used iron weapons to conquer the area that is now Turkey. They moved farther and took the ancient lands of Mesopotamia. When they moved to the south, they ran into the Egyptians. Neither side was able to defeat the other, however, so they decided to make peace.

The Hittites adopted many features of the culture that had grown in Mesopotamia before they arrived. Some they used without making any changes, but others they adapted to suit their own ideas. The Hittites ruled their Southeast Asia empire from about 2000 to 1190 B.C. Then they fell to a new wave of invasions.

Another group of Indo-European people named the Aryans moved into modern India. They first captured the land of the people of the Indus Valley. They were divided into three classes of people: priests, warriors, and peasants or traders. They came to see the non-Aryans living in the area as a fourth class. Over time, they developed complex rules for how people in these classes, or castes, could interact with one another. People were born into their caste for life. Some "impure" people lived in a group outside this class system. They were

butchers, grave diggers, and trash collectors. Because they did work that was thought to be not clean, they were called "untouchables." They were kept away from contact with the members of other classes.

Over many centuries, the Aryans took more and more of what is now India. Eventually many powerful people tried to create their own kingdoms. They fought each other until one kingdom, Magadha, won control over almost all of India. Around this time, an epic poem *Mahabharata* was written. It tells the story of a war. The poem reveals the blending of cultures at the time and sets down ideals that were to become important in Hindu life.

❷ Hinduism and Buddhism Develop

KEY IDEA *Religious beliefs arose in India during the age of Aryan settlement. Later these ideas developed into the religions of Hinduism and Buddhism.*

Hinduism is a collection of religious beliefs that forms no one system. Unlike many religions, it was not founded by just a single person. It is a religion that allows great variety for its followers. Certain ideas became common to the beliefs of all Hindus.

Hindus believe that each person has a soul. However, there is also a larger soul, called Brahman, that brings together all the individual souls. A person's goal is to become free of desire and not bothered by suffering. When that takes place, the person's soul wins escape from life on Earth. It can take a long time to reach that understanding. Hindus believe that the soul is born again into another body after death. In the next life, the soul has another chance to learn its lessons. According to Hindus, how a person behaves in one life has an effect on the person's next life. Someone who was evil will be reborn into a poor position. Someone who did good deeds, however, will benefit in the next life.

Another religion that arose in India was Jainism. It was started by Mahavira, a man who lived from about 599 to 527 B.C. He believed that every creature in the world—even animals—has a soul. Because of that, people must be sure not to harm any creature. Today, Jains take jobs that are certain not to hurt living things.

Another new religion, Buddhism, arose about the same time as Hinduism and Jainism. Buddhism has millions and millions of followers all around the world. It was started around 528 B.C. by Siddhartha Gautama.

Siddhartha searched for a way that would allow him to escape the suffering of human life. He spent many years searching for this answer and tried learning from many different teachers. Finally, he sat down and meditated under a tree. After 49 days of this meditation, he had his answer. He was now called the Buddha, which means the "enlightened one," and he began to teach others.

The new teaching was based on the Four Noble Truths:

1. Life is filled with suffering and sorrow.
2. Suffering is caused by people pursuing the immediate pleasures of the world.
3. The way to end suffering is to end all desires.
4. The way to end all desires is to follow the Eightfold Path leading to nirvana—release from selfishness.

As with Hinduism, the Buddha taught that the soul would be reborn into a new life. This chain of new lives would continue until the soul, like the Buddha, reached understanding.

These ideas attracted many followers. Many people who lived in the lower classes of Indian society saw these ideas as a chance to escape from the limits placed on them. His teaching also spread in southern India, where the Aryans did not have much influence. Some followers took the ideas to other lands. In the centuries after Buddha's death in 483 B.C., Buddhism appeared in Southeast Asia. Later it was carried to China and then to Korea and Japan. Merchants and traders played an important role in spreading the religion. Strangely, in India where Buddhism was founded, the religion faded. It was possibly just absorbed into Hinduism. Many places that are important to Buddhism remain in India, however. Buddhists from around the world travel there to visit locations connected to the life of Buddha.

❸ Seafaring Traders

KEY IDEA *Trading societies developed civilizations beyond the Fertile Crescent region.*

In the Mediterranean area, a new culture arose on the island of Crete. It is called the Minoan culture after a legendary king. The Minoans were peaceful people who lived in rich cities that were safe from invaders. They controlled trade in their area and sent their fine pottery, swords, and metal drinking cups to other lands. They also sent other countries their style of art and architecture. This style later had influence on the art of Greece.

Archaeologists have explored the ruins of ancient cities of the Minoans. They have found beautiful wall paintings that offer looks into Minoan culture. One interesting feature of life on the island was the high position that women seem to have held. An earth goddess seems to have headed all the gods of Crete, and women ruled over some important religious places. Among other peoples who lived nearby, women did not play such important roles.

Minoan cities were damaged in 1470 B.C. by a series of disasters. First, a number of earthquakes rocked the island, destroying buildings. Then a volcano exploded on a nearby island. That was followed by huge waves and clouds of white ash from the volcano's fire. These shocks seem to have been too much for the Minoans. The Minoan civilization ended about 1200 B.C.

Another people arose on the eastern shore of the Mediterranean because of their role as traders. Living in several city-states in what is today Lebanon, they traded far and wide. Some may have even sailed as far as Britain—and perhaps around Africa. They were the Phoenicians.

The Phoenicians put colonies all along the coast of the Mediterranean Sea. Colonies were 30 miles apart because that was the distance that one of their ships could travel in a day. One of those colonies, Carthage, in North Africa, later became a major power in the Mediterranean world. Phoenicians traded such goods as wine, weapons, metals, ivory, slaves, and objects made of wood and glass. They also made a red-purple dye that was highly valued.

The important achievement of the Phoenicians was their alphabet. They used symbols to stand for the sounds of consonants. They wanted a way of writing so they could make records of their trade agreements. They brought their system of writing to other lands such as Greece, where Greeks changed the form of some letters. The alphabet that we use today, however, had its beginnings in Phoenician writing.

❹ The Origins of Judaism

KEY IDEA *The Hebrews became the only ancient people in their region to believe in one god.*

Another people entered the world scene. They made a claim to an important piece of land, the area now called Palestine. This region sat on the eastern edge of the Mediterranean Sea and on the Red Sea, which led to the Indian Ocean. As a result, it opened to the trade of many lands. The people who settled here were the Hebrews, and they believed that the land had been promised to them by God. Today the Jewish people are the descendants of the ancient Hebrews.

The Hebrews were among the world's earliest peoples to believe in one god. Their story began in Mesopotamia, where a man named Abraham lived. God told him to move his family to Canaan, where he would prosper. Abraham promised that he and his people would always obey God. God, in turn, promised to always protect them from their enemies.

Later the Hebrews suffered from the failure of their crops. They moved to Egypt, but over time they were made into slaves. After many years, they left in a mass departure that Jews called the Exodus. According to the sacred book of the Jews, a man named Moses led them out of Egypt. They wandered 40 years in a wilderness. During that time, the story says, Moses received from God the Ten Commandments. These were the laws that the Hebrews were to follow. For the second time, God promised to protect these people in return for their obedience to his laws.

After Moses died, the people finally reached Palestine and settled down. They began to adopt new ways of life. They often fought with other peoples living in the area, as each group tried to control the best land and other resources. The Hebrews were organized into twelve groups, called tribes. Each tribe was separate from the others, but in times of danger they would all get together under leaders called judges. One of those judges was a woman named Deborah. This was unusual for women in Hebrew society, who were expected to stay home and raise children.

The Hebrews had other leaders called prophets. They said that they were messengers sent by God to tell the people how he wanted them to act. These prophets told the people that they had two duties: to worship God and to deal in just and fair ways with each other. With this message, religion was changing. Instead of being a part of life run by priests who followed certain rituals, it was now a matter of each person living a moral life.

From about 1020 to 922 B.C., the Hebrews were united under three kings. The first, Saul, drove off enemy peoples; the second, David, made Jerusalem the capital; and the third, Solomon, built a magnificent temple to be used to worship God. After his death, though, the kingdom split into two parts. For the next two centuries, these kingdoms had their ups and downs. Finally, though, they were conquered by outside forces. The Chaldeans destroyed Solomon's great temple and forced the Hebrews to leave the land and settle in Babylon. They lived there for several decades, until the Chaldeans themselves were conquered. The new ruler allowed 40,000 of the Hebrews to return home. They rebuilt the temple and the walls of the city of Jerusalem.

Review

1. *Clarifying* What were the social groups of the Aryan people who entered India?
2. *Summarizing* Explain the beliefs of Hindus about life and death.
3. *Developing Historical Perspective* Where did the ideas of the Buddha have appeal?
4. *Drawing Conclusions* What kind of movement is represented by the Minoans and Phoenicians? Why was it important?
5. *Comparing and Contrasting* What was unusual about the religion of the Hebrews?

Answer Key
Chapter 3
SUMMARY

People and Ideas on the Move, 2000 B.C.–250 B.C.

Responses will vary but should include points similar to the following:

1. The three original groups were the priests, warriors, and peasants or traders. Later, the non-Aryan people became a fourth group, and still later a group called the "untouchables," who were thought to be impure, was added.

2. Hindus believe that the soul can be born into different bodies. The position in life depends on how a person behaved in the previous life. The goal is to reach the understanding that will allow escape from life on earth.

3. They appealed to the lower levels of Hindu society, who saw a way to escape from the limits placed on their lives. They also appealed to the people who lived in the south of India, who were not Aryans.

4. The Minoans and Phoenicians both engaged in trade, which moved goods and ideas from one place to another. As a result, new ideas came to be adopted, such as the alphabet.

5. They believed in only one god. Later they developed the idea that religion was a matter of living a moral life.

CHAPTER 4 Summary

CHAPTERS IN BRIEF *First Age of Empires, 1570 B.C.–200 B.C.*

CHAPTER OVERVIEW *Egypt becomes an empire by conquering other lands. It later falls to the Assyrians, who are highly skilled at war. When they fall, Persians become the power in Southwest Asia. Their empire treats conquered peoples less harshly. In China, thinkers develop different ideas to restore values after the warring Zhou Dynasty falls. However, the new Qin Dynasty is just as cruel.*

❶ The Egyptian and Nubian Empires

KEY IDEA *After Egypt conquered Nubia, these two empires along the Nile began trading and cultural ties.*

At the end of its second period of glory, Egypt was weakened by internal power struggles. New invaders, the Hyksos, soon swept into Egypt. They had the chariot, a new machine of war that the Egyptians had never seen before. The Hyksos ruled Egypt for many years until the pharaohs took back their land. Then they began some conquests of their own. The time from 1570 to 1075 B.C. is called the New Kingdom. In this third period, Egypt was richer, more powerful than ever.

The pharaohs of this New Kingdom brought Egyptian rule to Syria and Palestine in the east. They also moved south into Nubia, a part of Africa that lay near where the Nile began. Egypt had traded with and influenced Nubia for centuries. During the New Kingdom, the rulers of the Nubian kingdom of Kush accepted many traditions and ideas from Egypt. They began to build pyramids, to worship Egyptian gods, to wear Egyptian clothing, and to use a form of writing that was similar to the writing used in Egypt.

The pharaohs of the New Kingdom also wanted to create great tombs for themselves. They did not build pyramids, like those who had come before, however, because these tombs were often looted for their precious goods. Instead, they built their tombs in a secret place called the Valley of the Kings. Some pharaohs also built huge palaces for themselves or temples to the Egyptian gods.

Eventually, though, the pharaohs became weaker. Starting around 1200 B.C., a new group of people reached the eastern Mediterranean, and they brought trouble with them. As the power of Egypt fell, the land broke into many small kingdoms. Soon people from Libya took control of the land. The rulers in Kush felt that they were the pro-

tectors of Egyptian civilization. They moved into Egypt to force the Libyans out.

The Kushites ruled Egypt for a few decades until another people—the Assyrians—invaded and forced them back to their home. There the Kushite kings settled in the city of Meroë, south of Egypt. Their kingdom entered a golden age. The city was far enough from Egypt to protect it from attack. Yet, it was close enough to trade routes to play an important role in trade. Meroë also became an important center for making iron—and weapons of iron.

Traders in the city brought their iron to the ports of the Red Sea. They were taken on ships to Arabia and India. The traders from Meroë, in the meantime, brought back jewelry, cloth, silver lamps, and glass bottles. The city thrived from about 250 B.C. to about A.D. 150. By A.D. 350 Meroë had fallen to rival Aksum, a seaport farther south.

❷ The Assyrian Empire

KEY IDEA *Assyria created a powerful army and conquered its neighbors. Rulers built an empire and formed a government to run it.*

The Assyrians who took Egypt had started their career of conquest hundreds of years earlier and farther to the east. They came from the northern part of Mesopotamia. Their homes were open to attack, however. The Assyrians decided to form a strong fighting force to defend their homes. Soon, though, they turned to conquest.

The Assyrians used many different methods to win their battles. Their soldiers wore leather or metal armor and carried strong iron-tipped spears and iron swords. They used troops for rapid attacks and large numbers of men with bows to shower an enemy with arrows. Some opponents hoped city walls would stop the Assyrian army, but they could not. The Assyrians simply dug tunnels under the walls to weaken them. They used heavy battering rams to knock down the wooden gates of the city. The Assyrians conquered almost everything in their path. They usually killed or enslaved those they defeated.

Between 850 and 650 B.C., the Assyrians conquered all of Mesopotamia along with Syria and Palestine. Then they took modern Turkey and Egypt. They ruled by putting kings in power who would support them. They also collected taxes and tribute—yearly payments a people make to a stronger power. If a city did not hand over the year's tribute, the Assyrian army moved in and destroyed it.

The Assyrian kings were builders, too. One built the city of Nineveh on the north branch of the Tigris River. It was the largest city of its day. Another gathered thousands and thousands of writing tablets from the lands that had been taken. When these were found in modern times, they gave historians much information about the ancient world.

The Assyrians' cruelty had made many enemies over the years, however. Eventually those enemies banded together and struck back. In 612 B.C., an army captured Nineveh. To pay the Assyrians back for their past actions, it destroyed the city.

The Chaldeans, who had ruled the area earlier, took control of Mesopotamia again. They rebuilt the city of Babylon, and once more they made it one of the greatest cities of the world. The city included famous gardens that brought many different plants from the cool mountain regions to the dry desert where the city was. To keep the plants alive, slaves worked hidden pumps that brought water to the garden.

They also built a huge building called a ziggurat. This was a step-shaped pyramid that soared 300 feet into the air. At night, scientists would study the stars and the planets. What they saw and recorded became the beginnings of the science of astronomy.

❸ The Persian Empire

KEY IDEA *The Persian Empire accepted the differences of many different peoples as rulers tried to govern wisely.*

East of Mesopotamia, in modern Iran, arose a new power in the ancient world, Persia. The area had good farmland and was rich in such minerals as copper, lead, gold, and silver. About 550 B.C., the Persians began conquering neighboring kingdoms and founded a huge empire.

Their leader was King Cyrus, an excellent general. Cyrus led his army to conquer a huge empire that stretched from the Indus Valley in India all the way through Mesopotamia to Turkey. It covered about 2,000 miles, and he took all this land in just over 10 years.

Helping Cyrus win this vast land was the wise way he treated the people who lived in these lands. Unlike the Assyrians, who destroyed towns and cities, Cyrus made sure that his army did nothing to harm the people he conquered. He allowed the people to practice their old religions, too. It was Cyrus who let the Hebrews return to Jerusalem and rebuild their temple there.

Cyrus died in 530 B.C., and the kings who followed him had to decide how to run the vast new empire. His son was a failure, but the next king—Darius—proved as able as Cyrus had been. He put down several revolts, won more land for the empire, and created a government for the empire. Only Greece escaped Persian control.

Darius divided the land into 20 provinces, each holding a certain group of people. He allowed each group to practice its own religion, speak its own language, and obey many of its own laws. He also put royal governors in place to make sure that the people obeyed his laws. To bring his large empire together, Darius built a road that ran 1,677 miles and made it easy to move goods—and troops—from place to place. Also, Darius made metal coins that could be used for business anywhere in the empire. This was the first time that an empire so large shared a system of money.

During the Persian Empire, a new religion arose in Southwest Asia. A prophet named Zoroaster tried to explain why the world worked as it did. The earth is a battleground, he said, where the spirit of good and the spirit of evil fight. Each person is supposed to take part in the struggle. How a person would be judged depended on how well he or she fought for good. These ideas had influence on later religions.

❹ The Unification of China

KEY IDEA *War and turmoil in China helped produce new philosophies and a drive to bring together the Chinese people.*

In Chapter 2, you learned that China's Zhou Dynasty collapsed into the "warring states period." China became a land of troubles. Long-held Chinese values—social order, harmony among people, and respect for leaders—were forgotten.

Some thinkers, however, tried to find ways to restore these values.

One of the most important of these thinkers was Confucius. Born in 551 B.C., he became a well-educated man who thought deeply about the troubles of China. He believed that a time of peace could return if the people would work at five basic relationships: ruler and subject, father and son, husband and wife, older and younger brothers, and friend and friend. The family relationships, he thought, were the most important.

He also tried to change government for the better. Using his ideas, the Chinese built a system in which people could work in the government only if they had a good education. Over time, the ideas of Confucius spread to other countries of East Asia.

Another thinker of this period was Laozi, who was more interested in putting people in touch with the powerful forces of nature. Nature follows a universal force called the Dao, or "the Way," said Laozi. People do not follow this force, but they can learn to do so.

A third set of ideas came from a group of people called the Legalists. They said that the way to restore order in China was to have a strong government. A ruler should reward those who do what they are supposed to do, the Legalists said, and punish harshly those who do wrong.

These three ways to restore values were just philosophical debates. So, for practical advice in solving problems, people in China could consult a book called *I Ching*. Other people turned to the idea of Yin and Yang, two powers that balanced together to make harmony in the universe. Yang represented all that is warm, bright, hard, and clear. Yin stood for all that is cold, dark, soft, and mysterious. By having these two forces in balance, a person could reach harmony.

While these ideas moved through China, a new ruler arose to put an end to the troubles of the warring states period. At 13, he became king of a part of China called Qin (chihn), and he used the ideas of the Legalists to bring the different parts of China together. In 221 B.C., he took a new name—Shi Huangdi, which means "First Emperor."

Shi Huangdi defeated many leaders of different states and doubled the size of China. He also acted to extend his power within this land. He forced wealthy nobles to give up their land in the country and move to his capital city. There he kept a watchful eye on them, while he gave their land to members

of his government. The emperor wanted to control ideas, too. He ordered his government to burn many books—those that held ideas that he disagreed with.

Shi Huangdi also took steps to bring all parts of his empire together. He ordered the peasants to build a network of roads that linked one corner to another. The roads made trade grow, but the peasants hated the emperor for the forced work. He set standards for writing, law, money, and weights and measures that were to be followed throughout the empire.

Finally, he moved to protect his empire from foreign invaders. In the past, some Chinese rulers had built sections of wall to try to block attacks from northern nomads. Emperor Shi Huangdi had hundreds of thousands of poor people work to connect these sections of wall and make a huge barrier. When finished, the Great Wall of China stretched from the Yellow Sea to the Gobi Desert.

These steps won the emperor little support. When he died, his son took the throne. Just three years into his reign, peasants revolted and managed to overthrow the emperor. By 202 B.C., the Qin Dynasty had given way to the Han Dynasty.

Review

1. *Clarifying* Why did the Kushites move into Egypt, and where did they go after they were defeated?
2. *Drawing Conclusions* What made the Assyrians such a powerful army?
3. *Comparing and Contrasting* What was different about how Cyrus ruled his empire?
4. *Summarizing* Describe the three ways to restore values that were lost in China during the time of the warring states.
5. *Clarifying* What did Shi Huangdi do to unite his empire?

Answer Key

Chapter 4

SUMMARY

First Age of Empires, 1570 B.C.–200 B.C.

Responses will vary but should include points similar to the following:

1. The Kushites thought that they were the defenders of Egypt's heritage. After their defeat, they returned to their home in Nubia and enjoyed a golden age based in the city of Meroë.

2. Their soldiers wore leather or metal armor and carried iron weapons. They used troops for rapid attacks and men with bows and arrows. They used tunnels to weaken city walls and battering rams to knock down city gates.

3. Cyrus was less harsh than other rulers of other empires. He allowed the people he conquered to keep their own language, follow their own religion, and even keep their own laws.

4. The first way was that of Confucius, based on finding peace through building strong relationships. Second was that of Laozi, based on putting people in harmony with natural forces. Third was the Legalists, who wanted a strong government.

5. He defeated the rulers of other states and extended control over more land; he broke the power of nobles by taking their land; he burned books to control ideas; he forced the peasants to build roads and the Great Wall; and he created standards for writing, law, money, and weights and measures to be used throughout the empire.

CHAPTER 5

Summary

CHAPTERS IN BRIEF *Classical Greece, 2000 B.C.–300 B.C.*

CHAPTER OVERVIEW A rugged Greek landscape causes creation of independent city-states. They fight one another but unite to defeat invaders from Persia. Athens becomes the home of culture, but its empire collapses after years of war with Sparta. Alexander conquers Greece, the Persian Empire, and Egypt. After his death, a new culture blends influences from territory he conquered.

❶ Cultures of the Mountains and the Sea

KEY IDEA *The shape of the land caused separate groups of Greek-speaking peoples to develop societies in isolation from one another.*

The lives of the ancient Greeks were shaped by the geography of their land. Greece is a rocky land with high mountains and deep valleys. It was difficult to move over this land. So, Greeks living in different areas could not easily be united. Good farmland covered only a small part of Greece and could not support many people. The Greeks had easy access to the sea, however. They became excellent sailors, and trade became important. The climate is mild, which allowed Greek men to spend much time outdoors. They attended public events and were active in civic life.

The first culture to arise in Greece was that of the Mycenaeans. They were among the Indo-Europeans who invaded many areas around 2000 B.C. The Mycenaeans were ruled by powerful warrior-kings in their main city, Mycenae. Other rulers lived in palace-forts in other cities.

The Mycenaeans came in contact with the Minoan culture of Crete. They adopted many parts of this culture, including the form of writing and some religious beliefs. Because of this contact, the Mycenaeans also became interested in trade. According to ancient legend, Mycenaeans also had a long war with the people of Troy, a city in Anatolia. The famous Trojan Horse—a gigantic, hollow wooden horse hiding Greek soldiers—is part of that legend.

The culture of the Mycenaeans fell about 1200 B.C. Sea raiders destroyed their palaces. For the next 400 years, Greece went into decline—a decline so deep that no written records exist from this period. However, through spoken word, Greeks of this time continued to relate epic stories of the earlier age of heroes. One long poem, the *Iliad*, tells of the war with Troy. The Greeks also created a rich set of myths. Many of them tried to explain the world in terms of the actions of the Greek gods.

❷ Warring City-States

KEY IDEA *Greek culture produced many city-states. They had different forms of government, one of which is democracy.*

By 750 B.C., the center of Greek life was the polis, or city-state. This name was given to Greek cities and the countryside villages surrounding them. Each city-state was independent. The people who lived in them were fiercely proud of their homes. These city-states had different kinds of government. A monarch or king might rule some. A family of nobles might rule a few. A few wealthy merchants might rule others. Also, the idea of a government made of representatives chosen by the people took hold in some city-states. The most prominent of these city-states was Athens.

In Athens, as in other city-states, the wealthy and poor clashed in a contest for power. Athens, however, avoided major political upheaval by introducing reforms. Solon, an Athenian leader who came to power in 594 B.C., removed some of the laws that the poor did not like, such as debt slavery. He also opened the assembly, where laws were discussed and approved, to all Athenian citizens. Some 90 years later, the Athenian leader Cleisthenes introduced further reforms. The most important of these was the setting up of the Council of Five Hundred. This body proposed laws and advised the assembly. Council members were chosen by lot.

The reforms of Solon and Cleisthenes allowed Athenian citizens to take part in a limited democracy. But citizenship was limited to a small group of Athenians. Only free adult male property owners were considered citizens. Women, foreigners, and slaves were denied citizenship and played no role in Athenian political life.

Sparta, a very strong city-state in the south of Greece, developed in a very different way. The leaders of Sparta made their city a military state. Boys joined the army at age seven and went through a long period of training as soldiers. Spartan women ran the farms and other businesses, freeing their husbands to serve in the army. A small Council of Elders suggested laws that had to be approved by a vote of all Spartan citizens.

Over the years, the Greeks developed the ability to make iron weapons. Because these cost less than weapons made of bronze, more people could afford them. Soon each city-state had its own army. The soldiers were from all walks of life—armed with iron weapons and ready to defend their homes. This new citizen army proved itself in fending off an attack from the east. The powerful Persian Empire set its sights on conquering the Greeks. In 490 B.C., Persian ships landed 25,000 soldiers on the coast of Greece. At the Battle of Marathon, the Greeks won a tremendous victory that saved Athens.

The Persians returned ten years later. The Greeks lost a battle on land, despite the heroic efforts of a small band of Spartans. The Persians also burned Athens. However, the ships of Athens won a great sea battle. The Spartans followed it with another victory on land. The threat from Persia was over.

❸ Democracy and Greece's Golden Age

KEY IDEA During Greece's Golden Age, democratic ideas and Greek culture flourished.

Athens chose Pericles as its leader, and he served in that role for more than three decades. In that time, he took many steps to make Athens better. He had three main goals:

1. He wanted to make Athens more democratic. So he created more positions in government that paid a salary. Poor people could hold these jobs.
2. He wanted to make Athens stronger. The city was the head of a group of more than 200 Greek city-states called the Delian League. Pericles used the league's money to make sure that Athens had the strongest navy in the Mediterranean.
3. He wanted to make Athens beautiful. So he again used Delian League money to fund a great building program in his city.

Athens also became home to a group of very skilled playwrights. Some wrote tragedies, plays

about the pain and suffering of human life. Others wrote comedies, which often included important ideas. Some plays were critical of Athenians, proof that Athens was a free and open society.

After being rivals for many years, Sparta and Athens finally went to war beginning in 431 B.C. The conflict ended badly for Athens. In 430 B.C. a horrible plague killed a large portion of Athens' people. After several battles, the war dragged on until Athens finally gave up in 404 B.C. Athens had lost its empire.

In the time of uncertainty after Athens' defeat, several great philosophers appeared. They tried to understand human life. One, Socrates, believed deeply in truth and justice, but many people did not trust him. He was convicted of treason and forced to drink poison. His pupil, Plato, recorded many of his ideas and became an important thinker in his own right. A third was Aristotle. He wrote books that summarized all things known to the Greeks at the time. He also invented a way of thinking logically. His work was very influential for many centuries.

❹ Alexander's Empire

KEY IDEA Alexander the Great conquered Persia and Egypt. Then he moved as far east as the Indus River in northwest India.

North of Greece was the kingdom of Macedonia. The Greeks looked down on the people there because they lacked the great culture of Greece. The Macedonians were tough fighters, though, and had a strong leader in King Philip II. He decided to use his army to invade Greece. The Greek city-states united too late to save themselves. The Macedonians won, and Greek independence was now over. Philip did not enjoy his victory for long, though. He died just two years later, and his son Alexander became king at age 20.

Alexander was a brilliant general, just like his father. He had been taught well, and he prepared to carry out his father's dream of conquering the Persian Empire. In 334 B.C., Alexander invaded Persia. He won two stunning victories and then moved south to enter Egypt. He was crowned pharaoh and founded a city that he named for himself—Alexandria. He then turned back to Persia and won another great battle, which ended all Persian resistance. The empire was now his.

The young king pushed east, taking his army as far as India. He won another battle and moved deeper into India. However, after many years of marching and fighting, the soldiers wanted to return home. Alexander agreed, and turned back. On the way back, he began to make plans for how to govern his new empire. Then he suddenly fell ill and died. He was just 32 years old.

Three of Alexander's generals divided his empire. One ruled Macedonia and Greece. Another took control of Egypt. The third became ruler of the lands that used to be in the Persian Empire. Alexander's empire was not long-lasting, but it had important effects. After Alexander, the people of Greece and Persia and all the lands between mixed together and shared ideas and culture.

❺ The Spread of Hellenistic Culture

KEY IDEA *Hellenistic culture was formed of ideas from Greece and other lands. It flourished throughout Greece, Egypt, and Asia.*

A new culture arose—the Hellenistic culture. It blended Greek with Egyptian, Persian, and Indian influences. The center of this culture was Alexandria, Egypt. Located in the delta of the Nile River on the Mediterranean Sea, it had a ship harbor. Trade was lively and Alexandria had a large population from many different countries.

Alexandria was also a beautiful city. Its huge lighthouse towered over the harbor to show a light to incoming ships. Its famous museum had rooms with works of art, a zoo, and a garden. Its magnificent library held half a million scrolls of papyrus that contained everything known in the Hellenistic world. It was the first true research library, and scholars read through the scrolls.

These scholars kept alive what was known about science. Some used an observatory to look at the stars and the planets. One of these astronomers developed two important ideas. He argued that the sun was actually larger than the earth, which no one had thought to be the case before. He also suggested that the earth and other planets revolved around the sun. Other astronomers rejected these ideas, though, and their views remained common for many centuries. Another scientist tried to estimate the size of the earth. He came extremely close, figuring the earth to be about 16 percent larger than its actual size.

The thinkers in Alexandria also made advances in mathematics. Euclid wrote a book with the basic ideas of geometry; his approach is still used today. Archimedes was another important scientist and mathematician. He invented many clever machines, including the Archimedes screw, which could be used to bring water from a low level to a higher one. It was used to bring water to fields being farmed.

Two new schools of philosophy arose in these times. The Stoics argued that people should live a moral life to keep them in harmony with natural laws. Desire, power, and wealth, they thought, could hurt a person's moral well-being. The Epicureans said that people could rely only on what they learned from their five senses. They urged everyone to live moral lives. People should try to do things in moderate ways, rather than taking anything to an extreme.

The arts flourished in the Hellenistic age as well. Sculpture, in particular, had several notable achievements. The sculpture of this time differed from that of the earlier Greek style. In the past, figures had been idealized, as sculptors tried to show a perfect form. In the Hellenistic age, figures were more realistic and emotional.

Review

1. ***Recognizing Effects*** What effect did geography have on the way Greece developed?
2. ***Summarizing*** What were the different forms of government of the Greek city-states?
3. ***Comparing and Contrasting*** Compare and contrast Athens and Sparta.
4. ***Drawing Conclusions*** What happened to Alexander's empire, and why?
5. ***Synthesizing*** What was the long-lasting effect of Alexander's empire?

Answer Key
Chapter 5
SUMMARY

Classical Greece, 2000 B.C.–300 B.C.

Responses will vary but should include points similar to the following:

1. Because the land was rocky and mountainous, Greeks living in different areas could not easily be united. With poor soil and few resources, the land could not support many people. Because they had easy access to the sea, the Greeks became skilled sailors. The mild climate allowed them to spend a great amount of time outdoors. Much government business was handled outside.

2. Some city-states were ruled by kings, some by families of nobles, some by wealthy merchants, and some by representatives chosen by the people.

3. Sparta was a military society in which all men served as soldiers and women ran businesses. Athens was a limited democracy in which citizens had a say in the government. The Athenians were more interested in trade and art.

4. Alexander's empire split into three parts. He died so young that there was not enough time for him to organize a government for his empire.

5. Alexander's empire, although it ended quickly, was responsible for promoting a blending of the culture of the Greeks and the east.

CHAPTERS IN BRIEF *Ancient Rome and Early Christianity, 500 B.C.–A.D. 500*

CHAPTER OVERVIEW *The Romans make a republic in Italy and rise to power, but the internal struggle for control of their growing strength changes the government to an empire. The empire enjoys a long period of peace, during which a new religion, Christianity, arises. The empire finally collapses in the western part, but Rome leaves a legacy of many important ideas and achievements.*

❶ The Roman Republic

KEY IDEA *The early Romans made a republic. It grew in power and spread its influence.*

The city of Rome was founded by the Latin people on a river in the center of Italy. It was a good location, which gave them the chance to control all of Italy. It put them in the middle of the Mediterranean Sea. Two other groups lived in what is now Italy: the Greeks in the south, and the Etruscans in the north. The Romans borrowed some ideas from both peoples.

About 600 B.C., an Etruscan king ruled over his people and Rome. By this time, Rome had grown to be a wealthy and large city. The Romans resented the Etruscan rule. In 509 B.C., they finally overthrew the king. They declared that Rome would be a republic. The people would have the power to vote to choose the leaders of the government. They said that Rome would never again have a king.

Two groups struggled for power in the new republic—the nobles and the common people. At first, the nobles dominated the government. Over time, the common people won more rights. The basis for Roman law was a set of rules called the Twelve Tables. They said that all free citizens were protected by law. They were posted in a public place for all to see.

The government had three parts. Two consuls were elected each year to lead the government and the army. A person could not become consul a second time until after ten years had passed. In this way, the Romans hoped to prevent one person from having too much power. The second important part of the government was the Senate. It began by choosing 100 members from the upper classes. Later its size was expanded and some members were common people. The Senate passed laws. There were also assemblies that all people belonged to. They made laws that applied to all their members. All free-born males were citizens

and had the right to vote. Any citizen who owned property had to serve in the army.

In the fourth century B.C., Rome began to expand. Within 150 years, it had captured almost all of Italy. Rome allowed some of the conquered peoples to enjoy the benefits of citizenship. With its good location, Rome saw a growth in trade. This brought it into conflict with Carthage, a trading city in North Africa.

From 264 to 146 B.C., Rome and Carthage fought three bitter wars. In the first, Rome won control of the island of Sicily. In the second, an army from Carthage caused great destruction in Italy, although Rome itself was spared. In the third, Rome defeated Carthage once again and completely destroyed the city. In another few decades, Rome also conquered Greece, Macedonia, Spain, and parts of modern Turkey. It controlled the Mediterranean Sea.

❷ The Roman Empire

KEY IDEA *Rome became an empire. Its government, society, economy, and culture changed.*

Rome's victory brought conflict between rich and poor. When two brothers tried to pass laws that would help the poor, they were killed. Then Rome erupted in a civil war as leading generals fought for power.

Julius Caesar tried to take control. First he joined with two others—Crassius, a wealthy man, and Pompey, a successful general. For the next ten years, these three led Rome. Caesar gained fame with several victories in battle. Pompey now feared Caesar, and the two fought another civil war that lasted several years. After he won, Caesar took charge of the government. He made many changes that added to his popularity. However, he raised the mistrust of some members of the Senate who feared he wanted to become king. A group of them killed him.

Ancient Rome and Early Christianity 21

Once again Rome suffered civil war. The winner was the nephew of Caesar, who took over the government of Rome. He had the title Augustus, meaning "exalted one." The Roman Empire was now ruled by one man.

For about 200 years, through bad emperors and good, the Roman Empire was a great power. Its population of between 60 and 80 million enjoyed peace and prosperity. The empire stretched around the Mediterranean, from modern Syria and Turkey west and north to England and Germany. It depended on farming, which employed 90 percent of all workers. Trade was also important, bringing silk from China. Goods traveled by ship and along the Roman roads.

Defending all these people were the soldiers of the army. These included some troops recruited from the conquered peoples. Once they finished their time in the army, they became Roman citizens. This way, the empire extended its benefits to more and more people. Running the empire were government officials who reported to the emperor.

The quality of life in the empire depended on social position. The wealthy had rich lives full of luxury and huge meals. The poor—including many people in Rome itself—had no jobs and received handouts of food from the government. The government also entertained them, paying for spectacular—and bloody—shows of combat in public arenas.

About a third of the people in the empire were slaves. They were usually people from a land that had been conquered by the army. Many times slaves tried to organize a revolt to win their freedom, but they never could succeed.

❸ The Rise of Christianity

KEY IDEA *Christianity arose in the eastern part of the empire and spread throughout Roman lands.*

One of the groups whose land was taken into the empire was the Jews. Many Jews wanted to rid their land of the Romans. Others hoped for the coming of the Messiah—the savior. According to tradition, God promised that the Messiah would restore the kingdom of the Jews. In this time, Jesus was born.

At age 30, Jesus began to travel the countryside preaching his message of the love of God. According to close followers, he performed many miracles. He taught that those who regretted their sins would enter an eternal kingdom after death. His fame grew, and many people thought him the long-awaited Messiah.

Jewish church leaders did not believe that his teachings were those of God. Roman leaders feared his hold on the people. Jesus was arrested and sentenced to death. After his death, his followers said that he had appeared to them again and then gone to heaven. They said this proved he was the Messiah. They called him "Christ," which is Greek for "savior," and his followers came to be called Christians.

At first his followers were all Jewish. Later, under one follower, Paul, the Christians began to look to all people, even non-Jews, to join the church. The leaders of the early church traveled throughout the empire spreading the teachings of Jesus.

From time to time, Roman leaders tried to punish the Christians. They were angered when Christians refused to worship the Roman gods. Romans had them put to death or killed by wild animals in the arena. However, the religion spread until, after almost 200 years, millions of people across the empire believed. It spread because it accepted all believers, whether rich or poor, man or woman. It gave hope to those without power. It appealed to people who were bothered by the lack of morality in Roman life. It won followers because it offered a personal relationship with God and the promise of life after death.

As the early church grew, it developed an official structure. Priests led small groups of worshipers in individual churches. Bishops, based in most major cities, controlled all the churches in their area. The bishop of Rome headed the church.

In A.D. 313, Christianity entered a new era. The Roman emperor Constantine said that Christians would no longer be persecuted. He gave his official approval to Christianity. A few decades later, it became the empire's official religion. While Christianity grew in power, it also felt some growing pains. Church leaders sometimes disagreed over basic beliefs and argued about them. From time to time they met in councils to settle these matters.

❹ The Fall of the Roman Empire

KEY IDEA *The empire became weakened by internal problems and bothered by the arrival of warlike nomads. The empire was divided and later fell apart.*

Beginning about A.D. 180, Rome entered a period of decline. It suffered economic problems.

Trade slowed as raiders threatened the ships and caravans that carried goods over sea and land. The supply of gold and silver went down, and the price of goods increased. Food supplies dropped as tired soil, warfare, and high taxes cut the amount of grain and other foods produced on farms. On top of that, the empire had military problems. German tribes caused trouble on the frontiers while Roman generals fought one another for control of the empire.

After a century of these problems, a new emperor, Diocletian, took the throne. He passed many new laws trying to fix the economy. He tried to restore the status of the emperor by naming himself a son of the chief Roman god. He even divided the empire into eastern and western halves to make it easier to govern. Many of these changes were continued by Constantine, who in 324 became emperor of both halves of the empire. A few years later, Constantine moved the capital of the empire to Byzantium, a city in northwestern Turkey where Europe met Asia. The city was eventually renamed Constantinople after Constantine.

These reforms delayed the end of the Roman Empire but could not prevent its fall. The eastern part of the empire remained strong and unified, but in the west trouble continued. German tribes moved into the empire, all of them trying to escape fierce warriors—Mongol nomads from Central Asia—that were moving into their land. These were the Huns, and their arrival helped bring about the end of Rome. The Roman armies in the west collapsed, and German armies twice entered Rome itself, looting and burning the once-great city. After the death in 453 of their leader, Attila, the Huns went back to central Asia. However, the Germans had arrived for good. By 476 there were German people living in many areas of Europe. That year a German general removed the last western Roman emperor from the throne.

❺ Rome and the Roots of Western Civilization

KEY IDEA *The Romans developed many ideas and institutions that have become part of Western civilization.*

Rome took features of Greek culture and added ideas of its own. This combination of influences helped shape Europe and the Western world.

Roman sculpture, for instance, borrowed Greek practices but with a difference. Roman statues were more realistic. Romans perfected a kind of sculpture in which images stood out three-dimensionally from a flat background. Romans made pictures from tiny tiles, a process called mosaic, and enjoyed wall painting. Roman writing was based on Greek models, too.

Romans became famous for their skill at engineering. They used arches and domes to build large, impressive buildings. Many of these forms are still used today. They also built an excellent system of roads and built several aqueducts to carry water from distant lakes or rivers to large cities.

Rome left another mark on the world. Many languages, from Spanish to Romanian, are based on Latin. Even languages such as English have many words taken from Latin.

Rome's most lasting influence, though, was in setting certain standards of law that still influence people today. These include the ideas that

- all persons should be treated equally by the law;
- a person should be thought innocent of a crime until proven guilty;
- someone who accuses another person of a crime has to prove it; and
- a person should be punished only for actions, not for thoughts or opinions.

Review
Determining Main Ideas
1. Describe the government of the republic.
2. Describe the empire during the long time of peace.
3. *Analyzing Issues* What important change did Paul make to Christianity?
4. *Summarizing* How did Diocletian try to fix the empire?
5. *Clarifying* Give two examples of principles of Roman law that still influence people today.

Answer Key
Chapter 6
SUMMARY

Ancient Rome and Early Christianity,
500 B.C.–A.D. 500

Responses will vary but should include points similar to the following:

1. Two consuls were elected each year to lead the government and the army. The Senate passed laws. It had 100 members from the upper classes at first. Later its size was expanded and some members were common people. People belonged to assemblies, which made laws that applied to all their members.

2. The empire stretched around the Mediterranean Sea, from modern Syria and Turkey west and north to England and Germany. It depended on farming, which employed 90 percent of all workers. Trade was also important. Soldiers protected the empire, and officials who reported to the emperor governed it.

3. He looked to non-Jews to become new members of the church.

4. He passed laws trying to fix the economy. He tried to restore the status of the emperor. He even divided the empire into two parts.

5. Any two: all persons should be treated equally by the law; a person should be thought innocent of a crime until proven guilty; someone who accuses another person of a crime has to prove it; and a person should be punished only for actions, not for thoughts or opinions.

CHAPTER 7
Summary

CHAPTERS IN BRIEF *India and China Establish Empires, 300 B.C.–A.D. 550*

CHAPTER OVERVIEW *Skillful generals and rulers establish empires in northern India. They join together many different peoples and bring peace and prosperity to the land. During this time, the religions of India undergo changes in order to be more appealing to the common people. In China a great empire sets the patterns of Chinese government and culture that would be followed centuries later.*

❶ India's First Empires

KEY IDEA The Mauryas and the Guptas made empires in India. Neither family, though, united India for very long.

In 321 B.C., Chandragupta Maurya used his army to defeat the king of eastern India. He took the throne and started a dynasty named after him.

Chandragupta, not stopping with eastern India, moved west. In 305 B.C., he began to challenge Seleucus, one of Alexander the Great's generals. The two armies clashed for several years, and eventually Chandragupta won. For the first time, northern India, from west to east, was joined under the rule of one person.

Chandragupta was a harsh ruler. He charged a heavy tax on all the farmers who raised food—one-half of the crop they grew each year. He used the wealth he gained to build a huge army. He created a government that he controlled by carefully choosing officials and keeping a watchful eye on them. He split his empire into four provinces, each ruled by a prince. These areas, in turn, were divided into smaller pieces that were run by members of the government.

We know a great deal about life in Chandragupta's court because Seleucus sent a Greek there as an ambassador. He described the richness of the palace and the beauty of the capital city.

Chandragupta's grandson Asoka took the throne in 269 B.C. and brought the Mauryan Empire to its greatest height. At first he was a warlike king and fought many fierce battles with an enemy to the south. Then he decided to accept the teachings of the Buddha.

Asoka promised to rule in a fair and just way. He issued laws that urged his subjects to avoid violence. He made great roads so that people could travel easily—and then placed wells and rest stops all along these roads for travelers to refresh themselves. Soon after Asoka died, however, his empire collapsed.

For the next 500 years, India was a land of troubles. In the center of India, a new kingdom arose to dominate the scene. In the northwest, many Greeks, Persians, and Central Asians entered the land, fleeing the invasions of others. They added new ideas and languages to India's rich mix of culture. In the south, three different kingdoms fought each other off and on.

Around A.D. 320, a new power arose in the north. It was Chandra Gupta (not related to the first emperor), and he came to power by marrying the daughter of an important royal family. With this alliance, he took the title of king and began to conquer other areas.

His son, Samudra Gupta, followed the same policy and for 40 years fought to win new lands for the Gupta Empire. His son, Chandra Gupta II, brought the empire to its largest size. He managed to take parts of western India, including important ports on the Indian Ocean. With these, the Guptas were able to engage in the rich trade that connected India, Southwest Asia, and the world of the Mediterranean Sea. The Gupta Empire, like the Mauryan Empire before it, now stretched all across northern India.

Farmers worked their land, following the cycle of the seasons. Each family was led by the father, and all members of the family worked on the farm. Part of each crop had to be paid to the king each year. Farmers also had to set aside part of each month to work on community resources such as wells or dams. Craft workers and those who worked in trade lived in special sections of each village, town, or city.

The Gupta kings were patrons of the arts, and artists flourished during their rule. The people were happy, too, according to a Chinese traveler who spent many years in India. However, this period of calm ended soon after the death of Chandra Gupta II. Another wave of invaders, related to the Huns sacking Rome at this time, moved into India. Soon the great Gupta Empire had broken up into several smaller kingdoms.

❷ Trade Spreads Indian Religions and Culture

KEY IDEA *Indian religions, culture, and science developed and changed. Through trade, they reached other lands.*

Over time, the religions of Hinduism and Buddhism became more and more distant from the common people. The special class of priests controlled Hinduism. Followers of the Buddha found it difficult to find the promised goal of release from this world. As new peoples moved into India, they brought new ideas. These ideas had an impact on these religions.

The Buddha had taught that a tough course of spiritual life was the way to escape from the suffering of the world. Self-denial was difficult for many people to follow, however. Many people came to worship the Buddha himself as a god, even though he had forbidden it. Then they came to believe that other people could become Buddhas themselves through good works and sacrifice.

These ideas created a new kind of Buddhism, and the religion broke into two ways of belief. Some took the new doctrine, and others held on to the stricter beliefs. However, with this new approach, Buddhism became a popular religion. All believers had the chance to be saved. This change caused an increase in art. Buddhists with money built temples and shrines and then paid artists to decorate them with sculptures and paintings.

Hinduism changed too. By the time of the Mauryan Empire, only priests were involved in many rituals of the faith. For centuries, Hinduism had been a religion of many gods. Now other religions based on only one god were becoming more important. Many Hindus began to emphasize three gods in particular. By devoting themselves to these gods, people began to feel the religion more directly in their lives.

Indian art enjoyed a period of great vigor during these centuries. Poets and playwrights wrote beautiful works of literature, while other artists laid the foundations for the classical form of dance in India.

The scientists of India had many achievements. They proved that the earth was indeed round many hundred years before Europeans realized it. They made great advances in mathematics, too. They invented the idea of zero and of decimal numbers.

The doctors of India became highly skilled. They knew more than 1,000 diseases and used hundreds of medicines from plants to help their patients.

India was also a center of trade. It traded cotton cloth and animals to China for silk. Traders brought spices from Southeast Asia to India along caravan routes called the Silk Roads. Then they sold them to Rome and to other western peoples. This trade was so busy that large numbers of Roman coins have been found in India. The Indians also traded their own cotton cloth in Africa for ivory and gold. They sent rice and wheat to Arabia for dates and horses. They carried out this trade by land and sea.

Along with goods, Indians spread their culture. The art and architecture of many lands in Southeast Asia shows the influence of Indian art. Some adopted Hinduism, and many began to follow Buddhism.

❸ Han Emperors in China

KEY IDEA *The Han Dynasty made China larger. It also started a system of government that lasted for centuries.*

An empire also arose in China, one that would have long-lasting effects on Asia. The Chinese had been united briefly under the Qin Empire, but it fell apart in a period of civil war. Two leaders worked together to win control of China. Then one of them, Liu Bang, turned on the other and defeated him in battle. In 202 B.C., he named himself the first emperor of the Han Dynasty. The Han would rule parts of China for the next 400 years and set many patterns for Chinese culture for centuries to come.

Liu Bang made his government strong so that no one else could rival him for power. Local officials led the government throughout the land. They reported to the emperor in the capital. The rule of the previous emperor had been very harsh. Liu Bang took a different approach. He lowered taxes and had lighter penalties for crimes. Life became easier for the Chinese people.

After the death of Liu Bang, one of his wives, the Empress Lü took over. In this time, as in other parts of Han rule, court politics was a major part of life around the ruler. Each group tried to find a way of making sure that it could get and hold power. This game of political chess would take the ruler's attention from the people he was supposed to rule.

From 141 to 87 B.C., the emperor Wudi ruled Han China. He made the area of his empire much larger, pushing it almost to the size of modern

China. He began by defeating some nomads who lived in the north and bothered the people with constant attacks. He moved troops and settlers to the west. He sent soldiers to the north into modern Korea and to the south to modern Vietnam.

Wudi also changed the government in important ways. To run his government, he had a large number of officials who reached down to the smallest village. To find people to fill these posts, he introduced a new system. Those who wanted to work for the government had to earn the right by passing an exam. The exam tested them on their knowledge of the writings of Confucius, the Chinese philosopher who had lived 400 years earlier. He also built schools around the country that taught this knowledge. This system continued to work into the 20th century.

To support this large government, Wudi collected taxes. Farmers paid part of the crops they gathered each year. Merchants paid taxes on the goods they traded. Peasants also gave one month's worth of labor each year to the government to work on large public building projects such as dams and roads.

Under Han rule, the Chinese had many new inventions. One of the most important was paper. Before that invention, books were printed on silk. Because paper was much cheaper, using it meant that there were more books—and more learning in the country. The Chinese also improved farming by inventing a new two-bladed plow.

This change was important because the number of Chinese people had grown greatly. The Han emperors told their people that farming was the most important work to do—because they needed to grow much more food to feed so many people.

At the same time, several industries became important. The government took control of mining salt and making iron, coins, and alcohol. For a while the government went to work making silk. This expensive cloth was in great demand in India, Rome, and other lands. Only the Chinese knew how to make silk from the cocoons of the silkworm, and they kept their secret closely guarded. They wanted to be sure to control the trade.

China now included many different peoples, and the Han rulers tried to make sure that they learned Chinese ways. They urged their people to marry with people from these other groups. New books told the story of the history of China.

One group that did not do well in Han China was women. According to the teachings of Confucius, women were supposed to meet the needs of their husband and children and not become involved in other areas of life. Although some women in the emperor's family might wield power, this was rare.

The empire began to have problems as the rich people who owned large amounts of land grew more and more rich. The poor, at the same time, were being forced to pay heavy taxes. For about 40 years, China suffered in two ways. The members of the court were caught up in plots to try to gain power. Meanwhile, the peasants rebelled against their high taxes and poor lives. A government official named Wang Mang took the throne and tried to help the poor by taking land from the large landholders. In the middle of these changes, though, a terrible flood struck China and destroyed millions of homes. The peasants rebelled again, and Wang Mang was killed. At that time, a member of the old imperial Han family was put back on the throne. A new Han rule—called the Later Han Dynasty—was created.

For the next few decades, China enjoyed peace and wealth. Later, though, the same problems arose again—the gap between rich and poor was too great. By A.D. 220, the Han Dynasty had fallen for good.

Review

1. *Comparing and Contrasting* Compare and contrast the rule of Chandragupta Maurya and Asoka.
2. *Drawing Conclusions* How did Buddhism and Hinduism become more popular religions in this period?
3. *Summarizing* Describe two advances in the sciences in India of the Guptas.
4. *Forming and Supporting Opinions* Which Han emperor do you think was most important? Why?
5. *Analyzing Causes and Recognizing Effects* What basic problem was there in Han China, which led to its fall?

Answer Key
Chapter 7
SUMMARY

India and China Establish Empires,
300 B.C.–A.D. 550

Responses will vary but should include points similar to the following:

1. Chandragupta Maurya was a harsh ruler who put a heavy tax on farmers and kept tight control on his government. Asoka changed his own ways in an effort to be more fair and just. He built great roads and made them comfortable for travelers.

2. Buddhists came to believe that others could become Buddhas through good works and sacrifice. Hindus began to emphasize three gods, reducing the importance of so many gods. These changes gave the religion more impact on the lives of common people.

3. Any two: The scientists of India proved that the earth was round, invented the idea of zero, invented decimal numbers, and became skilled doctors.

4. Many students will choose Wudi, who made the empire larger and established the system of using tests to find people to work in the government.

5. The gap between rich and poor was too great.

CHAPTER

8

Summary

CHAPTERS IN BRIEF *African Civilizations, 1500 B.C.–A.D. 700*

CHAPTER OVERVIEW *African peoples develop different ways of adapting to the continent's many environments. Yet, African cultures share many characteristics. Africa's earliest known culture develops in West Africa. Bantu-speaking people begin south of the Sahara Desert. Over the centuries they move until they fill the southern half of Africa. In East Africa, the kingdom of Aksum rises and flourishes.*

❶ Diverse Societies in Africa

KEY IDEA *African peoples developed many different ways of life as they adapted to many different environments.*

Africa is the second largest continent in the world. It reaches 4,600 miles from east to west and 5,000 miles from north to south. It has about one-fifth of the earth's land. Much of the land is a high plateau, with lower land near the coasts. The rivers that flow along this high land often form waterfalls or rapids. As a result, boats cannot use these rivers to travel either to or from the coast. Also, the coast is not good for boats. It has relatively few harbors for so large a landmass.

Africa has many different environments. The Equator crosses Africa and much of the continent lies in the tropics, where the weather is hot all year round. Even in this area, though, the environments are widely different. There are hot, dry deserts; steamy, wet rain forests; and high, cool mountains.

About a third of Africa's land is desert. This harsh land holds few people. It also forms a barrier to people who want to move from one area to another. The Sahara Desert in the north of Africa is about one-third the size of the United States. Dense rainforests cover much of the central part of Africa. This area receives heavy rainfall. Trees grow to towering heights and block sunlight from the forest floor. As a result, few small plants grow underneath the tall trees.

The northern and southern regions of Africa have large numbers of people. They have good soil for farming and plenty of grass for animals to eat. They have pleasant climates. Most Africans live on the grasslands that cover almost half of the continent. They grow grains, including rice and wheat, and tend to cattle. Each year, though, the Sahara Desert expands and takes away a bit more of this grassland.

The first humans in Africa got food by hunting animals and gathering plants. Even today, some

African peoples still use this method for obtaining food. Men hunt animals with spears or bows and arrows. Women and children gather roots and berries.

Over time, these people learned to tame animals and raise them for food. These ancient herders kept cattle, goats, or sheep. Like the hunters and gatherers, these herders were nomadic people. As they moved, they looked for plentiful grass and for water for their animals. When food or water was used up in one area, they moved to another.

About 10,000 B.C., some people in Africa began to farm—growing their own food instead of gathering wild food. Later the climate changed, bringing more rainfall to the Sahara. People farmed there until the climate changed once again around 4000 B.C. and the desert returned. The people then left the desert and headed for many different areas. They went to farm in the Nile Valley and West Africa or on the grasslands. Some moved to the rain forest.

The grasslands had good soil, and the people could grow extra food. As in other areas, farming led to changes in African society. With more food, people lived longer and the population grew. Some people were able to specialize in tasks beyond raising food, such as making jewelry or pottery. Others became leaders. They organized the group's efforts to grow food, defend against invaders, or plan for the future.

African peoples had many differences because of the different environments in which they lived. The people who lived south of the Sahara, though, had these features in common:

- The family was the most important unit of society. In some groups, family was considered all people who come from common ancestors. This is called a clan.
- They believed that one god created the world. Also, they felt that plants, animals, and other

natural forces all have spirits that play an important role in life.

- They relied on oral storytelling, rather than writing, to pass on the traditions of their people.

The Nok culture, of West Africa, existed from about 500 B.C. to A.D. 200. The Nok people are known for their interesting pottery figures and for being the first people in Africa who knew how to make iron. Some styles of Nok pottery are still found in Africa today.

By looking for signs of the past, archaeologists found an ancient city in West Africa. Djenné-Djeno is the oldest known African city south of the Sahara. The city rested on the banks of the Niger River. Researchers have found thousands of objects such as pottery, toys, jewelry, and knives. The oldest pieces are from 250 B.C.

The city held about 50,000 people at its largest. At first, they lived in round huts made of reeds and covered with mud. Later they lived in houses of mud bricks. They grew rice, raised cattle, and made iron. They traded these goods for gold and copper.

❷ Migration Case Study: Bantu-Speaking Peoples

KEY IDEA *Throughout history, various peoples have desired to leave their homes and move to a new land.*

Throughout human history, many peoples have felt the urge to move from their homes to a new land. While there are many reasons that people make such a move, they can be grouped into three main causes:

1. *Environmental.* The climate of an area may change or its soil may become too poor for farming or all the water may be used up. Then, people move to a new area.
2. *Economic.* There are too many people in an area or too little food or too few jobs. Then, some people will move to another place to find the land, food, or jobs they need.
3. *Political.* Sometimes one group of people treats a different group harshly. They may capture their land and turn them into slaves. The people made to suffer in this way may end up moving to a new land. They may go by force—as when they are made slaves—or by choice—as they hope to escape their suffering.

Any of these factors can push people out of an area. Or they may pull people into an area. These are called push-pull factors. For example, available jobs will pull people into an area. But too few jobs willl push them out.

These reasons have pushed or pulled people to move from the beginning of human life on Earth, and they continue to do so today. The large-scale movement of people in modern times can be traced in written records. In studying times before written history, though, researchers need to look for other clues to these migrations. One clue they use is language.

People bring their language with them when they move to a new place. Languages do change over time. Suppose that historians find two languages from two distant areas that have words that are somewhat similar. They can conclude that those two languages may have both come from the same original language. They say that the original speakers of the language simply moved to the two different areas long before. Then, the two languages changed independently of one another. This kind of clue has given historians a way of understanding the early history of Africa. Many languages spoken in Africa today developed from the same parent language called Proto-Bantu. The people who spoke Bantu first lived in a part of modern Nigeria. In the first few centuries A.D., they began to move south and east. Over time, they spread throughout Africa south of the Sahara Desert, reaching the southern tip around 500 years ago. They brought their language and their culture with them.

One reason that these people moved had to do with how they farmed. Their method was to clear forest land by burning down trees. This left a plot of rich soil that was suitable for growing food—for a few years. After that, however, the soil no longer could produce good crops. The people then needed to move to a new area to clear a new patch of ground.

Another reason they moved was that their farming was so successful. Farming helped them produce more food than they could by hunting and gathering. With more to eat, groups became larger—and the land more crowded. They could not move north, where the Sahara Desert made a barrier. So they had to move farther and farther south.

As they reached new areas, the Bantu peoples met other peoples. Sometimes these meetings were violent. The Bantus, who knew how to make iron, had better weapons than those they met, who only had stone tools. Some of the peoples that they met are still found in Africa, but they live in small areas with very harsh environments. The Bantus took the better land.

❸ The Kingdom of Aksum

KEY IDEA *The kingdom of Aksum in East Africa became an important part of trade between different nations. It also adopted Christianity as its religion.*

The peoples in East Africa had far more contact with people from other areas. The Kushite kingdom of Nubia had close relations with Egypt, and its kings even ruled Egypt for a while. That kingdom continued for many centuries as a trading power. It was then replaced by the kingdom of Aksum in modern Ethiopia.

Aksum may have begun when Arabian traders mixed with the people of Kush about 1000 B.C. Its first mention in written records is in a Greek book from A.D. 100 that talks about the king of Aksum. About that time, the kingdom of Aksum began to grow, taking other lands. Some were in Africa, and some were on the Arabian peninsula.

With this growth, Aksum became an important part of world trade. Salt, emeralds, brass, copper, gold, cloth, olive oil, and wine all moved through Aksum. Its trade routes helped link Rome to India. In the early 300s, Aksum had a strong new king named Ezana. He captured more land on the Arabian peninsula. Then he conquered Kush and destroyed the ancient city of Meroë in 350. The action removed an old rival in trade.

Because it was a trading center, Aksum was home to peoples from many different cultures. At the time of King Ezana, these different peoples all spoke to one another in Greek in order to be understood. The mixing of these different peoples did more than bring a new language to Aksum. It also brought a new religion. During his rule, King Ezana decided to become a Christian. Slowly, the religion spread throughout the land. Even today, about 22 million people in modern Ethiopia are Christian.

The people of Aksum developed a special way of building. They made structures out of stone, not mud baked into bricks by the hot sun. Their kings built tall pillars of stone that reached as high as 60 feet. They were among the tallest structures in the ancient world.

Aksum had other advances as well. Outside of Egypt and Meroë, it was the only culture of ancient Africa to have a written language. The language of

Aksum had been brought to the land by Arab traders many hundreds of years before.

The people of Aksum also developed a new way of farming. They cut wide steps called terraces into the steep mountainsides in their country. The terraces helped the land hold water instead of letting it run down the mountain in a heavy rain. They also used dams and stone tanks to store water and used ditches to channel it to their fields.

Aksum remained an important power in East Africa for 800 years. It was first challenged in the 600s, though, after the new religion of Islam came to Arabia. The followers of Islam captured the lands that Aksum held in the Arabian peninsula. Within a few decades, they had taken much of North Africa, and Aksum remained an island of Christianity in a sea of Islam.

At first, these conquerors left Aksum alone. By 710, however, they had destroyed its chief port on the Red Sea. The Aksum kings moved their capital over the mountains to a hard-to-reach area. Cut off from other Christian lands and from the sea trade, though, Aksum went into decline.

Review

1. ***Analyzing Causes and Recognizing Effects*** What impact did geography have on the way human societies developed in Africa?
2. ***Determining Main Ideas*** What features of culture are common to people south of the Sahara?
3. ***Clarifying*** Give an example of one of the three reasons that people move from their home to a new land.
4. ***Analyzing Causes and Recognizing Effects*** Why did the Bantu peoples move their homes?
5. ***Drawing Conclusions*** Why was Aksum important?

Answer Key

Chapter 8

SUMMARY

African Civilizations, 1500 B.C.–A.D. 500

Responses will vary but should include points similar to the following:

1. Because of rivers that could not be taken by boats, people in the interior of Africa probably had little contact with those on the coast. The large deserts blocked the movement of people. Deserts and the rain forests were not good places to live. Most people live on the northern and southern coasts, which have good land and good climates, or on the grasslands.

2. The family is the most important unit of society. The people believed that one god created the world but that plants, animals, and other natural forces all have spirits that play an important role in life. They relied on people relating stories orally, rather than in writing, to pass on their traditions.

3. People move from their home to a new land when there are not enough jobs or when food runs out.

4. The Bantu peoples moved because their farming methods used up the soil and they needed to find new land to plant. Also, their farming produced more food, which led to more people, which in turn led to crowding.

5. It was a trading power. It changed to Christianity and was one of only three ancient African lands to have a written language.

CHAPTER
9
Summary

CHAPTERS IN BRIEF *The Americas: A Separate World, 40,000 B.C.–A.D. 700*

CHAPTER OVERVIEW *Long ago, huge ice sheets cover the land. The level of the oceans goes down, and a once-underwater bridge of land connects Asia and the Americas. Asian hunters cross this bridge and become the first Americans. They spread down the two continents. They develop more complex societies and new civilizations. The earliest of these new cultures are found in central Mexico and in the high Andes Mountains.*

❶ The Earliest Americans

KEY IDEA *The first Americans were separated from other parts of the world. Nevertheless, they developed in similar ways.*

North and South America form a single stretch of land that reaches from the freezing cold of the Arctic Circle in the north to the icy waters around Antarctica in the south. Two oceans on either side of these land masses separate them from Africa, Asia, and Europe.

That was not always the case, though. From around 1.6 million to about 10,000 years ago, the earth went through an Ice Age. During this time of severe cold, much water froze into huge sheets of ice called glaciers. With water trapped in ice, the level of the world's oceans went down. The lowered oceans exposed land that is today again covered by water.

One strip of this land, called Beringa, connected Asia and North America. Wild animals crossed this rocky land bridge and entered North America for the first time. Some of the Asians who hunted these animals followed them. Without knowing it, they became the first Americans.

No one knows for sure when these first people reached the Americas. Some historians say it took place as long ago as 40,000 B.C. Others say it happened as late as 10,000 B.C. A recent discovery in Chile suggests that people were well settled in that part of the Americas by 10,500 B.C. Since Chile lies far south of the land bridge, some experts say that people needed many thousands of years to travel that far. For this reason, they think that the first people over the land bridge must have arrived about 20,000 years ago.

Whenever it was that they arrived, these first Americans clearly lived as hunters. One of their favorite targets for the hunt was the huge mammoth. This creature was like an elephant covered

with thick, long hair to protect it from the bitter cold of the Ice Age. It was so large that one animal alone gave enough meat, hide, and bones to feed, clothe, and house many people.

Over time, all the mammoths died, and the people were forced to look for other food. They began to hunt smaller animals such as rabbits and deer and to fish. They also began to gather plants and fruits to eat. Because they no longer had to roam over large areas to search for the mastodon, they settled for part of the year in one spot.

Between 12,000 and 10,000 B.C., the climate changed. The Ice Age ended, and the world warmed up again. The huge sheets of ice melted, and the oceans rose again to cover the land bridge that connected Asia to the Americas. By this time, though, people lived from north to south in the Americas. They lived in many different environments and found special ways of life suited to the place where they lived.

About 7000 B.C., the people living in central Mexico started a quiet revolution—farming. It was the same kind of radical change that had happened in several spots in Asia and Africa. By 3400 B.C., they had several foods that they grew, including squashes, beans, chilies, and the most important one—corn. Corn grew so well that a family of three could, in four months, grow enough corn to feed it for two years.

Over many centuries, the practice of farming spread throughout the Americas. In what is now the eastern United States and in the region of the Andes Mountains, early Americans may have discovered the idea of farming on their own. In central Mexico, farmers became so skilled at growing corn that they could enjoy three harvests each year.

Farming had the same results in the Americas that it did in Asia and Africa. Growing food gave people a more reliable food supply—and more food, too. As a result, more people could be fed, they were healthier, and they lived longer. The population grew. Because farmers produced so much food, some people could concentrate on other ways of making a living. They began to work in different arts and crafts or to learn how to build buildings. Some people grew to be rich—to own more than others and to enjoy a higher position in society. Some people became rulers, and others became their subjects.

❷ Early Mesoamerican Civilizations

KEY IDEA *The Olmecs created the first civilization in the Americas. It influenced later civilizations in the area.*

These changes marked the beginnings of more complex societies. The first of the early American civilizations arose in southern Mexico, an area of hot rain forests. These people are called the Olmecs, and they flourished from about 1200 to 400 B.C. They were an important culture because they had influence on their neighbors and on peoples who lived long after them.

The Olmecs lived along the Gulf Coast of Mexico in a land of dense forests and heavy rains. The land gave them many benefits, though. It had good clay that could be used for pottery, wood and rubber that could be taken from the forest, and stone for building in the mountains to the north. The rivers could be used to move people and goods, and the soil was excellent for growing food.

Archaeologists have found earthen mounds, courtyards, and pyramids built of stones. Standing on top of the mounds were many monuments made of stone. Some are columns, others seem to be altars used in religious ceremonies, and still others are heads. Some of these stone structures are very large and weigh as much as 44 tons.

Researchers are not sure whether the Olmec sites were monuments to rulers or areas important for religious reasons. They do think that the Olmecs had many gods who stood for important forces of nature. The most important god, it seemed, was the jaguar spirit. Many stone monuments show figures that are half human and half jaguar.

The Olmec peoples busily traded with other people to the north and south. In return for the products they made, they received iron ore and different kinds of stone. Along with their trade goods, they spread their culture to other people. For some reason, the Olmecs disappeared around 400 B.C.

Historians still do not understand why. However, their influence lived on.

Another important early culture of Mexico was the Zapotec people. Their home was to the southwest of the Olmecs in a valley that had excellent soil for farming and plenty of rainfall. They began to rise about 1000 B.C. at a site that included stone platforms and temples. A few hundred years later, they developed a kind of writing and a calendar.

About 500 B.C., the Zapotecs began building the first city in the Americas. Called Monte Albán, it grew to hold as many as 25,000 people and lasted as late as A.D. 700. The city was an impressive sight with high pyramids, temples, and palaces made out of stone. It had an observatory that could be used to look at the stars. However, the Zapotec culture also collapsed, and, as with the Olmecs, historians do not know why.

Both of these cultures left their mark on later peoples, though. The jaguar figure of the Olmecs continued to appear in the sculpture and pottery of people who came later. Also, the look of Olmec towns—with pyramids, open space, and huge stone sculptures—was repeated in later times. The Olmecs developed a ritual game played with a ball that also continued to be used in the area.

The Zapotecs also shaped the lives of later peoples. Their way of writing and their calendar—based on the movements of the sun—were taken by other groups. The dramatic and beautiful city of Monte Albán also influenced later peoples, who built their own cities in similar ways. These cities combined religious purposes with the needs of the common people who lived in them.

❸ Early Civilizations of the Andes

KEY IDEA *In the rugged landscape of the Andes Mountains, various peoples created their own civilizations.*

Other interesting civilizations arose in the Americas far to the south of the Olmec and Zapotec peoples. This took place in an environment that was very harsh—the high Andes Mountains that snake down the western edge of South America. This range of mountains has many peaks that are more than 20,000 feet high.

Toward the northern part of South America, along these mountains, lies the modern country of Peru. In this area, the mountains are steep and very rocky. The area is also very cold, with many mountains covered by ice and snow during the entire year. It is very hard to travel this area, and the climate changes quickly from being hot during the day to bitter cold at night. The soil is poor as well, making it hard to grow food.

It was in this difficult land that a new civilization arose in the mountains. That culture is called Chavín. It takes its name from a major ruin, Chavín de Huántar, in the Andes Mountains. At this site, researchers have found pyramids, open spaces, and large mounds made of earth. The Chavín culture was at its height from 900 B.C. to 200 B.C. It is considered the first influential civilization in South America.

Scientists have found objects that suggest that the Chavín culture helped shape other people living to the north and south of this site. In these other sites, they see the art styles and symbols of religion that they had found at Chavín. They think that the main site was not the center of a political empire but was the chief site of a spiritual or religious movement. People from other areas may have made trips to the main site to pay their respects. The Chavín culture, like the Olmecs in Mexico, may have been a "mother culture," one that gave the first form to the ideas and styles of the area.

Two other important cultures arose in Peru. The Nazca culture developed along the coast of the Pacific Ocean in the south of Peru. It lasted from 200 B.C. to A.D. 600. The Nazca people built large and complex systems to bring water to their farmlands. They made beautiful cloth and pottery.

The Nazca are most famous for another of their features, though. Called the Nazca Lines, they are huge pictures scraped on the surface of a rocky plain. The drawings include a monkey, a spider, some birds, and other creatures. What is most remarkable is that the pictures are so large that they can be seen and appreciated only from high in the air. Some experts think that the Nazca drew these pictures to please their gods.

The other culture of early Peru arose along the Pacific Coast but far to the north. This was the Moche culture, and it lasted from A.D. 100 to A.D. 700. The Moche tapped into rivers that flowed down from the mountains. They built ditches to bring water to their fields, where they grew many different crops. They raised corn, beans, potatoes, squash, and peanuts. They also fished, caught wild ducks and pigs, and hunted deer.

Archaeologists have found some tombs of the Moche people, and they show that the culture had great wealth. They have found jewelry made of gold, silver, and jewels. The Moche people made beautiful pottery that showed scenes of everyday life. So, even though they never had a written language, it is possible to learn much about how they lived.

Eventually, though, the Moche culture also fell. As with the other peoples of the Americas, the reason for this fall is not known. For the next hundred years, other cultures would rise and fall in the Americas. Most of them remained separate from one another, however.

Review

Analyzing Causes and Recognizing Effects
1. What did the first Americans hunt, and what happened when that supply of food disappeared?
2. What happened when the early peoples of America began to farm?
3. ***Drawing Conclusions*** Why were the Olmecs and Zapotecs important?

Determining Main Ideas
4. How was the environment of the Andes Mountains difficult?
5. Write one important thing each about the Chavín, Nazca, and Moche peoples.

Answer Key
Chapter 9
SUMMARY

The Americas: A Separate World,
40,000 B.C.–A.D. 700

Responses will vary but should include points similar to the following:

1. The first Americans hunted mammoths. When all those animals died out, they began to catch and eat fish, hunt smaller animals such as rabbits and deer, and gather plants and fruits.

2. Growing food gave people a more reliable food supply and more food. The population grew. With more food available, some people began to work in other fields, such as arts and crafts. Some people became more rich and powerful than others.

3. Both the Olmecs and Zapotecs influenced the peoples who lived in the area after them.

4. The mountains are steep, rocky, and very cold. It is very hard to travel in the area, and the climate changes quickly from being hot during the day to bitter cold at night. The soil is poor.

5. Chavín: may have been the "mother culture" for the people of the Andes. Nazca: drew huge pictures of animals that could be seen only from above. Moche: had a varied diet that included many different kinds of food.

CHAPTERS IN BRIEF *The Muslim World, 600–1250*

CHAPTER OVERVIEW In the harsh environment of the Arabian Peninsula, a new religion arose. Muhammad united the Arab peoples in the belief that there was only one God. Strengthened by their faith, the Arabs began a conquest of parts of three continents. In ruling this vast empire, the Arabs preserved the achievements of many cultures and promoted learning in many fields of study.

❶ The Rise of Islam

KEY IDEA *Muhammad unified the Arabic people both politically and through the religion he founded, Islam.*

The harsh environment of the Arabian Peninsula left its mark on the society of the Arab peoples. Located at about where Africa, Asia, and Europe meet, the region felt the influence of cultures from all three continents. With the land almost completely covered by desert, making a living was difficult. The people who lived on the desert followed a nomadic way of life. They herded animals, which they led from one fertile spot—oasis—to another in search of precious water. Over time, many of these people, called Bedouins, began to live in towns and cities. People who lived in the towns engaged in local and long-distance trade.

The Bedouins developed a society based on family groups called clans. Courage and loyalty to the family, as well as warrior skills, were important values.

By the early 600s, trade had become an important activity in the Arabian Peninsula. Merchants from the Byzantine and Sassanid empires to the north brought goods to Arabia. They traded in the cities for spices and other goods. They also brought new ideas.

At this time, the Arab people believed in many gods. Religious pilgrims came to Mecca to worship at an ancient shrine called the Ka'aba. Over the years, Arabs had introduced the worship of many gods and spirits to the Ka'aba. It contained more than 360 idols brought there by several tribes.

Around the year A.D. 570, Muhammad was born into this Arab society. Though a member of a powerful family of Mecca, his early life was difficult. He was orphaned at age six and received little schooling. However, he became a successful merchant. Muhammad was always interested in religion. At around age 40, he took religion as his life's mission. One night, the angel Gabriel visited him and told him to proclaim the word of God to his people.

Muhammad began to teach that there was only one God—Allah. His religion was called Islam, and its followers took the name of Muslims. He converted a few friends and family members and then began to preach in public. At first, many people in Mecca violently opposed Muhammad's views. They feared Meccans would neglect traditional Arab gods. Muhammad and his followers were forced to leave Mecca for Yathrib (later called Medina) in 622. Muhammad became a leader of that city.

The forces of Mecca and Medina fought several times over the next few years. Finally, in 630, the leaders of Mecca surrendered to Muhammad. He went to the building that held the Ka'aba and destroyed the idols to other gods. Many of the people of Mecca adopted Islam. They began to worship Allah as the only God. Though Muhammad died shortly thereafter, in 632, much of the Arabian Peninsula was already united under Islam.

Muslims have five duties to perform. The duties show a person's accepting of the will of God:

- A person must state a belief that there is no God but Allah and that Muhammad is his prophet.
- A person must pray to Allah, facing Mecca, five times every day.
- A person must give aid to poor people through a tax.
- A person must eat only one meal a day, after sunset, every day during the holy month of Ramadan.
- A person should perform the hajj—a trip to the holy city of Mecca—at least once in his or her life.

Even today, for Muslims, their private and religious lives are the same. So, many religious laws tell Muslims how they must live. Some rules forbid them from eating pork or drinking alcohol. Every Friday afternoon they meet as a community for prayer. The central ideas of the Muslim religion are found in the Qur'an, which Muslims believe to be the will of Allah as revealed to Muhammad. The Qur'an is written in Arabic, and that language spread as the faith of Islam spread. Muslims are also guided by the example of Muhammad's life, called the Sunna, and by a set of laws and rules.

Muslims believe that Allah is the same God that Jews and Christians worship. To Muslims, the Qur'an perfects the earlier teachings of God found in the Jewish Torah and the Christian Bible. Because their holy books were related to the Qur'an, Jews and Christians enjoyed special status in Muslim societies.

❷ Islam Expands

KEY IDEA *In spite of internal conflicts, the Muslims created an empire of land on three continents.*

When Muhammad died, his followers elected a new leader, Abu-Bakr. He had been loyal to Muhammad. He was given the title caliph, which means "successor" or "deputy."

Abu-Bakr reacted quickly when a group of Arabs abandoned Islam. He defeated them in battle over a two-year period. Abu-Bakr died soon thereafter. However, his army became an effective fighting force that began to conquer new lands. The Arabs took Syria and lower Egypt from the Byzantine Empire. By 750, the Muslim Empire stretched from the Indus River in India west to the Atlantic Ocean.

The Muslims' faith helped them achieve this rapid expansion. They saw each victory as a sign of Allah's support of Islam. Other factors were the fighting skill of the armies and the strong leadership of their generals. The Byzantine and Sassanid empires to the north were also weak at this time, and the Arabs took advantage of that. Finally, many people who lived in those empires did not support the official religions. They often supported the Arabs, who they thought would liberate them from the harsh rule of these empires.

Many of these people accepted Islam. Some found the message of Islam appealing. Some liked the fact that by becoming Muslims they avoided paying a tax put only on non-Muslims. The Qur'an prevented Muslims from forcing others to accept the religion, however. Muslim rulers allowed people to follow whatever beliefs they chose.

After the murder of a ruling caliph in 656, different Muslim groups began to struggle for control of the empire. Ali, a cousin and son-in-law of Muhammad, was chosen caliph. After a few years, he, too, was killed. The system of electing caliphs died with him.

A family known as the Umayyads took power

over the vast empire. They did not follow the simple life of earlier caliphs and surrounded themselves with wealth. This created a division within the Muslim community.

Most Muslims accepted Umayyad rule. However, some did resist, and a different view of the office of caliph developed. The Shi'a group—the "party" of the deceased Ali—felt that caliphs needed to be relatives of Muhammad. Those who did not outwardly resist Umayyad rule became known as the Sunni. Another group, the Sufi, reacted to the Umayyads' life of luxury. The Sufis emphasized a more spiritual way of life.

After 750, Muslim caliphates existed on three continents. The Abbasids (750–1258) conquered the Umayyads and took over the east. They held the lands of modern Iraq, Iran, and central Asia. They built the city of Baghdad in central Iraq as their capital. They were powerful, using their location to control the rich trade between China and Europe. They formed a complex government to run their empire.

One Umayyad prince had escaped to Spain in 750. There Muslims known as Berbers already existed. The prince set up a Muslim state called al-Andalus. The Umayyads of al-Andalus (756–976) controlled parts of Spain and North Africa.

Another Muslim state—the Fatimid caliphate (909–1171)—sprang up in North Africa. It eventually spread to western Arabia and Syria.

The Muslims were divided politically. However, the Abbasids, Umayyads of al-Andalus, and Fatimids were linked by religion, language, culture, and trade. Muslim traders brought goods from China to Spain. They formed banks along the route. They also accepted a form of substitute money later known as checks.

❸ Muslim Culture

KEY IDEA *Muslims combined and preserved the traditions of many peoples and also advanced learning in a variety of areas.*

The vast Muslim Empire included people of many different lands and cultures. Muslims blended Arabic culture with these other traditions to create a new culture of great achievement. This new culture arose in the major cities of the Muslim world.

Damascus, in modern Syria, was the leading city and cultural center of Islamic learning. The cities of Córdoba and Cairo were centers of Muslim rule in Spain and North Africa. The Abbasid capital, Baghdad, was especially impressive. Its inner area was circular and had three sets of protective walls, each inside the other. In the center of the circle was the palace of the caliph, made of marble and stone. Nearly a million people lived in Baghdad.

Muslim society was divided into four groups. At the top were people who were Muslims from birth. Next came those who converted to Islam. The third group included Jews, Christians, and Zoroastrians—protected because Muslims shared some of their beliefs. The fourth group was slaves, none of whom were Muslims.

According to Muslim law, women should obey men. However, Muslim women still enjoyed more rights than did those living in European society of the time. They had some economic and property rights. In the early Muslim society, women could also have an education and take part in public life. Later they lost those rights.

Muslims placed a high value on learning. Muslim scholars added much to humans' store of knowledge. Europe was in chaos, and much that had been known in ancient Greece and Rome was lost. During this time, Muslim scholars kept much of this knowledge alive. They collected ancient Greek, Indian, and Persian works of science and philosophy and translated them into Arabic. One center of this study was the House of Wisdom built in Baghdad. Later, this ancient learning returned to Europe when the works of Muslim scholars were translated.

One area in which Muslim scholars made great advances was medicine. The physician al-Razi wrote an encyclopedia that collected all that was known about medicine from Greece to India.

Another area of advance was mathematics. A brilliant mathematician named al-Khwarizmi wrote a textbook that introduced a new branch of math. By developing algebra, he was able to use known quantities to find unknown quantities.

In science, Muslims studied the work of ancient Greek scientists but took a new approach. The Greeks had tried to learn about nature by using logic to reach conclusions. In contrast, Muslims used experiments to test ideas. Another field of advance was astronomy. One Muslim scientist made new discoveries about how people see. His findings helped lead later to the invention of the telescope and microscope.

In philosophy, the Muslim scholar Ibn Rushd tried to join together the thinking of ancient Greeks with Muslim ideas.

Muslim literature developed a strong tradition. The Qur'an is the standard for all Arabic literature and poetry. The collection *The Thousand and One Nights* included many entertaining stories, fairy tales, and legends. It was read and narrated throughout the Muslim world.

Muslims put to use the traditions in art that they found among the other peoples they met. Muslims had their own special practices in art, however. For instance, artists could not draw pictures of people. Only Allah, the religion said, could create life. Unable to draw these images, Muslims developed a new art form. They practiced calligraphy, or the art of beautiful handwriting. Some of this writing was used to decorate the beautiful buildings that Muslims built. These buildings often showed the blending of cultures that was a major part of the Muslim world.

Review

1. ***Drawing Conclusions*** What caused Muhammad to leave Mecca for Yathrib? What was the result?
2. ***Summarizing*** What are the five duties that a follower of Islam must perform?
3. ***Analyzing Causes and Recognizing Effects*** What factors contributed to the Muslims' success in capturing so much land?
4. ***Determining Main Ideas*** What was the most important factor in the division of Muslim society into four parts? What does that reveal about the place of Islam in this society?
5. ***Clarifying*** Describe two achievements of Muslim culture in art or learning. What contributed to them?

Answer Key
Chapter 10
SUMMARY

The Muslim World, 600–1250

Responses will vary but should include points similar to the following:

1. Muhammad left Mecca because he met opposition from the people there. He became a leader in Medina and then returned later to take control of Mecca.

2. The five duties of Muslims are to (a) state their belief that there is no God but Allah and that Muhammad is his prophet; (b) pray to Allah, facing Mecca, five times every day; (c) give aid to poorer people through a tax; (d) eat only one meal a day, after sunset, every day during the holy month of Ramadan; and (e) make a trip to the holy city of Mecca at least once in their lives.

3. Muslims were able to conquer so much land because their faith made them strong; they had skillful generals and armies; the Byzantine and Sassanid empires were weak; and many people who lived in those empires supported the Arabs, who they thought would liberate them from the harsh rule of the empires.

4. The most important factor was religion. The private and religious lives of Muslims are not separate.

5. Muslims developed the art of calligraphy, or decorative handwriting, because they were banned from making images of people or animals. They developed styles of architecture that blended Arab traditions with the local practices of the areas that they conquered.

CHAPTERS IN BRIEF *Byzantines, Russians, and Turks Interact, 500–1500*

CHAPTER OVERVIEW *The eastern part of the old Roman Empire maintained a brilliant civilization centered in Constantinople. With a separate Christian Church, it developed a culture different from that of western Europe. Slavs and Vikings joined to create a new culture in Russia, which was influenced by the Eastern Church. Turks entered the area, converted to Islam, and made their own empire.*

❶ The Byzantine Empire

KEY IDEA *Constantinople ruled an eastern empire that survived for over a thousand years.*

In the A.D. 300s, the Roman emperor Constantine was worried about the growing power of German tribes. He moved the Roman Empire's capital to the east, where he could better meet that threat. The location also put him closer to the eastern provinces of the empire, which were richer than those in the west. He built a great new capital city, Constantinople, on the site of the old port city of Byzantium. Constantinople became the center of an empire in the eastern area of the Mediterranean Sea that lasted for hundreds of years. It was called the Byzantine Empire.

The Roman Empire was officially divided in 395. The western area was overrun by German tribes. It ceased to exist after 476. However, the Byzantine eastern part remained strong. In 527, Justinian became the Byzantine emperor. He sent an army to try to regain control of Italy and restore the Roman Empire once again. His army managed to win almost all of Italy and much of Spain from the Germans. By around 550, Justinian ruled over almost all of the old Roman Empire's territory.

Under the direction of Justinian, legal experts created a complete code of laws based on the laws of ancient Rome. This body of civil law—the Justinian Code—served the empire for 900 years.

Justinian also worked at making Constantinople a strong and beautiful capital. He built high, strong walls to protect the city from attack by either land or sea. He built a huge palace, public baths, courts, schools, hospitals, and many churches. The main street of the city was lined with shops and open-air markets, where people bought and sold goods from Asia, Africa, and Europe. Another huge building was used to stage chariot races and circus acts.

In 532, the city erupted in riots against the emperor. Justinian thought about leaving the city,

but his wife, the empress Theodora, convinced him to use the army to fight back. The troops regained control of the city, killing thousands of rioters. A church called Hagia Sophia ("Holy Wisdom" in Greek) had been destroyed by the mobs. Justinian rebuilt it to become the most beautiful church in the Christian world.

The empire faced further dangers. A terrible plague broke out in 542. It killed thousands of people and returned every 8 to 12 years until about 700. The many deaths that this illness caused weakened the Byzantine Empire.

Many enemies attacked the empire time and time again over the centuries. German tribes, the Sassanid Persians, and later Muslim armies all tried to gain control of Byzantine land. Constantinople remained safe at this time despite many attacks. Eventually, though, the empire itself shrank. By 1350, the empire included only the capital city and lands in the Balkans—a part of southeastern Europe.

Although it was based on the Roman Empire, the Byzantine Empire had developed a culture all its own. Few people in the Byzantine Empire spoke the Latin of the old Roman Empire. They spoke Greek and belonged to the Eastern Orthodox Church, not the Catholic Church that was centered in Rome. The Eastern Church was led by an official named the patriarch, the leading bishop. However, even he had to obey the emperor. Slowly the Eastern and Roman churches grew further apart. In 1054, the split became permanent. Services in the Eastern Church were conducted in Greek, not in Latin as in the Roman Church. The Eastern Church also allowed priests to marry and let its members have divorces.

Some missionaries traveled from the Byzantine Empire to the north. They met a people known as the Slavs and converted them to the eastern form of Christianity. In this way, the influence of the Byzantine Empire entered Russia as that nation began to form.

❷ The Russian Empire

KEY IDEA *Russia grew out of a blending of Slavic and Byzantine cultures with Eastern Orthodox traditions.*

The Slavs lived in what is today eastern Russia. The area stretched from the Ural Mountains to the Black Sea on the south and the Baltic Sea in the north. The southern regions are hilly grasslands. The northern area is flat and covered with trees or swamps. Slow-moving rivers in the region have moved people and goods for centuries.

The Slavs lived in the forest areas, working as farmers and traders. In the 800s, some Vikings called the Rus came from the north. They built forts along the rivers and blended with the Slavs. They founded the cities of Novgorod and Kiev and became the rulers of the land. They began to trade in Constantinople, bringing furs, timber, and the Slavs who were their subjects. They sold these people as slaves—in fact, the word *slave* comes from *Slav*.

Over time, the Vikings adopted the Slavs' culture. While divisions between Vikings and Slavs disappeared, the society was sharply split between the great mass of peasants and the few nobles.

In the 980s, the ruler of Russia—Vladimir—converted to Byzantine Christianity. He also ordered all of his subjects to adopt this religion. Now more than trade linked Russia to the Byzantine Empire. Russia also looked to Constantinople for religious leadership. Teachers from the empire gave the Russian people instructions in the new religion. The king liked the idea that the ruler of the empire was also the head of the church.

Under the influence of Byzantine culture, Kiev grew to be a large, wealthy, and cultured city. The state grew, as Vladimir took land to the west and to the north. His son, Yaroslav the Wise, proved an able ruler as well. Under him, Kiev grew even more wealthy through trade and alliances made with western nations.

Then the state centered in Kiev began to have problems. The sons of Yaroslav fought one another for control of the land after his death in 1054. Trade declined, cutting the wealth of Kiev. Then deeper troubles appeared. Nomadic fighters from central Asia, the Mongols, began to conquer many different areas. In the middle 1200s, they reached Kiev. They quickly overran the Russian state, killing many people. The Mongols held control of the area for more than 200 years.

As long as the Russian people did not rebel, the Mongols allowed them to keep their customs. The Mongols allowed the Russians to continue following their Eastern Christian religion. The Church helped settle any differences between the Mongol rulers and the Russian people. The Mongols made the Russians pay tribute, a sum of money that was owed every year. They used Russian nobles to collect the tribute. One of those nobles, Alexander Nevsky, grew to power. His heirs became princes of the city of Moscow.

Control by the Mongols had important effects on Russia. First, it isolated the Russians from western Europe. As a result, Russian society developed in its own way. Second, rule by the Mongols united many different areas of Russia under one central authority. Before then, what is now Russia had been ruled by a number of different princes. Third, Mongol rule led to the rise of Moscow.

That city had a good location near three major rivers: the Dnieper, Don, and Volga. By the 1320s, under Prince Ivan I of Moscow, this position could be used to expand the power of Moscow. Ivan served the Mongols by crushing a local rebellion. In return, the Mongol ruler gave him the right to collect the tribute in all of European Russia. Now the most powerful Russian prince, Ivan I became known as "Ivan Moneybags."

He increased the influence of Moscow by persuading the leader of the Russian church in Kiev to move to Moscow. Over time, Ivan and his successors added to the land that Moscow controlled. In the late 1400s, under Ivan III, Russia grew to be a mighty empire. In 1453, the Byzantine Empire had fallen, defeated by the Turks. In 1472, Ivan married the niece of the last Byzantine emperor, linking himself to that historic throne. From then on, he called himself czar, which was the Russian version of Caesar. In 1480, Ivan finally broke with the Mongols. He refused to pay that year's tribute. Because the Mongols did not respond militarily, Russia had in effect won its independence from Mongol rule.

❸ Turkish Empires Rise in Anatolia

KEY IDEA *Turkish people converted to Islam and founded new empires that would renew Muslim civilization.*

The Turks were a nomadic people from the vast grasslands of central Asia. They lived by herding sheep and goats and engaging in raids and trade with the settled peoples of the Abbasid Empire.

Beginning in the 900s, they moved into the lands of that empire and began converting to Islam.

These fierce nomads were highly skilled fighters. The rulers of the empire began to buy them as children to train them for their armies. Turks became an important political factor in the empire. Turkish soldiers many times removed caliphs from the throne in Baghdad and put new rulers in place.

While this Turkish influence was growing, the empire itself was shrinking. Local leaders in several areas split off to establish their own states. In 945, a Persian army seized control of the empire. Members of the Abbasid family continued to hold the position of caliph and act as religious leaders. The new rulers of the government were from outside the dynasty. They were called sultans.

As these changes took place, larger and larger numbers of Turks settled in the empire. They were called Seljuk Turks after the name of the family that led them. In 1055, the Seljuks captured Baghdad and took control of the government. In the next few decades, the Seljuks used their force to take land away from another empire—the Byzantine Empire. They won almost all of Anatolia, the peninsula where modern Turkey now sits. In this position, they stood almost at the gates of Constantinople.

In ruling their empire, the Seljuks relied on the government experience of Persians. They placed their capital in Persian lands and gave Persians important positions in the government. In return, Persians became loyal supporters of Turkish rule.

The Turks also adopted Persian culture. They looked to Persian scholars to teach them the proper way to follow Islam. They began to use the Persian language for art and education. The Turkish rulers even took the Persian word for "king"—*shah*—as their title. One of the greatest Seljuk rulers, Malik Shah, became a patron of the arts. He made the capital city more beautiful by building many mosques, or Muslim houses of worship. Persian became so important that Arabic—the language of the Qur'an—almost died out in Seljuk lands.

The Seljuk Empire collapsed quickly, as a series of weak rulers were unable to maintain it. One reason was the growing pressure from western Europe, whose rulers sent armies on the Crusades in the effort to capture the lands of ancient Palestine, which were sacred to Christians. The First Crusade began in 1095, and the Christian armies captured Jerusalem. Not quite 100 years later, the Turks retook the city.

Just when the Crusades became less of a threat to the Muslim world, the Mongols moved in from the east. They overran vast stretches of territory and captured Baghdad in 1258. They killed the last caliph and took control of the government from the Seljuk Turks.

Review

1. ***Determining Main Ideas*** Describe two accomplishments of the emperor Justinian.
2. ***Contrasting*** What cultural factors separated the Byzantine Empire from western Europe?

Analyzing Causes and Recognizing Effects

3. What cultural influences combined to produce Russian culture?
4. What effects did Mongol rule have on Russian history?
5. ***Comparing*** How was the Turkish adoption of culture similar to the adoption of culture by the Russians?

Answer Key
Chapter 11
SUMMARY

Byzantines, Russians, and Turks Interact, 500–1500

Responses will vary but should include points similar to the following:

1. Any two: He recaptured lands in Italy and Spain that had belonged to the ancient Roman Empire; he sponsored creation of a body of laws; he built many buildings in the capital city of Constantinople; he suppressed the riots of 532.

2. People in the Byzantine Empire spoke Greek, not Latin. They also followed a different Christian Church.

3. Russian culture was formed by the culture of the Slavic people, the Vikings who came to the area, and the religion and culture of the Byzantine Empire.

4. Mongol rule isolated Russia from the rest of Europe, turned Russia into a unified state, and led to Moscow's position as the central power in the region.

5. The Russians adopted the culture of the Byzantine Empire, an advanced civilization. In a similar way, the Seljuk Turk rulers adopted the more advanced culture of the Persian lands that they conquered.

CHAPTER 12
Summary

CHAPTERS IN BRIEF *Empires in East Asia, 600–1350*

CHAPTER OVERVIEW Under Tang and Song rulers, China became the most advanced culture in the world. Then fierce warriors from Central Asia swept over China, creating a new empire that encouraged trade. In ruling China, the Mongols reached great heights. Japan developed its own culture based on ideas and practices borrowed from China. Chinese influence extended to Korea and Southeast Asia.

❶ Tang and Song China

KEY IDEA *During the Tang and Song dynasties, China experienced an era of prosperity and technological innovations.*

Starting in A.D. 220, China went through a long period of troubles during which no single ruler was strong enough to unite the entire area. In 589, Wendi changed that. He brought the northern and southern regions under his power and named himself emperor. His new dynasty—the Sui—lasted only during his rule and that of his successor. However, these two rulers were important. They built the Grand Canal, a long waterway that connected the two major rivers of China. It linked the people of the cities in the north to the rice-growing regions in the fertile south.

The Tang Dynasty followed and lasted for 300 years. Tang rulers retook northern and western lands that had been lost under the Han Dynasty. Under the Empress Wu—the only woman ever to rule China as emperor—the Tang captured parts of Korea as well.

Early Tang rulers made the government stronger. To run their empire, they revived the practice of using men educated in the writings of the philosopher Confucius. Schools were set up to train people in these works. Candidates for government jobs had to pass tests in order to win work.

The Tang Dynasty began to weaken when the rulers once again levied heavy taxes. While the Chinese people became angry over these burdens, nomads attacked the empire's western lands and began to capture some areas. In 907, the last Tang ruler was killed, and a new dynasty—the Song—took its place. It, too, lasted about 300 years. The Song Dynasty ruled a smaller area than did the Tang. However, China under its rule was strong.

During the Tang and Song periods, China made many advances in technology. The Chinese invented the use of movable type, allowing them to print books. They also invented gunpowder for use in fireworks and weapons. The Chinese grew more food, based on advances in farming and an improved variety of fast-growing rice. Trade increased, first through Central Asia on the land route called the Silk Road and later over the oceans. This allowed Buddhism to spread from China to Japan, Korea, and Vietnam. Tang and Song China became famous for their artistic advances.

These developments brought about changes in Chinese society. The old noble families lost power, while the scholar-government officials gained power. Below them was an urban middle class, laborers, and peasants. The status of women became worse.

❷ The Mongol Conquests

KEY IDEA *The Mongols, a nomadic people from the steppe, settled across much of Asia.*

Much of Central Asia is covered by flat grassland that cannot support farming. Nomadic herders lived in this area. They traveled from place to place seeking grass to feed herds of sheep and goats. From time to time over the centuries, these nomads struck out to attack the settled farming peoples to the east, south, and west. In the early 1200s, the Mongols began such an attack. Under the leadership of Genghis Khan, they met huge success. In just over 20 years, he led his people to conquer Central Asia.

Three factors contributed to the Mongols' military success. First, they organized their army in a logical, easy-to-control way with experienced fighters in command. Second, Genghis Khan was able to outthink and outwit his enemies. Finally, the Mongols used cruelty as a weapon. This helped convince other cities to surrender without a fight.

After Genghis Khan died in 1227, the Mongol armies continued to advance. Under Genghis's sons and grandsons, the armies conquered China, took parts of Korea, captured Russia, and threatened eastern Europe. By 1260, the remaining empire was divided into four areas called khanates. The rulers in these areas gradually adopted the culture of the people they ruled. Those in the west became Muslims. Those in China took on Chinese culture. In this way, the four khanates grew apart.

The Mongols proved able rulers who brought about a long period of peace in Central Asia. They promoted trade and the exchange of ideas between Asia and Europe. Along with this trade, they may have brought a deadly disease—the plague—that caused widespread death in Europe in the 1300s.

❸ The Mongol Empire

KEY IDEA *Kublai Khan ruled China and encouraged foreign contact and trade, but the Yuan Dynasty was beset by problems.*

The Mongols needed several decades to complete their conquest of China begun by Genghis Khan in 1215. In 1260 Kublai Khan, grandson of Genghis, took the title of Great Khan. Finally, in 1279, Kublai Khan managed to defeat the last Chinese army in the south. He became the first foreigner to gain complete control of China and rule the land.

Kublai Khan founded the Yuan Dynasty that ruled China for only about 100 years. The dynasty was important because it united China for the first time in several hundred years and opened China to trade with the west. The Mongols did not disrupt Chinese government or culture but, in fact, adopted it for themselves. Kublai Khan adopted Chinese ways and built a new capital in the city of Beijing.

However, the Mongols still wanted further conquests. Kublai Khan launched two attacks on Japan in 1274 and 1281, but both failed.

To rule his empire, Kublai Khan continued to follow Chinese practices. The Mongols kept the top government jobs for themselves. They also hired many people from other lands for these jobs, trusting them more than they did the Chinese.

Kublai Khan rebuilt the Great Canal. He promoted foreign trade, which took such Chinese inventions as printing, gunpowder, paper money, the compass, and playing cards to Europe. This activity led the European trader Marco Polo to journey to China. He lived there for many years and traveled throughout the Mongol Empire. When he returned to Italy in 1292, he told Europeans fantastic stories about Chinese wealth.

In the last years of his rule, Kublai Khan ran into trouble. Attacks on Southeast Asia failed, costing many lives and much treasure. After Kublai's death in 1294, Mongol leaders struggled for control of the empire. These fights helped weaken Mongol rule, which allowed parts of China to erupt in rebellion. In 1368, some rebels finally won control of the Chinese government from the Mongols. They established a new dynasty called the Ming.

By this time, the whole Mongol Empire had begun to collapse. Mongols lost control of Persia in the 1330s and Central Asia in the 1370s. They continued to rule Russia until the late 1400s, however.

❹ Feudal Powers in Japan

KEY IDEA *Japanese civilization was shaped by cultural borrowing from China and the rise of feudalism and military rulers.*

Japan gained from its location. It was near enough to China to benefit from the influence of Chinese culture. It was also far enough to be able to protect itself from complete Chinese domination.

Japan is not one island but several thousand islands of varying sizes. Most people, though, live on the four largest of them. The islands have few natural resources, such as coal and oil. Also, the many mountains leave little land that can be used for farming.

Early in its history, Japan was broken up into many small areas, each led by a clan. These clans believed in their own gods. Later, all these beliefs were combined to form Japan's religion, Shinto. The main ideas of Shinto were to respect the forces of nature and the ancestors of a family.

In the A.D. 400s, the Yamato became the most powerful of these clans. They claimed that they were descended from a sun goddess. Later, Yamato leaders began to call themselves emperors. The emperor remained an important figure in Japan. Even when other groups took control of the government, they retained the position of the emperor and said they were ruling in his name.

During the 400s, Japan began to feel the influence of Chinese culture. Buddhism traveled from China to Japan and became an important religion in the islands. The emperor sent people to

China to learn Chinese ways and bring them back to Japan. The Japanese also adopted the Chinese system of writing, painting, and other parts of Chinese culture. Around the late 800s, though, the Japanese stopped sending people to China to learn Chinese culture.

From 794 to 1185, Japan's noble family ruled the country from the capital at Heian. This era represented the peak of Japanese culture, when the people of the court led lives of complex rituals, careful manners, and artistic good taste. Women writers of the time provide a detailed view of this refined court life.

Over time the power of the emperor declined and nobles with large land holdings began to assert their power. They hired private armies, and these soldiers began to terrorize farmers. For protection, farmers gave up some of their land to the lords. Thus began a time of local power like Europe's Middle Ages. The local lords used a group of trained soldiers called samurai to protect them from attacks by other lords. These samurai followed a strict code of honor.

After a period of war, one of these lords arose as the most powerful. The emperor named him the shogun, or superior general of the emperor's army. While the emperor remained in power in name, the new shogun ran the country. This pattern was followed in Japan from 1192 to 1868. Shoguns led a defense of Japan against invasions of the Mongols from China.

❺ Kingdoms of Southeast Asia and Korea

KEY IDEA *Several smaller kingdoms prospered in East and Southeast Asia, a region culturally influenced by China and India.*

Southeast Asia lies between the Indian and Pacific oceans and stretches from China almost to Australia. It includes such mainland areas as modern Myanmar (Burma), Cambodia, and Vietnam and the islands of Sumatra, Java, and Borneo, among others. The region has never been united culturally or politically.

From about A.D. 800 to 1200, the Khmer empire of modern Cambodia was the main power on the mainland of Southeast Asia. The main source of wealth of this empire was the growing of rice. The Khmer had large irrigation works to bring water to their fields. Rulers built huge and beautiful temples

and palaces. At the same time, a trading empire called Srivijaya arose on Java and nearby islands. Its capital became a center for the study of Buddhism.

These two cultures were influenced by India. Another culture—Vietnam—fell under the influence of China. China controlled the area from about 100 B.C. to A.D. 900. Vietnam became an independent kingdom, known as Dai Viet, in 939. While taking Buddhism and other influences from China, the Vietnamese developed their own special culture. Women, for instance, enjoyed more rights in Vietnam than they did in China.

Korea, like Japan and Vietnam, was influenced by China but maintained its own traditions as well. From China, the Koreans learned Buddhism, the teachings of Confucius, the benefits of central government, and a system of writing. The Koryu Dynasty ruled Korea from 935 to 1392. It had a government similar to China's. However, Korea's method of using examinations to fill government jobs did not keep wealthy landowners from dominating society. The dynasty, though, produced many great artistic achievements in Korean culture.

Korea fell to the Mongols and was occupied until the 1350s. The heavy tax that they demanded made the country poor and led the people to revolt. When the Mongols lost power, a new dynasty took control of Korea and ruled for 518 years.

Review

1. *Clarifying* Identify two changes in technology or society that took place in Tang and Song China.
2. *Analyzing Causes* What factors helped create Mongol success in war?
3. *Determining Main Ideas* What kind of relations did the Mongols have with the Chinese?
4. *Summarizing* What pattern of government developed in Japan?
5. *Drawing Conclusions* What two cultures influenced the people of Southeast Asia? How does geography help explain why?

Answer Key
Chapter 12
SUMMARY

Empires in East Asia, 600–1350

Responses will vary but should include points similar to the following:

1. Any two: The use of movable type, allowing them to print books; gunpowder, used in fireworks and weapons; improvements in farming, enabling the Chinese to grow more food; trade increased, linking China to the west and opening it to the influence of foreign religions, including Buddhism; old noble families lost power, scholar-officials gained power, and women lost status.

2. They organized their army in a logical, easy-to-control way and placed experienced fighters in command of each unit; Genghis Khan could out-think his enemies; and they used cruelty to terrify their enemies into giving up.

3. The Mongols admired Chinese culture and adopted it, but they did not entirely trust the Chinese. They put Mongols or foreigners in top government positions.

4. In Japan for many centuries, the emperor held authority, but real political power rested in the hands of powerful nobles.

5. Southeast Asia was influenced by the cultures of India and China. The closeness of the region to those lands explains the influence.

CHAPTERS IN BRIEF *European Middle Ages, 500–1200*

CHAPTER OVERVIEW *German peoples invaded the Roman Empire, causing it to fall. Small Germanic kingdoms arose. The kingdom of Charlemagne finally reunited western Europe but split apart after his death. As different groups invaded Europe, people sought protection and gave up some rights to powerful lords, producing a system called feudalism. The Church proved an important spiritual and political force throughout the Middle Ages.*

❶ Charlemagne Unites Germanic Kingdoms

KEY IDEA *Many Germanic kingdoms that succeeded the Roman Empire were reunited under Charlemagne's empire.*

By the end of the fourth century, invaders from many different Germanic groups overran the Roman Empire in the west. Their arrival and the collapse of Roman rule had several effects. The attacks put a halt to all trade, as it was not safe to move goods from one place to another. The end of Roman government and the decline in trade made cities less important. As cities faded, nobles moved to the countryside. Poorer people followed, hoping to be able to grow their own food. The general level of education in society became lower. As Germanic people settled in different areas, they began to blend Latin with phrases of their own. Their language developed different dialects. Europe no longer had a single language understood by all.

From about A.D. 400 to 600, Europe was the scene of turmoil and chaos as small Germanic kingdoms fought each other for power. Long-held Roman ideas about law were replaced by Germanic ideas of society based on close personal ties. The Catholic Church provided the only sense of order. In 496, Clovis, the king of the Franks, became a Christian with all his warriors. From then on, the pope in Rome supported the military efforts of Clovis.

Clovis was one of many leaders to become Christian. The Church made an effort to bring these people to the religion. It also set up new communities called monasteries, where men called monks and women called nuns lived lives devoted to God. These monasteries became important because their libraries preserved some of the writings of the ancient world.

The Church also grew in importance when Gregory I became pope in 590. He made the pope the guardian of the spiritual lives of all Christians. He also made the pope an important power in governing part of Italy.

The kingdom of the Franks covered much of modern France. By the 700s, the most important official was the mayor of the palace, even more powerful than the king. He made laws and controlled the army. In 719 Charles Martel became mayor and expanded the lands controlled by the Franks. He also won a battle in 732 against a Muslim force moving north from Spain. That ended the Muslim threat to Europe and made Martel a Christian hero. His son, Pepin, was crowned king.

One of Pepin's sons, Charlemagne, became king of all the land of the Franks in 771. At six feet, four inches tall, Charlemagne towered over most people of his time. With military skill, he expanded his kingdom to make it larger than any known since ancient Rome. By 800, he held most of modern Italy, all of modern France, and parts of modern Spain and Germany. Pope Leo III crowned him emperor. With that, the power of the Church and the German kings joined the heritage of the old Roman Empire.

Charlemagne cut the power of the nobles in his empire and increased his own. He traveled throughout his lands, visiting the people and judging cases. He brought well-read men to his court and sponsored a revival of learning. However, Charlemagne's empire broke into pieces soon after his death.

❷ Feudalism in Europe

KEY IDEA *Feudalism, a political and military system of protective alliances and relationships, develops in Europe.*

Between 800 and 1000, Europe was threatened by new invasions. Muslims captured Sicily in southern Italy. Magyars struck from the east. From the north came the most feared fighters of all, the Vikings, or Norsemen.

The Vikings came from Scandinavia (now Sweden, Norway, and Denmark). In small, quick raiding parties, they attacked villages and monasteries. They took anything of value. The Vikings struck terror in the hearts of Western Europeans. By around the year 1000, though, the Vikings had adopted Christianity and stopped raiding to become traders and farmers.

The Magyars, Turkish nomads, attacked from the east and reached as far as Italy and western France. The Muslims invaded what are now Spain and Italy from the south. The worst years of the invaders' attacks were from 850 to 950. People in Western Europe suffered and feared for their futures. With no strong central government, they went to local leaders for protection. In this way, Europe's feudal system began.

The feudal system was based on rights and obligations. For example, a local leader, or lord, gave land to person of lower status, called a vassal. In return, the vassal promised to supply soldiers when the lord needed them. The structure of feudal society was like a pyramid. At the top was the king. Next came the most powerful vassals, such as nobles and bishops. Beneath them were knights, mounted horsemen who pledged to defend their lord's land. At the bottom were landless peasants who toiled in the fields.

Peasants were by far the largest group. Many of them were not free to move about as they wished. They were tied to the land of their lord.

The lord's land was called the manor, and manors became the centers of economic life. Lords gave peasants land, a home, and protection from raiders.

The peasants worked the land to grow food, giving part of each year's crop to the lord. They also paid taxes every year and had much of their lives controlled by the lord. Peasants lived in small villages of 15 to 30 families. They found everything they needed in that small community and rarely traveled far from their homes. Their cottages had only one or two rooms with only straw mats for sleeping. They had poor diets. They endured these lives, believing that God had set their place in society.

❸
The Age of Chivalry

KEY IDEA *The code of chivalry for knights glorified combat and romantic love.*

Nobles were constantly at war with one another. They employed knights, who were soldiers who fought on horseback. Using the saddle and stirrup to stay firmly in place on the horse, these knights became the most important military weapon of the time in Europe. By about the year 1000, nobles used their armies of mounted knights to fight one another for control of land. When they won battles, they gave some of the new land to their knights. The knights could use the income from this land to support their need for costly weapons, armor, and horses. They devoted much of their time to improving their skill at fighting.

By the 1100s, a new code of conduct for knights had developed. This code of chivalry said that a knight had to fight fiercely for three masters: his lord, God, and his chosen lady. Knights were also required to protect the weak and poor. While the code set high standards, few knights met all of them. For example, most treated peasants harshly.

The sons of nobles and knights began training to become knights at an early age. They gained experience by fighting in staged combats called tournaments. These fights were fierce, but real battles were very bloody and harsh. To protect their lands and homes, nobles built stone castles. When a castle was attacked, defenders poured hot oil or boiling water on people trying to attack.

The literature about knights did not reflect this bloody reality. Poems and stories stressed the code of chivalry, life in the castle, and the knight's loyalty to the woman he loved. Some long poems, called epics, told the story of regal or legendary heroes such as King Arthur and Charlemagne. Songs told the joys and sorrows of romantic love. Many of the writers of these songs traveled to the court of Eleanor of Aquitaine, the rich and powerful ruler of a land in southern France.

The knights' ideals of love and devotion to a noble lady seemed to give women a high position in the society of the Middle Ages. In fact, most women in feudal society had little power. The Church taught that they were inferior. They were limited to working in the home or living in convents. Noblewomen could sometimes rule the land when their husbands were away from home, but they could not inherit land. It usually passed from father to son.

Peasant women had to work in the fields with their husbands and children simply to grow enough food to survive—just as they had always done.

❹ The Power of the Church

KEY IDEA *Church leaders and political leaders competed for power and authority.*

With the central governments of Europe weak, the Church became the most important force unifying European society. An early pope had said that God had made two areas of influence in the world—religious and political. The pope was in charge of spiritual matters, he said. The emperor and other rulers were in charge of political affairs. Over the years, though, the difference was not so clear. Popes often tried to influence the actions of rulers, who clashed with them in a struggle for power.

The Church was organized into a structure that mirrored society. At the bottom were the priests who led services at local churches. Above them were bishops, who oversaw all the priests in a large area. At the top was the pope, the head of the Church.

The Middle Ages was an Age of Faith, when people were bound together by their belief in God and the teachings of the Church. Though life was hard, the peasants hoped that by obeying God and doing their work they would earn the reward of being saved and being taken into heaven after death. The local church served as both a religious and a social center for the community. Holidays such as Easter and Christmas were especially festive times of the year.

The Church developed a body of law called canon law. It set standards for the conduct of people and officials of the Church. These laws ruled over such matters as marriage and religious practices. They applied to all Christians, from kings to peasants. The Church also set up courts that took charge when people broke these laws.

Two punishments were especially harsh. If the Church excommunicated a person, he or she was banished from the Church. The person was denied the chance for eternal life in heaven. Popes often used this power as a threat to try to force rulers to do what they wanted. When a ruler refused to obey the pope, the Church leader could place his land under interdiction. That meant that no sacraments and religious services of the Church could officially take place in those lands. The ruler's subjects deeply feared this punishment, for without sacraments they were doomed to hell.

Otto I was the strongest ruler of medieval Germany. He set up an alliance with the Church. In 962, the pope crowned him emperor of what became the powerful Holy Roman Empire. It was made up of what are now Germany and Italy.

Eventually, popes and emperors came into conflict. Rulers had, for a long time, enjoyed the power to name the bishops who led the Church in their lands. In 1075, Pope Gregory VII banned this practice. Emperor Henry IV was angry and persuaded his bishops to say that this pope had no real authority. Gregory then excommunicated Henry. When Henry's nobles rebelled against him, he went to the pope and asked for forgiveness. But the larger issue of lay investiture was left open until 1122. Then an agreement stated that only the pope could name bishops. However, the emperor had the right to turn down any appointment that he did not like.

In the late 1100s, a new German ruler—Frederick I—tried to rebuild the power of the Holy Roman Empire. He invaded Italy but was defeated at an important battle in 1176. When he died in 1190, his empire fell to pieces. Later kings tried to revive the empire. However, real power in Germany was held by the German nobles.

Review

1. ***Analyzing Causes and Recognizing Effects*** What were the effects of the arrival of the Germans and the fall of the Roman Empire?
2. ***Determining Main Ideas*** Why was Charlemagne important? Did his achievements last long?
3. ***Synthesizing*** How did invasions contribute to the beginnings of the feudal system?
4. ***Determining Main Ideas*** What was the position of women during the Middle Ages?
5. ***Forming and Supporting Opinions*** How important do you think the Church was in the Middle Ages? Why?

European Middle Ages, 500–1200

Responses will vary but should include points similar to the following:

1. The Germans' attacks put a halt to all trade, which combined with the end of Roman government to make cities less important. Nobles and poor people moved to the countryside. The general level of education in western society became lower. Latin divided into several different languages.

2. Charlemagne was important because he created an empire that was larger than any since Rome's and because he sponsored a revival of learning. His achievement did not last long because his empire broke up soon after his death.

3. The invasions had made the world dangerous and less stable. With no strong central government, people looked to local leaders for protection. This was the origin of feudalism in Europe.

4. During the Middle Ages, women had little power whether they were noblewomen or peasants. The Church taught that they were inferior.

5. The Church was very important. It led people's spiritual lives, had laws that ruled over marriage and other religious issues, and had political as well as spiritual power.

CHAPTERS IN BRIEF *The Formation of Western Europe, 800–1500*

CHAPTER 14 Summary

CHAPTER OVERVIEW *A new spirit of religion led to reforms in the Catholic Church and to wars against Muslims. Prosperity followed improved farming and the growth of trade and cities. England and France developed as nations and included some government participation by the people. In the 1300s, however, a terrible plague, a long war, and religious conflict ended this Age of Faith.*

❶ Church Reform and the Crusades

KEY IDEA *The Catholic Church underwent reform and launched Crusades (religious wars) against Muslims and others.*

Beginning in the 1000s, a new sense of spiritual feeling arose in Europe, which led to changes in the Church. Popes began a reform movement. Launching the reform was the founding of the monastery at Cluny, France, in 910. During the 900s, about 300 related monasteries were begun in Europe.

Popes Leo IX and Gregory VII made other reforms. They enforced laws against the marriage of priests and the selling of Church offices. Later popes reorganized Church structure. To advise the pope, they created a group called the Curia, which made church law—canon law—and enforced it. The Church collected a tax from all believers, which it used to care for the sick and poor.

In the early 1200s, a new Church group arose. Called friars, they moved from place to place spreading the ideas of the Church. They owned nothing and begged for food. Some became scholars because they studied the Bible and other writings. Women joined in this spiritual revival as well. Many joined convents to dedicate themselves to God.

This new Age of Faith was shown in another way, as many towns in Europe built magnificent cathedrals. In the early 1100s, these huge churches used a new style of architecture called Gothic. These buildings were tall, reaching toward heaven. They had walls covered with windows of colorful stained glass, which let in beautiful light.

The renewed faith also led to war. In 1093, the Byzantine emperor asked for help against Muslim Turks who were threatening Constantinople, his capital. The pope urged the leaders of Western Europe to begin a holy war. He wanted Christians to gain control of Jerusalem and the entire Holy

Land. This was the first of several Crusades fought over the next 200 years. Rulers and the Church favored the Crusades because they sent warlike knights out of their lands. Common people joined the Crusades out of deep religious feeling.

The First Crusade, begun in 1096, was badly organized. Yet the Crusaders still captured some of the Holy Land, including Jerusalem. Muslims later won back some of this land, and other Crusades began to try to seize it again. Finally, a Fourth Crusade ended in disaster. The Western army attacked not the Muslims but the Byzantine Empire itself. In 1204, the Crusaders looted Constantinople. This helped make a lasting split between western and eastern Christian churches.

A later Crusade took place in Spain. Christian rulers tried to win back the land that Muslims had conquered in the 700s. This fight lasted from the 1100s until 1492, when the last Spanish Muslim land fell. Thousands of Jews had lived in Spanish Muslim lands. Many became Christians so that they could remain after the reconquest was completed.

The Crusades had many effects on Europe. The failure of later ones cut the power of the popes, and the deaths of many knights reduced the power of nobles. Contact with the East revived trade. However, the Christians' harsh treatment of Muslims in the Holy Land led to bitterness that has lasted to the present.

❷ Changes in Medieval Society

KEY IDEA *European cities challenged the feudal system as agriculture, trade, finance, and universities developed.*

At the same time, Europe enjoyed an improved food supply. The climate warmed between the years 800 and 1200, which helped farming. As farmers moved into areas that were once too cold, they also developed new ways of farming that produced better crops. One technique was to pull plows with horses that worked twice as fast as oxen. A new harness made the use of horses possible. Another new technique was a method of taking turns with the crops planted in an area. In the past, farmers had planted half their land and let the other half go unplanted each year. That prevented the soil from becoming overworked, but the new system was better. Farmers now planted two-thirds of their fields, leaving only one-third unplanted. This increased the amount of food they could grow.

Along with the growth in the food supply, trade and finance increased. Craft workers began to make goods that were sent all over Europe in trade. Fairs were held each year in towns, where merchants sold cloth, food, leather, and other goods.

Supporting the fairs were new organizations— the guilds. Guilds were formed in each town by the workers in the same craft, such as cloth makers, bakers, or glass makers. Members set standards for their products and set fair prices. They also made rules for how young people could enter the craft.

With more trade, merchants needed more cash. They had to borrow money to buy goods to sell. Christians didn't lend money because the Church had rules against charging a fee for loaning money. So, because Jews were outside the Christian Church, they became the chief sources of loans. Later, the Church relaxed its rules, and Christians began to form banks.

In the early 1100s, the population of western Europe grew rapidly. Towns grew larger and more important. Towns were dirty places, with narrow filthy streets. Built entirely of wood, they were fire hazards. Still, many peasants fled to the towns because, by living there a year and a day, they became free—no longer subject to the power of wealthy lords. Wealthier people in the towns fought for—and won—the right not to pay taxes to lords and to govern themselves.

Growing trade and wealth helped lead to a growing interest in learning. Many towns developed schools linked to the cathedrals, which taught religion and church law. These were called universities. Several writers also began to write in their native languages—not Latin, but English or Italian—producing great works of literature that many people still enjoy today.

Helping this new interest in learning was the contact with Muslims brought about by the Crusades. Muslim scholars had preserved books from ancient Rome and Greece, which came back

to Europe in this period. Christian thinkers became influenced by the thinking of these ancients. They tried to bring together the logic of old thinkers with the teachings of the Church.

❸ England and France Develop

KEY IDEA   As the kingdoms of England and France began to develop into nations, certain democratic traditions evolved.

England was formed by the blending of cultures. Danish Vikings came to the island in the 800s, uniting with the Anglo-Saxons who had come there from Germany hundreds of years earlier. Over time, these peoples became one kingdom. In 1066, the king died, and the duke of a land in northern France invaded and won control of the island. William the Conqueror, as he was called, declared England to be all his.

Later English kings, descendants of William, tried to expand the amount of land they still held in France. They also wanted to increase their control over the government. Henry II, who ruled from 1154 to 1189, was one of the strongest of these kings. He married Eleanor of Aquitaine, thus gaining control of more of France. At home, he began the practice of trial by jury.

One of Henry's sons, King John, had serious problems. Lack of money and his own harsh rule led nobles to rebel against him. They forced John to sign a paper called the Magna Carta that put limits on the power of the king. The document protected the power only of nobles, but later common people said that the protections applied to them as well. Another step toward limiting the king came in the 1200s. Edward I hoped to raise taxes to pay for a war in France. He called a meeting of representatives to approve his tax plan. His Model Parliament was famous because for the first time it included not only bishops and nobles but also common people from the towns.

In France, a new dynasty of kings, the Capetians, ruled from 987 to 1328. France was split into 30 separate small territories, each ruled by a different lord. The kings—who held only a small area centered in Paris—tried to gain control of all of the land.

One of the most successful kings was Philip II, who ruled from 1180 to 1223. He tripled the lands under his control, in part by seizing the French land held by the English King John. He also made a stronger central government, giving the king more control over his subjects. His grandson, Louis IX, ruled from 1226 to 1270, and carried on Philip's work. Louis set up royal courts where people could appeal decisions made by their lords. This increased the king's power. In 1302, Philip IV called for a meeting of the kingdom's most important groups. He, like Edward in England, invited commoners to this meeting of the Estates General, as the assembly was called.

❹ The Hundred Years' War and the Plague

KEY IDEA During the 1300s, Europe was torn apart by religious strife, the bubonic plague, and the Hundred Years' War.

In 1300, the pope challenged Philip IV of France, claiming to have supreme authority over the king. Philip held the pope as a prisoner for trial. He was rescued but died shortly thereafter. The king forced the election of a French cardinal as pope, and in 1305 the new pope moved to a city in France, to lead the Church from there. This action weakened the Church. In 1378 the French pope at that time died. An Italian was elected the next pope, but the French elected their own pope. Confusion resulted. Church officials had two popes—one in France and one in Rome. The situation, called the Great Schism, lasted 39 years.

At the same time, the pope's authority was being challenged. The English scholar John Wycliffe and the Bohemian John Huss argued that the Bible alone was the final authority for Christian teaching—not the pope.

People of the late 1300s experienced an even more severe shock. A fearful disease—the bubonic plague—swept across Europe starting in 1347 and lasting for decades. The disease killed millions of people—about one-third of the population of Europe.

The plague had a serious effect on Europe's economy. Trade declined, prices rose, and towns became smaller. Fewer people meant fewer workers. Peasants demanded wages or their freedom. When nobles resisted these demands, peasants often revolted. The Church lost prestige, as it was unable to stop the plague. The plague helped bring about the end of the Middle Ages.

A century-long war contributed as well. When the last Capetian king of France died in 1328, he left no heir. Edward III of England claimed the throne—he was a grandson of Philip IV of France. In 1337, he began a war, known as the Hundred Years' War, to win France.

English forces won three important battles. At one, their archers used longbows to launch arrows that destroyed the French troops—even armored knights. By 1429, the French were in desperate shape. Their army held the town of Orléans, which the English were about to capture. A teenage girl named Joan of Arc arrived on the scene. Convinced by voices of the saints that she could save the day, she persuaded French leaders to allow her to lead the army of France, which was victorious. With that, the French crowned a new king, Charles VII. Later, Joan of Arc was captured by English allies, turned over to the English, tried, and burned at the stake.

The Hundred Years' War finally ended in 1453. It had been fought mostly in France and brought much suffering to that nation. However, the war produced a strong national feeling in both England and France, a sense that the king was not just a feudal lord but also the leader of a nation. The English king's constant need for money led him to ask Parliament many times for taxes. This increased the power of Parliament.

Review

1. ***Determining Main Ideas*** How was the renewed religious feeling of the Middle Ages shown?
2. ***Analyzing Causes and Recognizing Effects*** What were the effects of the Crusades?
Clarifying
3. What social, economic, and cultural changes took place in the Middle Ages?
4. What changes occurred in England and France in the Middle Ages?
5. ***Forming and Supporting Opinions*** Which of the three problems that affected Europe—the Great Schism, the bubonic plague, or the Hundred Years' War—do you think was worst, and why?

The Formation of Western Europe, 800–1500

Responses will vary but should include points similar to the following:

1. the founding of new monasteries and reform in the Church, the building of magnificent cathedrals, and the launching of the Crusades

2. The Crusades resulted in the decline in prestige of the pope and nobles, a revival of trade, and bitterness felt by Muslims toward Christians.

3. In the late Middle Ages, improvements in farming led to more food being grown, which helped revive trade. Other changes included an increase in the use of money, the growth of towns and guilds, the weakening of manors, and the rise of universities.

4. In England and France, the central governments won more power, but some institutions arose that gave the people power as well.

5. Possible response: The bubonic plague was the worst because it resulted in the death of so many people, ended the economic revival of Europe, and contributed to the loss of prestige of the Church.

CHAPTER

15

Summary

CHAPTERS IN BRIEF *Societies and Empires of Africa, 800–1500*

CHAPTER OVERVIEW In north and central Africa, people lived by hunting and gathering. Later followers of Islam built states that joined religious and political power. In West Africa, empires built on wealth from trade rose and fell. In East Africa, a blend of African and Muslim cultures created several cities that enjoyed thriving trade. In Southern Africa, one trading empire gave way to another.

❶ North and Central African Societies

KEY IDEA North and central Africa developed hunting-gathering societies, stateless societies, and Muslim states.

People in early African societies began to get food by hunting and gathering. Some societies today use these methods as well. Scholars study them to obtain clues about the lives of people in the past. They recognize, though, that there is no exact relationship between how people lived then and now.

The Efe, who live in the rain forest of central Africa, are one group of hunter-gatherers that are studied. They live in groups of between 10 and 100 people, all being related to one another. Each family lives in its own shelter, made of grass and brush. They keep few possessions so that they can move often in the search for food.

Women perform the work of gathering. They travel through the forest looking for roots, yams, mushrooms, and seeds. Men and older boys do the hunting, killing small antelopes or monkeys. The group is led by an older male, but he does not give orders or act like a chief. Each family makes its own decisions, but they do ask the leader for his advice.

These African societies are organized along family ties. Families, however, are understood in broader terms than simply parents and children. Societies trace their families in terms of lineages, counting as related all people who share a common ancestor. The lineage includes not just living members but those born in the past and those yet to be born. In some societies, lineages are traced through mothers and in others they are traced through fathers.

In many African societies, lineage groups took the place of rulers. These societies are called state-less societies because they do not have central governments. Authority in these societies was spread among more than one lineage to prevent any one family from dominating. Within these societies, people use discussion to settle conflicts between groups.

Some African societies also have another set of relationships important to people. Children of similar ages form into groups called age sets. All members of the age set take part in ceremonies. These signal the movement from one stage of life to the next.

An important influence on the history of Africa was Islam, which arrived in the continent in the late 600s. By 670, Muslims ruled Egypt and most of North Africa. In their new states, the ruler served as both political and religious leader. The Islamic tradition of obeying the law helped promote order and support the government. The common influence of Islamic law also forged bonds between the different North African states.

Among the North Africans who converted to Islam were a group called the Berbers. In the 11th century, a group of Berbers became strongly committed to spreading Islam. They were called the Almoravids. They conquered modern Morocco around 1060, the empire of Ghana by 1076, and parts of Spain.

They were displaced in the 1100s by another group of Berbers, the Almohads. They arose in the Atlas Mountains of Morocco and opposed the Almoravids. They said Almoravids no longer followed strict Muslim teaching. Almohads, too, captured Morocco and then Spain. They extended their power as far east as the cities of Tripoli and Tunis. Within about 100 years, this empire broke up into smaller states.

❷ West African Civilizations

KEY IDEA *West Africa contained several powerful empires and states, including Ghana, Mali, and Songhai.*

Trade was conducted across the vast Sahara Desert of North Africa as early as A.D. 200, but it was not regular. The pack animals of the time—oxen, donkeys, and horses—could not travel far in the desert. Then Berbers began using camels. Since these animals were ideally suited to dry conditions, trade became regular and frequent.

By the 700s, the rulers of the kingdom of Ghana were growing rich. They taxed the goods that traders carried through their land. The two most important trade goods were gold and salt. Gold was taken from deep mines or from streams in the western and southern parts of West Africa. The people there were eager to trade for salt from the Sahara region. Arab traders brought cloth and manufactured goods from the cities on the Mediterranean Sea to the north.

The king of Ghana made sure that the price of gold stayed high. Only the king could own gold nuggets. As religious and military leader, as well as head of the government, the king was powerful. By the year 800, Ghana had become an empire, controlling the people of different regions nearby.

Over time, Muslim merchants and traders brought their religion to Ghana. By the 1000s, the kings converted to Islam and began to use Muslims as advisers. Many common people in the empire, though, stayed with their traditional beliefs. Later, Ghana fell to the Almoravids of North Africa. After that, Ghana never regained its former power.

By 1235, a new kingdom began—Mali. It arose south of Ghana, but its wealth and power was also based on the gold trade. Founder of the kingdom was Sundiata, who became the first emperor. After winning a series of battles, he set up a well-organized government to run his kingdom.

Later Mali rulers adopted Islam. One of them was Mansa Musa. He used his skill in leading an army to make Mali twice the size of the old empire of Ghana. To rule this large empire, he named governors to head several provinces. Mansa Musa was a devoted Muslim. He had new mosques, or houses of worship, built in two cities. One of those cities, Timbuktu, became known as a leading center of Muslim learning. A later traveler to the area named Ibn Battuta described how peaceful Mali was. Mali, though, declined in the 1400s and was replaced by another empire that grew wealthy from gold.

The next trading empire was Songhai, and it was farther to the east than Mali. It arose in the 1400s when Sunni Ali used river canoes and horses to strike quickly. He gained control of new areas—including the city of Timbuktu. He was followed by Askia Muhammad. He was a Muslim with a deep sense of religious feeling who was determined to run the empire in the way of Islam. The Songhai Empire fell, however, because other people had stronger weapons. In 1591, a Moroccan army used gunpowder and cannons to beat a Songhai army that had only swords and spears. This defeat ended the period when empires controlled West Africa.

In other parts of West Africa, people gathered in city-states that remained independent of these empires. In what is today northern Nigeria, the Hausa people built city-states between the years 1000 and 1200. They depended on the food raised by farmers and on trade in salt, grain, and cotton cloth. One city-state also traded people as slaves. No one city was powerful enough to control its neighbors for long.

In the southern part of Nigeria and modern Benin another people arose—the Yoruba. They lived in smaller communities that survived by farming. Some of these villages were joined together in small kingdoms. The people believed that the kings were gods. Kings surrounded themselves with a large court of musicians, magicians, and soldiers. At the same time, a secret society of religious and political leaders reviewed the king's actions and limited his power. Two powerful Yoruba kingdoms were called Ife and Oyo. Ife lasted from 1100 until the late 1600s, when Oyo arose. Both were centered in cities with high walls, and both were supported by highly productive farms. Ife had skilled artists who produced work in ivory, wood, pottery, bronze, brass, and copper.

To the south and west was another kingdom, Benin. The kingdom arose in the 1300s and reached its peak of power 100 years later. At that time, King Ewuare extended his control over an area from the delta of the Niger River as far east as the modern city of Lagos, Nigeria. He made Benin City, his capital, stronger by building high walls. He also built a huge palace full of works of art. In the 1480s, ships from Portugal arrived in the major port of Benin to trade. Their arrival marked the beginning of a long period of European interference in the history of Africa.

❸ Eastern City-States and Southern Empires

KEY IDEA *From 1000 to 1500, East African city-states and southern African empires gained wealth and power through trade.*

The east coast of Africa became an area marked by a blend of cultures. Africans speaking Bantu languages moved to the area from central Africa. Arab and Persian Muslims came from the north and east to make trading contacts. These peoples created a new blended language called Swahili. It became common in the port cities of the east coast of Africa.

The Persian and Arab traders brought porcelain bowls from China and jewels and cotton cloth from India. They bought ivory, gold, tortoise shells, and other goods in Africa to take back to Asia. By 1300, this thriving trade took place in more than 35 cities on the coast. Some cities became centers for manufactured goods, such as weaving and the making of iron tools.

One of the richest of these trading ports was Kilwa. It was located to the south—as far south as traders could reach from India and return in the same season. Thus all trade goods from farther south had to come through Kilwa. In 1488, though, the situation changed. Ships arrived on the east coast of Africa from Portugal. Portuguese sailors were looking for a route to India to join in the trade for spices and other goods desired in Europe. Soon the Portuguese used their cannon power to attack Kilwa and other trading centers in Africa. They burned parts of some cities and took control of others. For the next two centuries, the Portuguese remained a powerful force in the region.

On the east coast of Africa, as in West Africa, the growing contract with Muslim traders resulted in the adoption of Islam. A sultan, or governor, ruled each city. Most government officials and wealthy merchants were Muslims. As in West Africa, though, most common people kept their traditional beliefs.

Along with trade goods, the Muslim traders also engaged in the trade of human slaves. Enslaved persons did household tasks in such areas as Arabia and Persia. Some were sent to India to be used as soldiers. This slave trade was not large, however. Only about 1,000 people a year were traded as slaves. The later European-run slave trade was much broader.

In southern Africa, a great city-state arose in the 1000s. The Shona people lived in rich land, where they grew crops and raised cattle. Their city, called Great Zimbabwe, had a good location. It linked the gold fields inland with the trading cities on the coast. From the 1200s through the 1400s, the city controlled this trade and grew wealthy. Around 1450, though, the people left the city, although no one knows why. One explanation is that overuse had destroyed the grasslands, soil, and timber. It is thought the area could no longer support a large population. Acres of ruins remain as silent reminders of the past of Zimbabwe. They include stone buildings and a high wall carved with figures of birds.

Heir to Great Zimbabwe was the Mutapa Empire. It began around 1420 when a man named Mutota left the area and moved farther north looking for salt. He and his successors took control of a large area—almost all of the land of the modern country of Zimbabwe. This empire gained wealth from the gold in its land. The rulers forced people they had conquered to mine their gold, which they then sold on the coast. The southern region of the empire formed its own kingdom. In the 1500s, the Portuguese moved in. They tried to defeat the empire but could not. Later, through trickery, they gained control of the government.

Review

1. ***Comparing and Contrasting*** How did social groupings in north and central African societies differ from that of American society today?
2. ***Drawing Conclusions*** What religion had influence throughout Africa? Did that influence extend to all levels of society?
3. ***Determining Main Ideas*** What common feature linked the kingdoms and empires of West Africa?
4. ***Developing Historical Perspective*** How does Swahili symbolize the blending of cultures in East Africa?
5. ***Analyzing Causes and Recognizing Effects*** How did location add to the power of Kilwa?

Answer Key
Chapter 15
SUMMARY

Societies and Empires of Africa, 800–1500

Responses will vary but should include points similar to the following:

1. North and central African societies included family relationships based on lineages, or all the people descended from a common ancestor and age sets, which were all people of a similar age.

2. Islam was adopted by ruling peoples in North, West, and East Africa, but it did not go very deeply as many common people in these areas retained traditional beliefs.

3. The kingdoms and empires of West Africa gained their wealth through trade, especially of gold.

4. Swahili was a blend of languages of African and Muslim peoples, just as the culture of East Africa was a blend of these cultures.

5. Kilwa was the farthest south that traders could come from India and return in the same season. Thus all trade from southern Africa to Asia had to reach that port for sale to Asian merchants.

CHAPTERS IN BRIEF *People and Empires in the Americas, 500–1500*

CHAPTER 16

Summary

CHAPTER OVERVIEW Native North Americans followed several ways of life. Yet, they shared trade links and religious and social practices. The Maya of Central America developed a complex civilization of independent city-states. The Aztec of Mexico had a huge empire, but their harsh rule over conquered people caused bitterness. The Inca of South America built a vast empire in the Andes Mountains.

❶ North American Societies

KEY IDEA Complex North American societies were linked to each other through culture and economics.

Between about 40,000 and 12,000 years ago, hunter-gatherers moved from Asia to North America. (At that time the two continents had a land connection.) These were the first Americans, and they spread down throughout North and South America. They followed many different ways of life, each suited to the environment in which they lived.

The peoples of the Pacific Northwest, from modern Oregon to Alaska, lived in an area with many resources. They hunted whales in the sea and gathered food from the forests on the coast.

The peoples of the Southwest lived in a more difficult region. Still, they began farming the land. The Anasazi built cliff dwellings. Later, they built large apartment-style compounds. They used stone and clay baked in the sun for these buildings. They used irrigation to bring water to their crops. Later peoples living in this area continued the traditions of the Anasazi.

In the woods east of the Mississippi River, another culture arose. These people are called the Mound Builders. They built large mounds of earth that were filled with copper and stone objects. Some mounds were made in the shape of animals when seen from above. The Mississippians were a people who lived later in this area. They built a small city that was the center for their culture. It had a flat-topped pyramid with a temple on top.

The peoples of the eastern woodlands had many different cultures and spoke many different languages. They often fought over control of land. Some groups formed alliances to put an end to this fighting. The most successful of these was the Iroquois League, which linked together five different tribes in upper New York.

While these North American groups had many differences, they had some features in common, too. Trade linked people of all regions of North America. Religious ideas were similar across the continent as well. Nearly all native North Americans thought that the world was full of spirits and that people had to follow certain rituals and customs to live in peace. They also shared great respect for the land, which they did not believe that people could own. They also shared an emphasis on the family as the most important social unit. Family included parents, children, grandparents, and other relatives. In some tribes, families were linked together with others who shared a common ancestor. These larger groups, called clans, were identified with something in nature, such as an animal, called totems.

❷ Maya Kings and Cities

KEY IDEA The Maya developed a highly complex civilization based on city-states controlled by dynasties of kings.

A great civilization arose in what is today southern Mexico and northern Central America. This was the Maya civilization, and it appeared around A.D. 250. In their Classic Period—from 250 to 900—the Maya built large cities such as Tikal, Copán, and others. Each city was independent and ruled by a god-king. Each city was both a religious center and a trade center for the area around it. These cities were large, holding tens of thousands of people, and were full of palaces, temples, and pyramids. Archaeologists have found at least 50 Maya cities.

Trade linked these many cities. Among the trade goods were salt, flint, feathers, shells, cotton cloth, and ornaments made of jade. Cacao beans—which are used to make chocolate—were sometimes used as money. Farming of maize, or corn, beans, and squash provided the Maya's main source of food. Maya society was divided into social classes. The best warriors and priests were at the top, followed by merchants and craft workers. Peasant farmers—the majority of the people—were at the bottom.

The Maya had a complex religion that was the center of their society. There were many gods, including one for each day. The actions of the day's god could be predicted, they thought, by following a calendar. The Maya sometimes cut themselves to offer their blood to the gods in sacrifice. Sometimes they killed enemies and sacrificed them.

To understand their gods, the Maya developed knowledge of mathematics, calendars, and astronomy. Maya math included the idea of zero, which was used to help make calendars. They had two calendars, a religious one that had thirteen 20-day months and one based on the sun that had eighteen 20-day months. They linked the two together to identify days that would bring good fortune. Maya astronomy was very accurate. The Maya observed the sun, moon, and stars to make their calendars as accurate as possible. They calculated the length of the solar year—the time it takes the earth to revolve around the sun—almost perfectly.

In the late 800s, the Maya began to decline. Historians do not know why. One explanation may be growing war between the different city-states, which drove many people out of the cities into the jungle. Another may be that the soil became less productive due to intensive farming over a long time. Whatever the cause, the Maya became a less powerful people. They continued to live in the area, but their cities were no longer the thriving trade and religious centers they had been.

❸ The Aztecs Control Central Mexico

KEY IDEA *Through alliances and conquest, the Aztecs created a powerful empire in Mexico.*

The Valley of Mexico is a mountain valley more than a mile above sea level. Full of lakes and fertile soil, it was a good place for people to settle. In this area, an early city-state called Teotihaucán ("City of the Gods") arose in the first century A.D. At its peak in the sixth century, the city had as many as 200,000 people, many of whom were involved in the trade of obsidian. This hard green or black volcanic glass was found nearby and could be used to make very sharp weapons. In the city was the huge Pyramid of the Sun, larger at its base than the largest pyramid of Egypt. By 750, Teotihuacán was abandoned for reasons that are not clear.

The next people to dominate the area were the Toltecs, who rose to power around 900 and ruled over central Mexico for about 300 years. The Toltecs worshiped a fierce war god. They were very warlike and based their empire on conquest. Around 1000, a ruler named Topiltzin encouraged the Toltec people to worship a peaceful god, Quetzalcoatl. Followers of the war god rebelled, however, and drove Topiltzin away. In time, Topiltzin and Quetzalcoatl became one in the legends of the people of the Valley of Mexico. According to these legends, he would return one day, bringing a new reign of light and peace. The legend of Quetzalcoatl lived on in central Mexico for centuries.

Around 1200, as the Toltecs were losing control of the region, another people arrived on the scene—the Aztecs. The Aztecs founded a city and grew in power. By the early 1500s, they controlled a large empire that included somewhere between 5 and 15 million people. This empire was based on military conquest and collecting tribute from conquered peoples.

Military leaders, who owned huge amounts of land, led the Aztec nation along with government officials and priests. Below them were commoners—merchants, craft workers, soldiers, and farmers who owned their land. At the bottom of society were the slaves taken as captives in battle. At the top was the emperor, who was treated as a god as well as a ruler.

The capital city—Tenochtitlán—was built on an island in a lake. The Aztecs made long causeways to connect the city to the land. The city was large, with between 200,000 and 400,000 people. It was well-planned and had a huge government and religious complex at its center.

Religion played a major role in Aztec society. Their cities held many temples built for the different gods they believed in. Priests led rituals, and the most important was for the sun god. Priests had to make the sacrifice of human blood to ensure that the sun god was happy and the sun would rise every day. People taken captive in war were sacrificed. So the need for a steady supply of victims helped push the Aztecs to fight their neighbors.

When Montezuma II became emperor in 1502, the Aztec empire began to have problems. The Aztecs ordered the other peoples they had conquered to hand over even more people for sacrifice. These other peoples finally rebelled against the Aztecs. In the midst of this conflict, the Spanish arrived and made first contact with the Aztecs. Some Aztecs saw the Spaniards' arrival as the legendary return of Quetzalcoatl.

❹ The Inca Create a Mountain Empire

KEY IDEA *The Inca built a vast empire supported by taxes, governed by a bureaucracy, and linked by extensive road systems.*

Another great civilization—the Inca—arose in the Andes Mountains of South America. It was built on the foundations made by several earlier cultures. This culture, though, united much of the Andes under one rule.

The Inca first settled in the Valley of Cuzco, in modern Peru. It had a kingdom there by the 1200s. They believed that their ruler was related to the sun god, who would bring wealth and power to them. Only men from one of 11 noble families could serve as king.

In 1438, Pachacuti became the ruler of the Inca, and he launched a campaign of conquest that expanded the empire's size. By 1500, the Inca ruled an empire that stretched along the Andes Mountains from modern Ecuador all the way south to Chile and Argentina. It held about 16 million people. The empire did not grow only through military conquest. Often the Inca offered new peoples the chance to join the empire peacefully as long as they swore loyalty to the emperor. Many peoples became part of the empire in this way. When force was needed, though, the Inca were fierce fighters.

The Inca had a very organized system for the government of their empire. Families were placed in groups of 10, 100, 1,000, and so on. Each group was led by a chief. The Inca usually let local rulers stay in place when they conquered a people—as long as the ruler and the people met key Inca demands. The most important was the need for all adult workers to spend some days each year working for the state. They might work on state farms or state building programs.

The Inca built a complex network of roads to link all parts of the empire. The Inca also built all government buildings in the same style to create a common identity for the government throughout the empire. They made all people speak a common language—the Inca tongue, called Quechua.

The Inca controlled the economy, telling people what to grow or make and how it would be distributed. They used irrigation to ensure that farmlands got enough water. They also found a way to freeze-dry potatoes—a staple crop—for times when food was scarce. The government also took care of people who needed help, such as the very old or ill.

In spite of all these advances, the Inca never developed a system of writing. All records were kept in peoples' memories. They did have a system of counting. They also had day and night calendars for information about their gods.

The Inca religion played a central role in Inca life. They believed in fewer gods than the peoples of Mexico. The most important of them were the creator god and the sun god. Cuzco, the capital, was the most important religious center. It was decorated with gold and other precious objects.

Review

1. ***Clarifying*** What divided and what linked native North Americans?
2. ***Determining Main Ideas*** What Maya cultural advances were connected to their religious beliefs? Why?
3. ***Comparing and Contrasting*** Compare and contrast the Maya and the Aztec in terms of government.
4. ***Drawing Conclusions*** Were the Aztec people good engineers? Explain your answer.
5. ***Summarizing*** What steps did the Inca take to unify the different peoples in their empire?

Answer Key
Chapter 16
SUMMARY

People and Empires in the Americas, 900–1500

Responses will vary but should include points similar to the following:

1. Native North Americans were divided by their ways of life, which were adapted to their particular environments, but they were linked by trade, by religious beliefs, and by social practices.

2. Maya advances in mathematics, calendar-making, and astronomy were all connected to their religious beliefs. They used them to try to understand and predict the behavior of their gods.

3. The Maya had independent city-states. The Aztec had a tightly controlled empire that required conquered peoples to pay tribute.

4. The Aztec peoples must have been skillful engineers since they built their city on a lake.

5. To unify their empire, the Inca built a road system, built government buildings using the same style, required people to speak the same language, and kept tight control of economic life.

CHAPTER

17

Summary

European Renaissance and Reformation, 1300–1600

CHAPTER OVERVIEW *In the 1300s, a renewed interest in classical learning and the arts arose in Italy. Thinkers in northern Europe adopted these ideas as well but with a spiritual focus. The desire for a more satisfying spiritual life led some to revolt against the Catholic Church, as new churches were founded. In response, the Catholic Church undertook some reforms of its own, strengthening the faith.*

❶ Italy: Birthplace of the Renaissance

KEY IDEA *The European Renaissance, a rebirth of learning and the arts, began in Italy in the 1300s.*

The years 1300 to 1600 saw a rebirth of learning and culture in Europe. Called the Renaissance, it spread north from Italy. It began there for three reasons. First, Italy had several important cities, whereas most of northern Europe was still rural. Second, these cities included a class of merchants and bankers who were becoming wealthy and powerful. Third, Italian artists and scholars were inspired by the ruined buildings and other reminders of classical Rome.

That new interest in the classical past led to an important value in Renaissance culture—humanism. This was a deep interest in what people have already achieved as well as what they could achieve in the future. Scholars did not try to connect classical writings to Christian teaching but tried to understand them on their own terms. Renaissance thinkers stressed the things of the world. In the Middle Ages, the emphasis had been mostly on spiritual values. One way that powerful or wealthy people showed this interest in worldly things was by paying artists, writers, and musicians to create beautiful works of art.

Men tried to show that they could master many fields of study or work. Someone who succeeded in many fields was admired greatly. The artist Leonardo da Vinci was an example of this ideal. He was a painter, a scientist, and an inventor. Men were expected to be charming, witty, well-educated, well-mannered, athletic, and self-controlled. Women were expected not to create art but to inspire artists.

Renaissance artists sometimes used new methods. Sculptors made figures more realistic than those from the Middle Ages. Painters used perspective to create the illusion that their paintings

were three-dimensional. The subject of artwork changed also. Art in the Middle Ages was mostly religious, but Renaissance artists reproduced other views of life. Michelangelo showed great skill as an architect, a sculptor, and a painter.

Renaissance writers reached high achievements as well. Several wrote in their native languages, whereas most writing in the Middle Ages had been in Latin. Writers also changed their subject matter. They wrote to express their own thoughts and feelings or to portray in detail an individual. Dante and others wrote poetry, letters, and stories that were self-expressive and more realistic. Niccolò Machiavelli took a new approach to understanding government. He focused on telling rulers how to expand their power, even if that meant taking steps that the Church might view as evil.

❷ The Northern Renaissance

KEY IDEA *In the 1400s, northern Europeans began to adopt the ideas of the Renaissance.*

By 1450, the bubonic plague had ended in northern Europe and the population was recovering. Also, the Hundred Years' War between France and England was ending. The suffering caused by these two events was fading, and the new ideas from Italy spread to northern Europe, where they were quickly adopted. The northern Renaissance had a difference, however. While the educated people there became interested in classical learning, they were more likely to combine that with interest in religious ideas.

Major artists appeared in parts of Germany, France, Belgium, and the Netherlands. The use of oil-based paints became popular. Dürer painted religious subjects and realistic landscapes. Holbein, van Eyck, and Bruegel painted lifelike portraits and scenes of peasant life. They revealed much about the times.

The new ideas of Italian art moved to the north, where artists began to use them. Painters in Flanders were deeply interested in showing life in realistic ways. They painted members of the rising merchant class and peasants, revealing much about life of the period. One pioneered in the use of oil-based paints.

Writers of the northern Renaissance combined humanism with deep Christian faith. They urged reforms in the Church and society to try to make people more devoted to God and more just. Thomas More wrote a book about an imaginary ideal society where greed, war, and conflict did not exist.

William Shakespeare is widely viewed as the greatest playwright of all time. His plays showed a brilliant command of the English language and a deep understanding of people and how they interact with one another.

One reason that learning spread so rapidly during the Renaissance was the invention of movable type. The Chinese had invented the process of carving characters onto wooden blocks. They then arranged them in words, inked the blocks, and pressed them against paper to print pages. In 1440, a German, Johann Gutenberg, adopted this practice. He produced his first book—a Bible—in 1455. The technology then spread rapidly. By 1500, presses in Europe had printed nearly 10 million books.

Printing made it easier to make many copies of a book. As a result, written works became available far and wide. Fewer books were printed in Latin, and more books were printed in languages such as English, French, Spanish, Italian, or German. As a result, more people began to read the Bible on their own. Some formed ideas about Christianity that differed from those of the Church.

❸ Luther Leads the Reformation

KEY IDEA *Martin Luther's protest over abuses in the Catholic Church led to the founding of Protestant churches.*

By 1500, Renaissance values emphasizing the individual and worldly life weakened the influence of the Church. At the same time, many people sharply criticized the Church for some of its practices. Popes seemed more concerned with luxury and political power than with spiritual matters. Critics resented the fact that they paid taxes to support the Church in Rome. The lower clergy had

faults. Many local priests lacked education and couldn't teach people. Others took actions that broke their vows as priests.

In the past, reformers had urged that the Church change its ways to become more spiritual and humble. Christian humanists such as Erasmus and More added their voices to calls for change. In the early 1500s, the calls grew louder.

In 1517, a German monk and professor named Martin Luther protested some actions of a Church official. That person was selling what were called indulgences. By paying money to the Church, people thought they could win salvation. Luther challenged this practice and others. He posted a written protest on the door of a castle church. His words were quickly printed and began to spread throughout Germany. Thus began the Reformation, the movement for reform that led to the founding of new Christian churches.

Soon Luther pushed for broader changes. He said that people could win salvation only through faith, not good works. He said that religious beliefs should be based on the Bible alone and that the pope had no real authority. He said that each person was equal before God. He or she did not need a priest to explain the Bible to them.

The pope punished Luther for his views, but he refused to take them back. The Holy Roman Emperor, a strong Catholic, called Luther an outlaw. His books were to be burned. No one was to shelter him. Meanwhile, many of his ideas were being put into practice. The Lutheran Church was born around 1522.

In 1524, peasants in Germany hoped to use Luther's ideas to change society. They demanded an end to serfdom—a condition like slavery. When it was not granted, they revolted. Luther disagreed with this revolt, and the German princes killed thousands in putting the revolt down. Some nobles supported Luther because they saw a chance to weaken the emperor's power. German princes joined forces against Luther. Some princes protested this. War broke out between Catholics and these Protestant forces in Germany. It finally ended in 1555 with the Peace of Augsburg. That treaty granted each prince the right to decide whether his subjects would be Catholic or Protestant.

The Catholic Church faced another challenge to its power in England. Henry VIII, the king, was married to a princess of Spain. She had borne him a daughter, but he wanted a son. This could prevent a civil war erupting when he died. His wife was too old to have another child, but the pope refused to grant him a divorce. In 1534, Henry had the English Parliament pass a number of laws that took England out of the Catholic Church. The laws made the king or queen, not the pope, head of the Church of England. Henry remarried four times, gaining his only son from his third wife.

One of Henry's daughters, Elizabeth, became queen in 1558 and completed the task of creating a separate English church. New laws gave the new religion some traits that would appeal to both Protestants and Catholics. In this way, Elizabeth hoped to end religious conflict in England.

❹ The Reformation Continues

KEY IDEA *John Calvin and other Reformation leaders began new Protestant churches. The Catholic Church also made reforms.*

Protestantism arose elsewhere in the 1530s under the leadership of John Calvin. Calvin wrote an important book that gave structure to Protestant beliefs. He taught that people are sinful by nature and only those God chooses—"the elect"—will be saved. He said that God knew from the beginning which people would be saved and which would not.

Calvin created a government run by religious leaders in a city in Switzerland. The city had strict rules of behavior that urged people to live deeply religious lives. Anyone who preached different religious ideas might be burned at the stake.

A preacher named John Knox was impressed by Calvin's high moral ideals. Knox put these ideas into practice in Scotland. This was the beginning of the Presbyterian Church. Others in Switzerland, Holland, and France adopted Calvin's ideas as well. In France, his followers were called Huguenots. Conflict between them and Catholics often turned to violence. In 1572, mobs killed about 12,000 Huguenots. Another Protestant church that arose was the Anabaptists. They preached that people should be baptized into the faith as adults. They influenced some later groups.

Protestant churches grew, but millions remained true to the Catholic faith. Still, the Catholic Church took steps to reform itself. A Spanish noble named Ignatius founded a new group in the Church based on deep devotion to Jesus. Members started schools across Europe. They tried to convert people to Catholicism who were not Christians. In addition, they tried to stop the spread of Protestant faiths in Europe.

Two popes of the 1500s helped bring about changes in the Church. Paul III took several steps, including calling a great council of church leaders at Trent, in northern Italy. The council, which met in 1545, passed these doctrines:

- the Church's interpretation of the Bible was final;
- Christians needed good works as well as faith to win salvation;
- the Bible and the Church had equal authority in setting out Christian beliefs; and
- indulgences could be sold.

Paul also put in action a kind of court called the Inquisition. It was charged with finding, trying, and punishing people who broke the rules of the Church. His successor, Paul IV, put these policies into practice. These actions helped revive the Church and allowed it to survive the challenge of the Protestants.

Review

1. *Analyzing Causes and Recognizing Effects* Why did the Renaissance arise in Italy?
2. *Making Inferences* Why do you think that a person who is accomplished in many fields is called a "Renaissance" man or woman?
3. *Contrasting* How did the northern Renaissance differ from the Italian Renaissance?
4. *Drawing Conclusions* What role did political concerns play in the Reformation?
5. *Forming and Supporting Opinions* Which leader—Calvin or Luther—do you think had a greater impact? Explain why.

Answer Key
Chapter 17
SUMMARY

European Renaissance and Reformation, 1300–1600

Responses will vary but should include points similar to the following:

1. The Renaissance arose in Italy because of the strong element of city life, the merchants who had wealth and power, and the presence of reminders of ancient classical heritage.

2. Such a person is called a "Renaissance" man or woman because to be accomplished in many fields was an ideal of the Renaissance.

3. The northern Renaissance was more interested in spiritual matters along with classical studies than was the Italian Renaissance.

4. Some German princes backed Luther's ideas because they wanted to weaken the power of the emperor, who was Catholic. Also, Henry VIII's desire to have a son—and avoid a possible civil war—led to the break between the English church and Catholicism.

5. Luther launched the Reformation, but Calvin's ideas had impact on the Protestant churches of many different countries.

18

Summary

The Muslim World Expands, 1300–1700

CHAPTER OVERVIEW *A group of Turks called Ottomans set up a new empire in what is now modern Turkey. Farther to the east, the Safavid Empire arose in modern Iran, where rulers embraced a special type of Islam that made them different from their neighbors. Meanwhile, India saw the rise of yet another empire as Muslims created a powerful state there.*

❶ The Ottomans Build a Vast Empire

KEY IDEA *The Ottomans established a Muslim Empire that combined many cultures and lasted for more than 600 years.*

In 1300, the world of the eastern Mediterranean was seeing changes. The Byzantine Empire was fading. The Seljuk Turk state had been destroyed by the Mongols. Anatolia, the area of modern Turkey, was now inhabited by groups of nomadic Turks. They saw themselves as ghazis, or warriors for Islam. They formed military groups and raided the lands where non-Muslims lived.

The most successful ghazi was Osman. Western Europeans took his name to be Othman and called his followers Ottomans. Between 1300 and 1326, Osman built a strong but small kingdom in Anatolia. Leaders who came after Osman called themselves sultans, or "ones with power." They extended the kingdom by buying land, forming alliances with other chieftains, and conquering everyone they could. The military success of the Ottomans was aided by gunpowder—especially as used in cannons.

The Ottomans ruled kindly through local officials appointed by the sultan. Muslims had to serve in the army but paid no taxes. Non-Muslims paid the tax but did not have to serve in the army. Many joined Islam simply to avoid the tax. Most people in their empire adjusted quickly to their easy rule.

One warrior did not. Timur the Lame, called Tamerlane in the west, arose in central Asia. He claimed to be descended from Genghis Khan. The claim probably is not true—but he was as fierce as the Mongol conqueror. He conquered Russia and Persia, where he burned the city of Baghdad to the ground. In 1402, he defeated the Ottomans in battle and captured the sultan. Timur died three years later on his way to conquer China.

Back in Anatolia, the four sons of the last sultan fought for control of the empire. Mehmed I won

control, and his son and the four following sultans brought the Ottoman Empire to its greatest power. One of them—Mehmed II—took power in 1451 and captured Constantinople. At first, his ships were unable to sail near the city because barriers blocked the way. So he had his soldiers drag the ships over hills so they could be launched on another side of Constantinople. After several weeks of fighting, the Ottoman force was simply too strong for the tiny army left in the city. In 1453, Constantinople finally fell to the Ottomans. Mehmed made the city his capital, which was renamed Istanbul. The famous and beautiful church of the Hagia Sophia became a mosque. The rebuilt city became home to people from all over the Ottoman Empire.

Other emperors used conquest to make the empire grow. After 1514, Selim the Grim took Persia, Syria, and Palestine. He then captured Arabia, took the Muslim holy cities of Medina and Mecca, and gained control of Egypt.

His son, Suleyman I, brought the Ottoman Empire to its greatest size and most impressive achievements. He conquered parts of southeastern Europe by 1525. He won control of the entire eastern Mediterranean Sea and took North Africa as far west as Tripoli. Although he was defeated in a battle for Vienna in 1529, his Ottoman Empire remained huge.

Suleyman ruled his empire with a highly structured government. Serving the royal family and the government were thousands of slaves. Among them was an elite group of soldiers called janissaries. They were Christians taken as children and made slaves with personal loyalty to the sultan. They were trained as soldiers and fought fiercely for the sultan. Other slaves held important government jobs. The empire allowed people to follow their own religion. Jews and Christians were not mistreated by the Ottomans. Suleyman revised the laws of the empire, which won him the name Suleyman the Lawgiver. Suleyman also oversaw an empire that was full of accomplished works of art. Using an excellent architect, he built many fine buildings in his capital.

The empire lasted long after Suleyman but spent the next few hundred years in decline. None of the sultans were as accomplished as he had been, and the Ottoman Empire's power slipped.

❷ Cultural Blending Case Study: The Safavid Empire

KEY IDEA *Many world cultures incorporate influences from various peoples and traditions.*

Throughout history, different peoples have lived together, and their cultures have influenced one another. Often these people have blended one culture with another. This can be due to trade, conquest, movement of people from one area to another, or conversion to a new religion.

Changes often happen in places where cultural blending takes place. Changes in language, arts and architecture or religion are examples. For example in the Safavid empire the spoken language was Persian. But after Muslims came to live in the empire, Arabic words appeared in the Persian language.

Cultural blending took place in the Safavid Empire of Persia. The Safavids began as members of an Islamic group that claimed to be related to the prophet Muhammad. In the 1400s, they became allied with the Shi'a, a branch of Islam. The major group of Muslims, the Sunnis, persecuted the Shi'a for their views. The Safavids, fearing their strong neighbors who were Sunni Muslims, decided to build a strong army to protect themselves.

In 1499, a 14-year-old leader named Isma'il led this army to conquer Iran. He took the traditional Persian title of shah, or king, and made the new empire a state of Shi'a. He destroyed Baghdad's Sunni population. Ottoman Turk rulers—who were Sunni Muslims—in turn killed all the Shi'a that they met. This conflict between the two groups of Muslims continues today.

The Safavids reached their height in the late 1500s under Shah Abbas. He reformed the military, making two armies that were loyal to him and him alone. He also gave new weapons to the army to make them better fighters. He reformed the government, getting rid of corrupt officials. He also brought gifted artists to his empire, who helped make his capital and other cities very beautiful. In taking these steps, Shah Abbas drew on good ideas from other cultures. He used Chinese artists and enjoyed good relations with nations of Europe. Through this contact, the demand for Persian rugs increased greatly in Europe. In this period, rug-making, which had simply been a local craft in Persia, was changed into a major industry for the country.

As with the Ottoman Empire, the Safavid Empire began to decline soon after it had reached its greatest height. Shah Abbas had killed or injured his most talented sons—just as Suleiman had done—fearing that they would seize power from him. As a result, a weak and ineffective grandson became shah after him. Under his poor leadership, the empire lost power.

While the empire fell, the blended culture that the Safavid Empire had created continued. The main elements of that culture were the joining together of the Persian tradition of learning and sophistication and the devout faith of the Shi'a. These elements are found in Iran even today.

❸ The Mughal Empire in India

KEY IDEA *The Mughal Empire brought Turks, Persians, and Indians together in a vast empire.*

Starting in the 600s, India went through a long period of unsettled life and trouble. After the Gupta Empire fell, nomads from central Asia invaded the area and created many small kingdoms. In the 700s, Muslims arrived on the scene. Their arrival launched a long history of fighting between them and the Hindus who had lived in India for centuries.

The Hindus were able to prevent the Muslims from taking their land for about 300 years. Then a group of Muslim Turks conquered a region around the city of Delhi and set up a new empire there. They treated the Hindus in their area harshly. Their rule ended in 1398, when Timur the Lame totally destroyed Delhi.

A little over a hundred years later, a new power arose. Babur had a small kingdom north of India. He raised an army and began to win large parts of India. Babur had many talents. He was a lover of poetry and gardens and a sensitive man who used his feelings for others to become a superb leader. He was also an excellent general. He once led a force of only 12,000 soldiers to victory over an enemy army of 100,000. His empire was called the Mughal

Empire because he and his families were related to the Mongols.

Babur's grandson, Akbar, was equally talented. His name means "Greatest One," and the name seems suitable to the man. He ruled with great wisdom and fairness for almost 40 years.

Akbar was a Muslim, but he believed strongly that people should be allowed to follow the religion they chose. He set an example by letting his wives practice whatever religion they chose. In his government, too, Akbar hired people based on their ability and not their religion. Both Hindus and Muslims gained jobs as government workers.

Akbar ruled fairly. He ended the tax that Hindu pilgrims had to pay. He also ended the tax that all non-Muslims had to pay. To raise money, he imposed a tax based on a percentage of the food grown. This made it easier for peasants to pay the tax. His land policy was less wise. He generously gave land to government officials. However, when they died he took it back and handed it to someone else. As a result, workers did not see any point in caring for the land because they were not preserving it for their children.

He had a strong, well-equipped army that helped him win and maintain control of more lands. His empire held about 100 million people—more than lived in all of Europe at the time.

During Akbar's reign, many changes in culture took place. His policy of blending different cultures produced two new languages. Hindi blended Persian and local languages. It is still widely spoken in India today. Urdu grew out of a mixture of Arabic, Persian, and Hindi and was spoken by the soldiers in Akbar's camp. Today it is the official language of Pakistan. The empire became famous for its book illustrations, which were adapted from the art of Persia. Akbar—who could not read—had a huge library of books and served as a patron to many writers. He also sponsored the building of a new capital city and many buildings.

After Akbar's death in 1605, the empire began to decline. During the reign of Jahangir, the real power was his wife, Nur Jahan. She was an able ruler but had a bitter political battle with one of Jahangir's sons. Since that son found help from the Sikhs—members of a separate religion—that group became the target of attacks by the government.

Jahangir's successor was Shah Jahan, and he too chose not to follow Akbar's policy of religious toleration. Shah Jahan was a great patron of the arts and built many beautiful buildings, including the famous Taj Mahal. It was a tomb for his beloved wife. However, his ambitious building plans required high taxes, and the people suffered under his rule.

His son Aurangzeb ruled for almost 50 years and made the empire grow once again with new conquests. However, his rule brought about new problems. A serious Muslim, the new ruler put harsh new laws in place. He punished Hindus and destroyed their temples, which produced a rebellion that managed to take control of part of his empire. At the same time, the Sikhs had become skilled fighters, and they won control of another part of the empire. To fight these battles, Aurangzeb had to increase taxes. Since he only taxed Hindus, not Muslims, this move only made large numbers of people more and more angry.

After his death, the empire fell apart, and local leaders took control of small areas. There continued to be a Mughal emperor, but he was only a figurehead, not a ruler with any real power.

Review

1. *Clarifying* How did the Ottomans treat non-Muslims?
2. *Summary* What were Suleyman's major accomplishments?
3. *Determining Main Ideas* Despite their brilliant rule, what critical mistake did Suleiman and Shah Abbas make?
4. *Drawing Conclusions* What evidence of cultural blending can you find in Akbar's rule?
5. *Analyzing Causes and Recognizing Effects* How did Akbar's successors contribute to the end of the Mughal Empire?

Answer Key
Chapter 18
SUMMARY

The Muslim World Expands, 1300–1700

Responses will vary but should include points similar to the following:

1. The Ottomans treated non-Muslims well, allowing them to practice their own religion, although they did put a tax on them. They also placed some Christians into slavery, to serve as soldiers or government officials.

2. Suleyman brought the Ottoman Empire to its greatest size; revised the laws of the empire; had accomplished works of art and architecture created.

3. Both Suleiman and Shah Abbas weakened their empires by killing or hurting their sons who were able, leaving only weak rulers to follow them.

4. Akbar's policy of blending produced two new languages, Hindi and Urdu. The art of illustrating books, which became refined under his rule, was adapted from Persian art. He also gave government jobs to either Muslims or Hindus based on ability, not religion.

5. Akbar's successors did not continue his policy of religious toleration, which led to conflict between Hindus and Muslims. Ambitious building programs and military campaigns produced high taxes, which were unfairly paid only by Hindus. This added to the conflict between groups.

CHAPTER

19

Summary

CHAPTERS IN BRIEF *An Age of Exploration and Isolation, 1400–1800*

CHAPTER OVERVIEW *"God, glory, and gold" drove Europeans' early exploration of Asia. They took control of Asian trade, with Portugal leading the way. Eventually, nations of northern Europe displaced the Portuguese. Two dynasties in China resisted the growing power of Europeans in Asia, limiting Chinese contact with foreigners. In Japan, a new system of government brought peace and isolation.*

❶ Europeans Explore the East

KEY IDEA Driven by the desire for wealth and to spread Christianity, Europeans began an age of exploration.

For many centuries, Europeans had been largely, though not completely, isolated from contact with people from other lands. That changed in the 1400s. One reason for this change was that Europeans hoped to gain new sources of wealth. By exploring the seas far from Europe, traders hoped to find new, faster routes to Asia—the source of spices and luxury goods. Their goal was to win access to these lands and bypass the Muslims and Italians who currently controlled this trade. Another reason was the desire to spread Christianity to new lands. The Crusades had ended, but bad feelings between Christians and Muslims remained. The Christians of Europe wanted to convert the people of Asia.

Advances in technology made these voyages possible. A new kind of ship, the caravel, was stronger built than earlier ships. It had triangle-shaped sails that allowed it to sail against the wind. Ships could now travel far out into the ocean. The magnetic compass allowed sea captains to better stay on course.

The first nation to develop and use these new technologies was Portugal. Prince Henry of Portugal was deeply committed to the idea of exploring beyond the seas. In 1419, he started a school of navigation where sea captains, mapmakers, and navigators could meet, learn, and exchange ideas. Over the next few decades, Portuguese captains sailed farther and farther down the west coast of Africa. In 1488, Bartolomeu Dias led the first voyage to reach the southern tip of Africa. Ten years later, Vasco da Gama led a ship 27,000 miles around Africa, to India, and back. The Portuguese had found a sea route to Asia.

The Spanish, meanwhile, had plans of their own. Italian sailor Christopher Columbus convinced the king and queen that he could reach Asia by sailing west. In 1492, instead of landing in Asia, Columbus touched land in the islands of the Americas, land unknown to Europeans. At first, though, people still thought that he had landed in Asia. Spain and Portugal argued over which nation had the rights to the land that Columbus had claimed. In 1494, they signed the Treaty of Tordesillas. It divided the world into two areas. Portugal won the right to control the eastern parts and Spain the western parts—including most of the Americas.

Portugal moved quickly to make the new Indian Ocean route pay off. In 1509, it defeated a Muslim fleet off the coast of India and thus became the master of Indian trade. Soon, it captured cities in India and on the Malay peninsula. Portugal now had power over islands that were so rich in desirable spices that they were called the Spice Islands. Spices now cost Europeans one-fifth of what they had cost before, while still making Portugal very wealthy.

Other European nations joined in this trade. In the 1600s, the English and Dutch entered the East Indies to challenge Portugal. The Dutch fleet—about 20,000 ships—was the largest in the world. These two nations quickly broke Portuguese power in the area. Then both nations set up an East India Company to control Asian trade. These companies were more than businesses. They were like governments, with the power to make money, sign treaties, and raise their own armies. The Dutch managed to drive out the English and grab the Asian trade for themselves.

The Dutch made their trading headquarters on the island of Java in the East Indies. By 1700, the Dutch ruled much of Indonesia. They had trading posts in many other Asian countries and commanded the southern tip of Africa. At the same time, both England and France finally gained footholds in India.

While the Europeans controlled the trade between Asia and Europe, they had little impact on most people living in these areas. From 1500 to 1800, the people of Asia were largely untouched by the European traders.

❷ China Limits European Contacts

KEY IDEA *Advances under the Ming and Qing dynasties left China self-contained and uninterested in European contact.*

Mongol rule in China ended in 1368 when Hongwu led a rebel army that took control of the country. He declared himself the first emperor of the Ming Dynasty, which was to last for almost 300 years. Hongwu began his rule by increasing the amount of food produced, improving irrigation, and raising cotton and sugar cane. He also made changes that improved the government of China. Later he grew suspicious and untrusting. He caused the deaths of many people whom he suspected of plotting against him.

His son Yonglo continued his better policies and also launched a major effort at making contact with other Asian peoples. Beginning in 1405, an admiral named Zheng He led several voyages to Southeast Asia, India, Arabia, and Africa. The goal was to impress other people with the power and wealth of China. He also wanted to convince them to pay tribute to China each year. By sending gifts each year, these peoples would recognize that China was superior to them. Gifts did flow to China, but scholar-officials said that the voyages wasted valuable resources. Zheng He's journeys were stopped after seven years.

China allowed Europeans to trade officially at only three ports. China became isolated. However, illegal trade took place all along the coast. Because Europeans wanted Chinese silk and ceramics, the people began making large amounts of these goods. Europeans paid silver for them. Manufacturing never grew very large in China, however. The Confucian ideas that shaped Chinese thinking said that farming was a better way of life, so manufacturing was heavily taxed. European missionaries entered China at this time, bringing both Christianity and new technology.

The power of the Ming Dynasty declined because the government could not solve several problems. Rebels from Manchuria—a land to the north of China—took control of the country in 1644 and started a new dynasty called the Qing. At first, the Chinese people did not accept the new rulers, who were not Chinese. However, the Qing emperors won their support by taking steps to improve conditions in the country and by preserving Chinese traditions.

Two emperors were the most effective. Kangxi ruled from 1661 to 1721 and his grandson Qian-long served from 1736 to 1795. They brought China to its largest size, increased its wealth, and sponsored an increase in artistic production.

Qian-long had problems to face, however. One was the matter of trade. The Chinese insisted that Europeans had to follow certain rules in order to continue trading with them. The Dutch were willing to do so, and they carried on the largest share of trade with China. The British, though, did not agree to following these rules. This disagreement later led to conflict that broke up China's empire.

In China, the production of rice and the long period of peace gave the people better lives. In the 1600s and 1700s, the number of people in China almost doubled, rising to more than 300 million by 1800. The huge majority of these people were farmers. Because of the use of fertilizer and better irrigation, they could grow more food. They also began to grow new crops brought over from the Americas, such as corn and sweet potatoes. As a result, the level of nutrition improved, which led to the growth in population.

Women suffered in this period, however. Sons were valued over daughters. It was felt only sons could carry out family religious duties and tend to the family farm. For that reason, many infant girls were killed, and adult women were given few rights.

The invasions by the foreigners from Manchuria and the pressure from European traders bothered the Chinese. Artists created books and paintings that showed traditional Chinese values and ideas. Plays about Chinese history and heroes were popular. They helped to unify the Chinese people. At the same time, a feeling of national pride also was rising in neighboring Korea, a land that had long been dominated by China.

❸ Japan Returns to Isolation

KEY IDEA *The Tokugawa regime unified Japan and began a 200-year period of isolation, autocracy, and economic growth.*

From 1467 to 1568, Japan entered a long, dark period of civil war. Powerful warriors took control of large areas of land. They were called daimyo. They became the most important powers in the country in a feudal system similar to that of Europe's Middle Ages. The daimyo built strong castles. They also had small armies of samurai warriors on horses and soldiers on foot with guns. They fought each other constantly to gain more land for themselves.

In 1568, one of the daimyo took control of Kyoto, the site of the emperor's capital. He was unable to win complete control of Japan, however. Another general, Toyotomi Hideyoshi, continued the work of bringing all of Japan under one rule. Using military conquest and clever diplomacy, he won that goal in 1590. He failed in his effort to capture Korea, however, and died in 1598.

The work of unifying Japan was completed by Tokugawa Ieyasu, who became the shogun, or sole ruler. He moved the capital of Japan to a small fishing village named Edo. Later, it grew to become the city of Tokyo. While all of Japan was ruled by Tokugawa, the daimyo still held much power in their lands. Tokugawa solved that problem by forcing them to follow his orders. He required them to live every other year in his capital—and leave their families in the capital with him during the other years. As a result, no daimyo was able to rebel against his power. Tokugawa died in 1616. All of the shoguns to follow him were from his family. They maintained a strong central government in Japan. This system of rule, called the Tokugawa Shogunate, lasted until 1867.

The new government brought about a long period of peace and prosperity for most people. Peasant farmers suffered greatly during this time, however. They worked long and hard on the farms and paid heavy taxes. Many left the countryside to move to the cities. By the mid-1700s, Edo had more than a million people and was perhaps the largest city in the world. Women found more opportunities for work in this and other cities than they had in the country.

A traditional culture thrived. It preferred ceremonial Noh dramas, stories of ancient warriors, and paintings of classical scenes. However, in cities, new styles emerged. Townspeople attended kabuki theater dramas of urban life. They hung woodblock prints of city scenes in their homes.

Europeans began to arrive in Japan. In 1543, the Portuguese were first. They brought such goods as clocks, eyeglasses, and guns. Japanese merchants and the daimyo welcomed them at first. They even welcomed the Christian missionaries who came after 1549, hoping to convert the Japanese to Christianity.

Some missionaries scorned traditional Japanese beliefs, though. Tokugawa became worried. In 1612, he banned Christianity from the country. Over the next 20 years or so, Japan managed to rid the country of all Christians. This effort became part of a larger plan to protect the country from European influence. In 1639, leaders sealed Japan's borders except for one port city. It was open to only the Chinese and the Dutch. The Tokugawa shoguns controlled that port city, so they had tight control over all foreign contact. For the next 200 years, Japan remained closed to virtually all European contact.

Review

Analyzing Causes and Recognizing Effects

1. Why did the Europeans begin to explore overseas, and what technological changes made it possible?
2. Why did the Chinese stop the voyages of Zheng He?
3. What factors led to the growth in the Chinese population?
4. ***Determining Main Ideas*** What social changes took place in Tokugawa Japan?

Answer Key
Chapter 19
SUMMARY

An Age of Exploration and Isolation, 1400–1800

Responses will vary but should include points similar to the following:

1. Europeans began to explore overseas in search of wealth and converts to Christianity. Their voyages were made possible by a new, stronger ship design, triangular sails that allowed the ships to sail against the wind, and magnetic compasses that helped them stay on course.

2. The Chinese stopped the voyages of Zheng He because the emperor's scholar-officials said they were too costly.

3. The Chinese population grew because of better farming—due to use of fertilizer, better irrigation, and the introduction of crops from the Americas—and a long period of peace.

4. In Tokugawa Japan, the country became more urban and less rural. This development led to the creation of two separate cultures—the traditional culture and an urban-based culture.

CHAPTERS IN BRIEF *The Atlantic World, 1492–1800*

CHAPTER OVERVIEW Starting in 1492, the Spanish built a large empire in the Americas, but the native peoples suffered. In North America, the Dutch, French, and English fought for control. England finally won. The labor of enslaved persons brought from Africa supported the American colonies. The contact between the Old World and the New produced an exchange of new ideas.

❶ Spain Builds an American Empire

KEY IDEA *The voyages of Columbus prompted the Spanish to carve out the first European colonies in the Americas.*

In 1492, Christopher Columbus, an Italian sailor, led a voyage on behalf of Spain. He sailed west from Europe intending to reach Asia but instead landed in the Americas. This was land that Europeans had not known existed before. Columbus thought at first that he had reached Asia, or the Indies. He misnamed the natives he met Indians and claimed the land for Spain. The king and queen agreed to let him lead another voyage. This one was an expedition to form colonies, or controlled lands, that Spain would rule.

In 1500, a Portuguese explorer landed in Brazil and claimed that land for his country. In 1501, another Italian sailor on behalf of Spain, Amerigo Vespucci, explored the eastern coast of South America. He said that these lands were not Asia but a new world. Soon after, a mapmaker showed the lands as a separate continent. He named them America after Vespucci.

Other voyages gave Europeans more knowledge about the world. One explorer reached the west coast of Central America and first saw the Pacific Ocean. Another, Ferdinand Magellan, led a bold expedition from Spain that sailed completely around the world. Magellan himself died about halfway around. However, a few members of his crew survived. They returned to Spain after sailing for almost three years.

Spanish conquistadors, or conquerors, also began to explore the lands of the Americas. There they found great riches. In 1519, Hernando Cortés came to Mexico and defeated the powerful Aztec Empire. The Spanish had the advantage of rifles and cannons. They also had the aid of several native groups who were angry over harsh Aztec

rule. In addition, the Aztec were seriously weakened by new diseases brought to the Americas with the Spanish. Native peoples had no resistance to measles, mumps, and smallpox, which killed them by the hundreds of thousands.

About 15 years later, another Spanish force, led by Francisco Pizarro, conquered the mighty Inca Empire of South America. Once again, the Spanish gained access to huge amounts of gold and silver. By the mid-1500s, Spain had formed an American empire that stretched from modern-day Mexico to Peru. After 1540, the Spanish looked north of Mexico and explored the future United States. However, one large area of the Americas—Brazil—remained outside the control of Spain. Brazil was the possession of Portugal. Colonists there built huge farms called plantations to grow sugar, which was in demand in Europe.

The Spanish had a pattern of living among the people they conquered. Because few Spanish settlers in the Americas were women, Spanish men had children with native women. These children and their descendants formed a large mestizo population, people with mixed Spanish and Native American blood. The Spanish also formed large farms and mines that used natives as slave labor. Many landowners treated the native workers harshly. Some Spanish priests criticized this treatment. In 1542, the Spanish stopped making slaves of native peoples. They soon, however, would bring enslaved Africans to the Americas to meet labor demands.

❷ European Nations Settle North America

KEY IDEA *Several European nations fought for control of North America, and England eventually emerged victorious.*

In the early 1500s, the French began to explore North America. Jacques Cartier came across and named the St. Lawrence River. He then followed it inward to reach the site of modern Montreal. In 1608, Samuel de Champlain sailed as far as modern Quebec. In the next 100 years, the French explored and claimed the area around the Great Lakes and the Mississippi River all the way to its mouth at the Gulf of Mexico. The area became known as New France. The main activity in this colony was trade in beaver fur.

The English also began to colonize North America. The first permanent settlement came at Jamestown, in modern Virginia, in 1607. The colony struggled at first. Many settlers died from disease, hunger, or war with the native peoples. Soon farmers began to grow tobacco to meet the high demand for it in Europe.

In the 1620s and 1630s, other groups from England began to settle in modern Massachusetts. These settlers were deeply religious people who did not agree with the practices of the Church of England. They wanted to purify the church and were called Puritans. They hoped to build a model community dedicated to God. They succeeded over time in part because many families settled there.

Meanwhile, the Dutch also started a new colony. They settled in the location of modern New York City and called it New Netherland. Like the French, they engaged in the fur trade and set up trading posts along the Hudson River. The colony did not grow very large, but it did attract people from other European countries. New Netherland became known as a home to people of many different cultures. Europeans also took possession of many islands of the Caribbean. There they built tobacco and sugar plantations that used enslaved Africans as workers.

The European powers began to fight for control of North America. First, the English forced the Dutch to give up their colony. New Amsterdam was renamed New York. The English also planted other colonies along the Atlantic coast, from Maine to Georgia. These colonists came in conflict with the French settlers in Canada on many occasions. The final fight started in 1754 and was called the French and Indian War. When it ended in 1763, France was forced to give up all its land in North America to Britain.

The native peoples responded to these events in many different ways. Many worked closely with the French and Dutch, joining in the fur trade and benefiting from it. Those who lived near the English, though, had stormier relations with colonists. More than just trade, the English were interested in

acquiring land for settlers' living and farming. This was land that Native Americans would not be able to use for hunting or growing their own food. This conflict erupted into war several times. Natives, though, could not overcome the settlers' guns and cannons. As in Spanish lands, the native peoples suffered even more from disease. Thousands upon thousands of natives died from European illnesses, making it impossible for them to resist the growth of the colonies.

❸ The Atlantic Slave Trade

KEY IDEA *To meet their growing labor needs, Europeans enslaved millions of Africans in forced labor in the Americas.*

Slavery has a long history in Africa and in the world. For most of that history in Africa, though, no large numbers of people were enslaved. That changed in the 600s, when Muslim traders started to take large numbers of slaves. Between 650 and 1600, Muslims took about 17 million Africans to North Africa and Southwest Asia. Most did have certain rights. The European slave trade that began in the 1500s was larger. Also, the enslaved Africans were treated far more harshly.

In the Americas, when the natives began dying from disease, the Europeans brought in Africans, for three reasons. Africans had resistance to European diseases, so they would not get sick and die. Also, many Africans knew about farming so they would be accustomed to the work involved. Third, Africans were strangers to the Americas and would know no places to hide from slavery. From 1500 to 1870, when the slave trade in the Americas finally ended, about 9.5 million Africans had been imported as slaves.

The Spanish first began the practice of bringing Africans to the Americas. However, the Portuguese—looking for workers for sugar plantations in Brazil—increased the demand for slaves. During the 1600s, Brazil received more than 40 percent of all the Africans sent to the Americas. Other European colonies also brought slaves to work on tobacco, sugar, and coffee plantations. About 400,000 slaves were brought to the English colonies in North America. Their population increased over time, though, to number about 2 million in 1830.

Many African rulers joined in the slave trade. They moved inland to capture people and brought them to the coast to sell to European traders.

This trade was part of a triangular trade that linked Europe, Africa, and the Americas. European ships brought manufactured goods to Africa, trading them for people. They carried Africans across the Atlantic to the Americas, where they were sold into slavery. The traders then bought sugar, coffee, and tobacco, which they carried back to Europe. Another triangle involved ships sailing from the northern English colonies in North America. They carried rum to Africa, people to the West Indies, and sugar and molasses back to the colonies to make more rum.

The part of the voyage that brought people to the Americas was called the middle passage. It was harsh and cruel. People were crammed into ships, beaten, and given little food. Many died, and many others simply jumped overboard trying to escape. About 20 percent of the people on these ships died.

Life on the plantations was harsh as well. People were sold to the highest bidder and then worked from dawn to dusk in the fields of the plantations. They were given little food and lived in small huts. Africans kept alive their traditional music and beliefs to try to maintain their spirits. Sometimes they arose in rebellion. From North America to Brazil, from 1522 to the 1800s, there were small-scale slave revolts.

❹ The Columbian Exchange and Global Trade

KEY IDEA *The colonization of the Americas introduced new and different items into the Eastern and Western hemispheres.*

There was constant movement of people from Europe and Africa to the Americas. This large-scale mixing of people and culture was called the Columbian Exchange. Important foods such as corn and potatoes were taken from the Americas, where they originated, to Europe, Africa, and Asia.

Some foods moved from the Old World to the New. Bananas, black-eyed peas, and yams were taken from Africa to the Americas. Cattle, pigs, and horses had never been seen in the Americas until the Europeans brought them. Of course, deadly illnesses also moved to the Americas. They killed a large portion of the Native American population.

The settling of the Americas and the growth of trade led to a new set of business practices still followed today. One was the rise of an economic system called capitalism. It is based on private owner-ship of property and the right of a business to earn a profit. Another new business idea was the joint-stock company. With this, many investors pooled their money to start a business and share in the profits. European governments began to follow an idea called mercantilism. In this theory, a country's power depended on its wealth. Getting more gold and silver increased its wealth, as would selling more goods than it bought. Colonies played an important role because they provided goods that could be sold in trade.

With the American colonies, European society saw changes. Merchants grew wealthy and powerful, and towns and cities grew larger. Still, most people lived in the countryside, farmed for a living, and were poor.

Review

1. ***Drawing Conclusions*** What single factor was most devastating for the native peoples of the Americas and what effect did it have?

Analyzing Causes and Recognizing Effects

2. How did settlement patterns in the Spanish colonies lead to a mixing of Spanish and native cultures?

3. Why did the French and Dutch have better relations with the native peoples than the English?

4. ***Comparing and Contrasting*** Compare and contrast the Muslim slave trade in Africa with the European slave trade that began in the 1500s.

5. ***Summarizing*** What was exchanged in the Columbian Exchange?

The Atlantic World, 1492–1800

Responses will vary but should include points similar to the following:

1. European diseases, to which the native peoples had no resistance; the diseases killed millions of Native Americans and weakened their ability to resist European power.

2. The Spanish had a pattern of living among the people they conquered. So when few Spanish women came to the Americas to settle, Spanish men had children with native women, mixing the cultures.

3. The French and Dutch wanted mostly to trade with the native peoples. The English, though, wanted land for farming and to expand their settlers' populations.

4. The Muslim slave trade was smaller and less harsh. Enslaved Africans worked in Muslim lands and kept some rights. The European slave trade was nearly twice as large, the passage to the New World was harsh and cruel, and work on the plantations was difficult.

5. Food—such as corn and potatoes—moved from the New World to the Old. Bananas, yams, and black-eyed peas as well as large animals such as cattle and horses moved from the Old World to the New. Diseases came from the Old World to the New, which had a devastating effect on the population of Native Americans.

CHAPTERS IN BRIEF *Absolute Monarchs in Europe, 1500–1800*

Summary

CHAPTER OVERVIEW *Spain lost territory and money. The Netherlands split from Spain and grew rich from trade. For a time, France was Europe's most powerful country, where King Louis XIV ruled with total control. Austria's queen resisted a Prussian land grab. Peter the Great modernized Russia. England's Parliament struggled with different kings and became the greatest power in the country.*

❶ Spain's Empire and European Absolutism

KEY IDEA *During a time of religious and economic instability, Philip II ruled Spain with a strong hand.*

Charles V ruled the Holy Roman Empire and various other European countries. In 1556, he retired from the throne and split his holdings. His brother Ferdinand received Austria and the Holy Roman Empire. His son, Philip II, got Spain and its colonies.

Philip expanded his holdings by taking Portugal and gaining its global territories. When he tried to invade England in 1588, though, he failed. The defeat made Spain weaker. However, Spain still seemed strong because of its wealth—gold and silver—that flowed in from the colonies in the Americas.

This wealth led to some serious problems, however. The prices of goods constantly rose. Also, unfair taxes hit the poor, keeping them from building up any wealth of their own. As prices rose, Spaniards bought more goods from other lands. The silver from the colonies, then, began to flow to Spain's enemies.

In the middle of these troubles, Spain lost land. Seven provinces of the Spanish Netherlands rose in protest against high taxes. Also, they were Protestant and Spain was strongly Catholic. In 1579, these seven provinces declared their independence from Spain.

In the new Dutch republic, each province had a leader elected by the people. The Dutch also practiced religious tolerance, letting people worship as they wished. Dutch merchants established a trading empire. They had the largest fleet of merchant ships in the world and were the most important bankers in Europe.

Though he lost possessions, Philip held tight control over Spain. He and others who ruled in the same way were called absolute monarchs. They believed in holding all power. The Church's power had weakened, which helped make this possible. Some absolute rulers ended conflict within their countries by increasing their power. That is what happened in France.

❷ The Reign of Louis XIV

KEY IDEA *After a century of wars and riots, Louis XIV, the most powerful monarch of his time, ruled France.*

France was torn by eight religious wars between Catholics and Protestants from 1562 to 1598. In 1589, a Protestant prince, Henry of Navarre, became King Henry IV. He changed religions in 1593, becoming a Catholic to please the majority of his people. In 1598, he issued an order called the Edict of Nantes. It gave Huguenots—French Protestants—the right to live in peace and have their own churches in some cities.

Henry rebuilt the French economy and brought peace to the land. He was followed by his son, a weak king. However, that son had a very capable chief minister, Cardinal Richelieu. He ruled the land for him and increased the power of the crown.

The cardinal ordered that Huguenots could not build walls for their cities. He also said nobles had to destroy their castles. As a result, Protestants and nobles could not hide within walls to defy the king's power. Richelieu used people from the middle class—not nobles—to work in his government. That also cut nobles' power.

French thinkers had reacted to the religious wars with horror. They developed a new attitude—skepticism. Nothing could be known for certain, they argued. Doubting old ideas was the first step to learning the truth, they said.

In 1643, Louis XIV, age four, became king. Cardinal Mazarin ruled for him until Louis was 22. Louis became a powerful ruler, with total control.

Louis determined never to let nobles challenge him. He froze the nobles out of his government. He gave more power to government officials and made sure that they answered only to him. He also worked hard to increase the wealth of France. His chief minister of finance, Jean Baptiste Colbert, tried to build French industry. Colbert aimed to convince French people to buy French-made goods and not those from other countries. He urged people to settle in the new French colony in Canada. The fur trade there brought wealth to France.

Louis enjoyed a life of luxury at his court. He built a huge and beautiful palace at Versailles near Paris. He also made sure that nobles had to depend on his favor in order to advance in society.

Louis made France the most powerful nation in Europe. France had more people and a larger army than any other country. However, Louis made some mistakes that later proved costly. After winning some wars against neighboring countries, he became bolder and tried to seize more land. Other nations joined together to stop France by the late 1680s. The high cost of these wars combined with poor harvests to produce problems at home in France.

The final war fought in Louis's time lasted from 1700 to 1714. In this War of the Spanish Succession, France and Spain attempted to set up united thrones. The rest of Europe felt threatened and joined in war against them. Both France and Spain were forced to give up some of their American and European colonies to England, the new rising power.

❸ Central European Monarchs Clash

KEY IDEA *After a period of turmoil, absolute monarchs ruled Austria and the German state of Prussia.*

Germany had suffered from religious wars that ended in 1555. Rulers of each state agreed that they would decide whether their lands would be Catholic or Protestant. Over the next decades, though, the two sides had tense relations. In 1618, a new war broke out and lasted for 30 terrible years.

In the first half of the war, Catholic forces led by Ferdinand, the Holy Roman Emperor, won. However, Germany suffered, because he allowed his large army to loot towns. Then the Protestant king of Sweden won several battles against him. In the last years of the war, France helped the Protestants. Although France was a Catholic nation,

Richelieu feared growing Hapsburg family power.

The Thirty Years' War ended in 1648 with the Peace of Westphalia. It had been a disaster for Germany. About 4 million people had died, and the economy was in ruins. It took Germany two centuries to recover. The peace weakened the power of Austria and Spain and made France stronger. Because of this war, each nation of Europe was seen as having an equal right to negotiate with all the others.

While strong states arose in western Europe, none emerged in central Europe. The economies there were less developed than in the West. Most people were still peasants. This region had not built an economy based in towns. Nobles enjoyed great power, which kept the power of rulers in check. Still, two important powers arose.

The Hapsburg family ruled Austria, Hungary, and Bohemia in an empire that linked many different peoples. Maria Theresa, Queen of Austria, managed to increase her power and cut that of the nobles. She was opposed by the kings of Prussia, a new state in northern Germany. Those kings built a strong state with much power given to the large, well-trained army. In 1740, Frederick the Great of Prussia invaded one of Maria Theresa's lands. The queen fought hard to keep the territory, but lost. Still, in fighting this War of the Austrian Succession, she managed to keep the rest of her empire intact. The two sides fought again beginning in 1756. In this Seven Years' War, Austria abandoned Britain, its old ally, for France and Russia. Prussia joined with Britain. The Prussians and British won. In that victory, Britain gained complete control over France's colonies in North America and India.

❹ Absolute Rulers of Russia

KEY IDEA *Peter the Great made many changes in Russia to try to make it more like western Europe.*

Ivan III had made Moscow the center of a new Russian state with a central government. His son continued that work. His grandson, Ivan IV—called Ivan the Terrible—began as a successful ruler. He added lands to Russia and gave the country a code of laws. After his wife died, however, he ruled harshly. He used secret police to hunt down opponents and kill them. Ivan even killed his own oldest son. A few years after he died, Russian nobles met to name a new ruler. They chose Michael Romanov, the grandnephew of Ivan IV's wife. He began a dynasty that ruled Russia for about 300 years.

The Romanovs restored order to Russia. In the late 1600s, Peter I—called Peter the Great—began an intense program of trying to modernize Russia. Peter admired the nations of western Europe. He traveled in Europe to learn about new technology and ways of working. He returned to Russia determined to make his country more advanced. His first steps were to increase the powers of the czar, or ruler, so he could force people to make the changes he wanted. He put the Russian Orthodox Church under his own control. He cut the power of nobles. He built up the army and made it better trained.

He took several steps to make Russia more western. He brought potatoes as a new food, began Russia's first newspaper, gave more social status to women, and told the nobles to adopt Western clothes. He promoted education and built a grand new capital city, St. Petersburg, on the shores of the Baltic Sea.

❺ Parliament Limits the English Monarchy

KEY IDEA *Absolute monarchs in England were overthrown, and Parliament gained power.*

When Queen Elizabeth I died, her cousin James, king of Scotland, became king of England. James fought with Parliament over money. His religious policies also angered the Puritans in Parliament. They wanted to reform the English church to rid it of Catholic practices. James was unwilling to make these changes.

His son, Charles I, continued the tension between king and Parliament. Parliament forced him to sign a Petition of Right in 1628. By signing, Charles allowed that the king was answerable to Parliament. Then he dissolved the Parliament and tried to raise money without it—going directly against the Petition of Right.

Other actions of Charles had caused Scotland to threaten to invade England. To meet the danger, Charles needed some money, and to raise taxes he needed Parliament. When Charles called a new Parliament, it quickly passed laws to limit his power. Charles responded by trying to arrest its leaders. Soon England was plunged into a civil war: Charles and his Royalists against the supporters of Parliament, many of whom were Puritans.

The English Civil War lasted from 1642 to 1649. Under the leadership of Oliver Cromwell, the forces of the Puritans won. They tried and executed Charles for treason—the first time a king had ever been executed in public. Cromwell became a military dictator, ruling until 1658. He crushed a rebellion in Ireland and tried to reform society at home. Soon after his death, though, the government collapsed. The new Parliament asked Charles's older son to restore the monarchy. Charles II began to rule in 1660.

Charles II's reign was a period of calm after turmoil. After his death in 1685, James II became king. His pro-Catholic policies angered and worried the English, who feared that he would restore Catholicism. Finally, in 1688, seven members of Parliament contacted James's older daughter, Mary, and her husband, William of Orange, prince of the Netherlands—both Protestants. They wanted them to replace James II on the throne. The event was called the Glorious Revolution, a bloodless revolution that forced James to flee to France. William and Mary agreed, swearing to rule according to the laws made by Parliament. They agreed to accept the Bill of Rights, which guaranteed English people certain rights. From then on, no king or queen could rule England without the consent of Parliament.

Review

1. ***Analyzing Causes and Recognizing Effects*** Why did Spain weaken in power?
2. ***Summarizing*** How did Richelieu and Louis XIV increase the power of the French king?
3. ***Analyzing Causes and Recognizing Effects*** How did the Thirty Years' War affect Germany?
4. ***Clarifying*** What did Peter the Great do to modernize Russia?
5. ***Drawing Conclusions*** How did England develop away from an absolute monarchy?

Answer Key
Chapter 21
SUMMARY

Absolute Monarchs in Europe, 1500–1800

Responses will vary but should include points similar to the following:

1. Spain weakened in part because it lost the effort to invade England and because it lost the Spanish Netherlands. Also, the economy was weakened by several factors, including the constant rising of prices, overtaxing of the poor, and loss of silver to other nations.

2. Richelieu and Louis XIV broke the power of nobles, reduced the power of the French Protestants, and hired people from the middle-class—not nobles—for the government and then kept in close communication with those officials.

3. The Thirty Years' War devastated Germany, killing about 4 million people and weakening the economy. Germany would take about 200 years to recover.

4. Peter first increased the power of the czar by gaining control over the Russian Orthodox Church and by cutting the power of nobles. He built up the army and made it better trained, brought potatoes as a new food, began Russia's first newspaper, gave more social status to women, told the nobles to adopt Western clothes, and promoted education.

5. The Petition of Right of 1628 put some limits on the ruler's power. With the English Civil War and the execution of Charles I, Parliament showed that it had more power than did the king. That was also established firmly by the Glorious Revolution of 1688 and by the Bill of Rights.

CHAPTER 22 Summary

CHAPTERS IN BRIEF *Enlightenment and Revolution, 1550–1789*

CHAPTER OVERVIEW *Starting in the 1500s, European thinkers overturned old ideas about the physical world with a new approach to science. Thinkers of the Enlightenment hoped to use reason to make a better society in which people were free. Enlightenment ideas spread throughout Europe. They had a profound effect in North America, forming the basis of the new government of the United States.*

❶ The Scientific Revolution

KEY IDEA *In the mid-1500s, scientists began to question accepted beliefs and make new theories based on experimentation.*

During the Middle Ages, few scholars questioned ideas that had always been accepted. Europeans based ideas about the physical world on what ancient Greeks and Romans believed or what was said in the Bible. Therefore, people still thought that the earth was the center of the universe. To them, the sun, moon, other planets, and stars moved around it.

In the mid-1500s, however, attitudes changed. Scholars now started a scientific revolution drawn from a spirit of curiosity. One factor was the new focus on careful observation. Another was the willingness to question old beliefs. European explorations were a third factor. When they reached new lands, Europeans saw new plants and animals never seen by ancient writers. These discoveries led to the opening of new courses of study in universities.

The first challenge came in astronomy. In the early 1500s, Nicolaus Copernicus studied the stars and planets for many years. He concluded that the earth, like the other planets, revolved around the sun, and the moon revolved around the earth. Fearing attack, he did not publish his findings until just before his death. In the early 1600s, Johannes Kepler used mathematics to confirm Copernicus's basic idea.

An Italian scientist—Galileo Galilei—made several discoveries that undercut ancient ideas. He made one of the first telescopes and used it to study the planets. He found that Jupiter had moons, the sun had spots, and Earth's moon was rough. These statements went against church teaching, and Galileo was forced to deny their truth. Still, his ideas spread.

Interest in science led to a new approach, the scientific method. With this method, scientists ask a question based on something they have seen in the physical world. They form a hypothesis, or an attempt to answer the question. Then they test the hypothesis by making experiments or checking other facts. Finally, they change the hypothesis if needed. The English writer Francis Bacon helped foster this new approach to knowledge by telling scientists they should base their ideas on what they can see and test in the world. The French mathematician René Descartes also had great influence. His thinking was based on logic and mathematics.

In the mid-1600s, the English scientist Isaac Newton described the law of gravity. Using mathematics, Newton showed that the same force ruled the motion of planets and the action of bodies on the earth.

Scientists made new tools to study the world around them. One invented a microscope to study creatures too small for the naked eye to see. Others invented tools for understanding weather.

Doctors also made advances. One made drawings that showed the different parts of the human body. Another learned how the heart pumped blood through the body. In the late 1700s, Edward Jenner first used the process called vaccination to prevent disease. By giving a person the germs from a cattle disease called cowpox, he helped that person avoid getting the more serious human disease of smallpox. Scientists made advances in chemistry as well. One challenged the old idea that things were made of only four elements—earth, air, fire, and water. He and other scientists were able to separate oxygen from air.

❷ The Enlightenment in Europe

KEY IDEA *A revolution in intellectual activity changed Europeans' view of government and society.*

New ways of thinking arose in other areas. In the intellectual movement called the

Enlightenment, thinkers tried to apply reason and scientific method to laws that shaped human actions. They hoped to build a society founded on ideas of the Scientific Revolution.

Two English writers were important to this movement. Thomas Hobbes wrote that without a government, there would be a war of "every man against every man." As a result, Hobbes said, people formed a social contract—an agreement—in which they gave up their rights so they could secure order and safety. The best government, he said, is that of a strong king who can force people to obey. John Locke believed that all people have the rights to life, liberty, and property. The purpose of government is to protect those rights. When it fails to do so, he said, people have a right to overthrow the government.

A group of French thinkers had wide influence. They had five main beliefs: (1) thinkers can find the truth by using reason; (2) what is natural is good and reasonable, and human actions are shaped by natural laws; (3) acting according to nature can bring happiness; (4) by taking a scientific view, people and society can make progress and advance to a better life; and (5) by using reason, people can gain freedom.

Three French thinkers had great influence. Voltaire wrote against intolerance and criticized the laws and customs of France. The Baron de Montesquieu made a long study of laws and governments. He thought government power should be separated into different branches. Each should be able to check the other branches to prevent them from abusing their power. Jean Jacques Rousseau wrote strongly in favor of human freedom. He wanted a society in which all people were equal. The Italian Cesare Beccaria wrote about crime and justice. Trials should be fair, he said, and punishments should be made to fit the crime.

Many Enlightenment thinkers held traditional views about women's place in society. They urged equal rights for all men but ignored the fact that women did not enjoy such rights. Some women protested this unfairness. "If all men are born free," wrote one, "how is it that all women are born slaves?"

Enlightenment ideas had strong influence on the American and French Revolutions, which came at the end of the 1700s. They had three other effects. They helped spread the idea of progress. By using reason, people thought, it is possible to make soci-

ety better. These ideas also helped make Western society more secular—that is, more worldly and less spiritual. Finally, Enlightenment ideas promoted the notion that the individual person was important.

❸ The Enlightenment Spreads

KEY IDEA *Enlightenment ideas spread through the Western world, and influenced the arts and government.*

In the 1700s, Paris was the cultural center of Europe. People came there from other countries in Europe and from the Americas to hear the new ideas of the Enlightenment. Writers and artists gathered in the homes of wealthy people to talk about ideas. A woman named Marie-Thérèse Geoffrin became famous for hosting these discussions. She also supplied the money for one of the major projects of the Enlightenment. With her funds, Denis Diderot and other thinkers wrote and published a huge set of books called the *Encyclopedia*. Their aim was to gather together all that was known about the world. The French government and officials in the Catholic Church did not like many of the ideas that were published in the *Encyclopedia*. They banned the books at first, but later they revoked the ban.

Through the meetings in homes and works like the *Encyclopedia*, the ideas of the Enlightenment spread throughout Europe. The ideas also spread to the growing middle class. This group of people was becoming wealthy but had less social status than nobles and had very little political power. Ideas about equality sounded good to them.

Art moved in new directions, inspired by the Enlightenment ideas of order and reason. Artists and architects worked to show balance and elegance. Composers wrote music of great appeal for their creative richness. In this period, the novel became a popular form of literature. This new form told lengthy stories with many twists of plot that explored the thoughts and feelings of characters.

Some Enlightenment thinkers believed that the best form of government was a monarchy. In it, a ruler respected the rights of people. They tried to influence rulers to rule fairly. Rulers followed these ideas in part but were unwilling to give up much power. Frederick the Great made changes in Prussia. He gave his people religious freedom, improved schooling, and reformed the justice system. However, he did nothing to end serfdom, which made peasants slaves to the wealthy landowners. Joseph II of Austria did end serfdom. Once he died, though, the nobles who owned the land were able to undo his reform.

Catherine the Great of Russia was another of the rulers influenced by Enlightenment ideas. She tried to reform Russia's laws but met resistance. She hoped to end serfdom, but a bloody peasants' revolt convinced her to change her mind. Instead, she gave the nobles even more power over serfs. Catherine did manage to gain new land for Russia. Russia, Prussia, and Austria agreed to divide Poland among themselves. As a result, Poland disappeared as a separate nation for almost 150 years.

❹ The American Revolution

KEY IDEA *Enlightenment ideas help spur the American colonies to create a new nation.*

The British colonies in North America grew in population and wealth during the 1700s. The 13 colonies also enjoyed a kind of self-government. People in the colonies began to see themselves less and less as British subjects. Still, Parliament passed laws that governed the colonies. One set of laws banned trade with any nation other than Britain.

The high cost of the French and Indian War, which ended in 1763, led Parliament to pass laws that put taxes on the colonists. The colonists became very angry. They had never paid taxes directly to the British government before. They said that the taxes violated their rights. Since Parliament had no members from the colonies, they said, Parliament had no right to pass tax laws that affected the colonies. They met the first tax, passed in 1765, with a boycott of British goods. Their refusal to buy British products was very effective and forced Parliament to repeal the law.

Over the next decade, colonists and Britain grew further apart. Some colonists wanted to push the colonies to independence. They took actions that caused Britain to act harshly. These harsh responses, in turn, angered some moderate colonists. Eventually, the conflict led to shooting. Representatives of the colonists met in a congress and formed an army. In July of 1776, they announced that they were independent of Britain. They issued a Declaration of Independence that was based on the ideas of the Enlightenment.

From 1775 to 1781, the colonists and Britain fought a war in North America. The colonists had a poorly equipped army and the British were pow-

erful. However, in the end, they won their independence. The British people grew tired of the cost of the war and pushed Parliament to agree to a peace. The Americans were also helped greatly by aid from France. In 1783, the two sides signed a treaty in which Britain recognized the independent United States.

The 13 states formed a new government that was very weak. It struggled for a few years, but states held all the power and the central government had little. In 1787, many leaders met again and wrote a new framework of government.

The Constitution of the United States drew on many Enlightenment ideas. From Montesquieu, it put in effect the separation of powers into three branches of government. Each branch was able to prevent other branches from abusing their power. From Locke, it put power in the hands of the people. From Voltaire, it protected the rights of people to free speech and freedom of religion. From Beccaria, it set up a fair system of justice. Many of these rights were ensured in a set of additions to the Constitution called the Bill of Rights. Approval of these additions helped win approval of the Constitution as a whole.

Review

1. **Contrasting** Contrast how people in the Middle Ages and people in the scientific revolution looked at the physical world.
2. **Determining Main Ideas** How is the scientific revolution connected to the Enlightenment?
3. **Drawing Conclusions** What were three major ideas of the Enlightenment?
4. **Analyzing Causes and Recognizing Effects** What factors led to the spread of the Enlightenment?
5. **Analyzing Issues** How did the government of the United States reflect Enlightenment ideas?

Answer Key
Chapter 22
SUMMARY

Enlightenment and Revolution, 1550–1789

Responses will vary but should include points similar to the following:

1. In the Middle Ages, scholars based their ideas on what had been written by ancient writers and what was in the Bible. In the scientific revolution, scholars based their ideas on what they had observed firsthand and a willingness to question old beliefs.

2. The Enlightenment thought that advances in science were due to the use of reason. They hoped to apply reason to social and political issues, rather than the description of nature.

3. Enlightenment ideas included the rights to life, liberty, and property; that reason can gain people freedom; that government power should be separate and balanced; that trials should be fair; and that all men should have equal rights.

4. The discussions held in fashionable French homes and publication of the *Encyclopedia* helped spread the ideas of the Enlightenment.

5. From Montesquieu, the Constitution of the United States put in effect the separation of powers into three branches of government. Each branch was able to prevent other branches from abusing their power. From Locke, it put power in the hands of the people. From Voltaire, it protected the rights of people to free speech and freedom of religion. From Beccaria, it set up a fair system of justice. Many of these rights were ensured in a set of additions to the Constitution called the Bill of Rights.

CHAPTER 23 Summary

CHAPTERS IN BRIEF *The French Revolution and Napoleon, 1789–1815*

CHAPTER OVERVIEW *France's lower classes revolted against the king. Thousands died. Napoleon took control of France and created an empire. After his defeat, European leaders restored the rule of monarchs to the continent.*

❶ The French Revolution Begins

KEY IDEA *Economic and social inequalities in the Old Regime helped cause the French Revolution.*

In the 1700s, France was the leading country of Europe. It was the center of the new ideas of the Enlightenment. However, beneath the surface there were major problems causing unrest. Soon the nation would be torn by a violent revolution.

One problem was that people were not treated equally in French society. The French were divided into three classes, or estates. The First Estate consisted of the Roman Catholic clergy. The Second Estate was made up of rich nobles. Only about two percent of the people belonged to these two estates. Yet they owned 20 percent of the land and paid little or no taxes. They had easy lives.

Everybody else belonged to the Third Estate. This huge group included three types of people:

- the bourgeoisie—mostly well-off merchants and skilled workers who lacked the status of nobles
- city workers—cooks, servants, and others who were poorly paid and often out of work
- peasants—farm workers, making up more than 80 percent of the French people

Members of the Third Estate were angry. They had few rights. They paid up to half of their income in taxes, while the rich paid almost none.

Three factors led to revolution. First, the Enlightenment spread the idea that everyone should be equal. The powerless people in the Third Estate liked that. Second, the French economy was failing. High taxes kept profits low, and food supplies were short. The government owed money. Third, King Louis XVI was a weak, unconcerned leader. His wife, Marie Antoinette, was a big spender and was disliked.

In the 1780s, deeply in debt, France needed money. Louis tried to tax the nobles. Instead, they forced the king to call a meeting of delegates of the three estates to decide tax issues. The meeting began in May 1789 with arguments over how to count votes. In the past, each estate had cast one vote. The top two estates always voted together and got their way. Now the Third Estate delegates wanted to change the system. The Third Estate had as many delegates as the other two estates combined. They wanted each delegate to have a vote. The king and the other estates did not agree to the plan.

The Third Estate then broke with the others and met separately. In June 1789, its delegates voted to rename themselves the National Assembly. They claimed to represent all the people. This was the beginning of representative government for France.

Louis tried to make peace. He ordered the clergy and nobles to join the National Assembly. However, trouble erupted. Rumors flew that Swiss soldiers paid by Louis were going to attack French citizens. On July 14, an angry crowd captured the Bastille, a Paris prison. The mob wanted to get gunpowder for their weapons in order to defend the city.

A wave of violence called the Great Fear swept the country. Peasants broke into and burned nobles' houses. They tore up documents that had forced them to pay fees to the nobles. Late in 1789, a mob of women marched from Paris to the king's palace at Versailles. They were angry about high bread prices and demanded that the king move to Paris. They hoped he would end hunger in the city. The king and queen left Versailles, never to return.

❷ Revolution Brings Reform and Terror

KEY IDEA *The revolutionary government of France made reforms but also used terror and violence to retain power.*

In August 1789, the National Assembly took steps to change France. One new law ended all the special privileges that members of the First and Second Estates had enjoyed. Another law gave all French men equal rights. Though women did not get these rights, it was a bold step. Other laws cut the power of the Catholic Church. The government took over church lands, hoping to sell them and raise money.

The new laws about the church divided people who had backed the Revolution. Catholic peasants remained loyal to the church. They were angry that the church would be part of the state. Thereafter, many of them opposed the Revolution's reforms.

For months the assembly worked on plans for a new government. During this time, Louis was fearful for his safety in France. One night he and his family tried to escape the country. They were caught, brought back to Paris, and lived under guard. After this, the king and queen were even less popular.

In the fall of 1791, the assembly drew up a new constitution that gave the king very little power. The assembly then handed over its power to a new assembly, the Legislative Assembly. After the new assembly began to meet, however, it divided into opposing groups. Some wanted an end to revolutionary changes. Others wanted even more radical changes.

At the same time, France faced serious trouble on its borders. Kings in other countries feared that the French Revolution would spread to their lands. They wanted to use force to restore control of France to Louis XVI. Soon France found itself at war—a war it quickly began to lose. Foreign soldiers were coming near to Paris. Many people thought that the king and queen were ready to help the enemy. Angry French citizens imprisoned them. Many nobles were killed in other mob action.

The government took strong steps to meet the danger from foreign troops. It took away the king's powers. In 1792, the National Convention—another new government—was formed. It declared Louis a common citizen and then put him to death. It also ordered thousands of French people into the army.

Soon one man, Maximilien Robespierre, began to lead France. He made many changes. He ordered the death of many people who did not agree with him. His rule, which began in 1793, was called the Reign of Terror. It ended in July 1794, when Robespierre himself was put to death.

France got a new, but less revolutionary, plan of government. Tired of the killing and unrest, the French people wanted a return to order.

❸ Napoleon Forges an Empire

KEY IDEA *Napoleon Bonaparte, a military genius, seized power in France and made himself emperor.*

Napoleon Bonaparte became the master of France. In 1795, he led soldiers against French royalists who were attacking the National Convention. For this, he was hailed as the savior of the French republic. Later he invaded Italy to end the threat from Austrian troops located there.

By 1799, the unsettled French government had lost the people's support. In a bold move, Napoleon used troops to seize control of the government. He then wielded complete power over the country. Other nations feared his power and attacked France again. Napoleon led his armies into battle. In 1802, the three nations fighting him agreed to a peace. Napoleon went back to solve problems at home.

He made several changes that were meant to build on the Revolution's good ideas:

1. He made tax collection more fair and orderly. As a result, the government could count on a steady supply of money.
2. He removed dishonest government workers.
3. He started new public schools for ordinary citizens.
4. He gave the church back some of its power.
5. He wrote a new set of laws that gave all French citizens the same rights. However, the new laws took away many individual rights won during the Revolution. For example, they limited free speech and restored slavery in French colonies.

Napoleon had hoped to make his empire larger in both Europe and the New World. In 1801, he had sent soldiers to retake the island of present-day Haiti. During a civil war, slaves on the island had seized power. But Napoleon had to give up on his plan. Too many of his soldiers died in battle or from disease. Napoleon eventually abandoned his New World plans. In 1803, he sold the largest part of France's North American land—the huge Louisiana Territory—to the United States.

Stopped in the Americas, Napoleon moved to add to his power in Europe. In 1804, he made himself emperor of France. He quickly captured country after country. Other nations joined against him. However, after Napoleon won a major battle in Austria in 1805, almost all of his European enemies agreed to a peace treaty. Napoleon's only loss during this time was to the British navy off the southwest coast of Spain. This loss prevented him from invading and conquering Britain. That failure would be costly.

❹ Napoleon's Empire Collapses

KEY IDEA *Napoleon's conquests aroused nationalistic feelings across Europe and contributed to his downfall.*

Napoleon loved power. He took steps to make his empire larger. However, these steps led to mistakes that brought about his downfall.

Napoleon's first mistake was caused by his desire to crush Britain. He wanted to hurt the British economy. So in 1806 he tried stopping all trade between Britain and the lands he controlled. The effort failed, for some Europeans secretly brought in British goods. At the same time, the British put their own blockade around Europe. Because their navy was so strong, it worked very well. Soon the French economy, along with others, began to grow weak.

Napoleon's second mistake was to make his brother king of Spain in 1808. The Spanish people were loyal to their own king. With help from Britain, they fought back against Napoleon for five years. Napoleon lost 300,000 troops.

Napoleon's third mistake was perhaps his worst. In 1812, he tried to conquer Russia, far to the east. He entered Russia with more than 400,000 soldiers. He got as far as Moscow, which was deserted and on fire. His soldiers found no food or supplies there. Winter was coming, and Napoleon ordered them to head back to France. As the soldiers marched west, bitter cold, hunger, and attacks by Russian troops killed thousands. Thousands more deserted. By the time the army exited Russian territory, only 10,000 of its men were able to fight.

Other leaders saw that Napoleon was weaker now, and they moved to attack. He was defeated in Germany in 1813. In 1814, Napoleon gave up his throne and was sent away. Nevertheless, in March 1815, he boldly returned to France. He took power and raised another army. By June, though, Napoleon had lost his final battle near a Belgian town called Waterloo. This time he was sent to a far-off island in the southern Atlantic Ocean. He died there in 1821.

❺ The Congress of Vienna

KEY IDEA *After exiling Napoleon, European leaders at the Congress of Vienna tried to restore order and reestablish peace.*

After Napoleon's first defeat, in 1814, leaders of many nations met for months. They tried to draw up a peace plan for Europe that would last many years. They called the meeting the Congress of Vienna. The key person there was the foreign minister of Austria, Klemens von Metternich. He shaped the peace conditions that were accepted.

Metternich insisted on three goals. First, he wanted to make sure that the French would not attack another country again. Second, he wanted a balance of power in which no one nation was too strong. Third, he wanted to put kings back in charge of the countries from which they had been removed. The leaders agreed with Metternich's ideas. An age of European peace began.

Across Europe, kings and princes reclaimed their thrones. Most of them were conservatives and did not encourage individual liberties. They did not want any calls for equal rights. However, many people still believed in the ideals of the French Revolution. They thought that all people should be equal and share in power. Later they would fight for these rights again.

People in the Americas also felt the desire for freedom. Spanish colonies in the Americas revolted against the restored Spanish king. Many nations won independence from Spain. National feeling grew in many places in Europe, too. Soon people in areas such as Italy, Germany, and Greece would rebel and form new countries. The French Revolution had changed the politics of Europe and beyond.

Review

1. *Analyzing Causes* What factors led to the French Revolution?
2. *Following Chronological Order* Trace the fate of Louis XVI during the Revolution.
3. *Summarizing* What did Napoleon do to restore order in France?
4. *Making Inferences* Why did Napoleon's empire collapse?
5. *Determining Main Ideas* What were the goals of the Congress of Vienna?

Answer Key
Chapter 23
SUMMARY

The French Revolution and Napoleon, 1789–1815

Responses will vary but should include points similar to the following:

1. The members of the Third Estate, nearly 98 percent of France's population, were angry about their high taxes and lack of privileges. Enlightenment thinkers spread ideas about basic rights and equality. The French economy was failing, with low profits, shortages of food, and government debt. The king was weak and the queen was unpopular.

2. Louis and his family attempted to flee France but were captured. The National Assembly took away most of his powers. Other countries hoped to restore Louis to the French throne. He was imprisoned when it was thought he would help those countries. Finally, his powers were removed entirely, and he was executed as a common person.

3. He made taxes more equal and their collection more orderly; he removed dishonest government workers; he set up new public schools for ordinary citizens; he restored some church power; and he made new laws that gave citizens equal rights, though some rights were restricted.

4. He made three mistakes: trying to blockade Britain, which reacted by putting a stronger blockade on Europe; putting his brother on the Spanish throne, which caused the Spanish people to fight back; and invading Russia, where his army was nearly destroyed by brutal winter weather.

5. The congress weakened France so that it could not attack another country; created a balance of power in which no nation would be too strong; and restored monarchs to their throne.

CHAPTER
24
Summary

CHAPTERS IN BRIEF *Nationalist Revolutions Sweep the West, 1789–1900*

CHAPTER OVERVIEW *Spurred by the French Revolution, Latin American colonies won independence. In Europe, liberals and radicals pushed for change but conservatives resisted. Nationalism spread throughout Europe, and Germany and Italy formed as nations. Artistic and intellectual movements emphasized nature and feelings, true life, and "impressions" of a subject or moment.*

❶ Latin American Peoples Win Independence

KEY IDEA *Spurred by discontent and Enlightenment ideas, peoples in Latin America fought colonial rule.*

In the early 1800s, colonial peoples throughout Latin America followed the example of the French Revolution. In the name of freedom and equality, they fought for their independence.

In Latin America, society was divided into six classes of people. *Peninsulares*—those born in Spain—were at the top. Next came creoles, or Spaniards who had been born in Latin America. Below them were mestizos, with mixed European and Indian ancestry. Next were mulattos, with mixed European and African ancestry, and Africans. At the bottom were Indians.

The first movement for independence was the French colony of Saint Domingue, on the island of Hispaniola. Almost all of the people who lived in the colony were slaves of African origin. In 1791, about 100,000 of them rose in revolt. Toussaint L'Ouverture became the leader. By 1801, he had moved to the eastern part of the island and freed the slaves there. In 1804, the former colony declared its independence as Haiti.

Meanwhile in other parts of Latin America, creoles felt that they were unfairly treated by the government and the *peninsulares*. This bad feeling boiled over when Napoleon overthrew the king of Spain and named his own brother as king. Creoles in Latin America had no loyalty to the new king and revolted. However, even after the old king was restored, they did not give up their fight for freedom.

Two leaders pushed much of South America to independence. Simón Bolívar was a writer, fighter, and political thinker. He survived defeats and exile to win independence for Venezuela in 1821. José de San Martín helped win independence for Argentina in 1816 and Chile in 1818. Bolívar led their combined armies to a great victory in 1824

that gave independence to all the former Spanish colonies.

Turmoil continued in the region. Local leaders disagreed and split the new countries up into smaller units. In 1830, the territory of Gran Colombia divided into Colombia, Ecuador, and Venezuela.

In Mexico, mestizos and Indians led the fight for independence. The struggle began in 1810 when Miguel Hidalgo, a village priest, called for a revolt against Spanish rule. Creoles united with the Spanish government to put down this revolt by the lower classes, whom they feared. Fighting continued until 1815, when the creoles won. In 1820, a new government took charge in Spain. Fearing that they would lose their rights this time, the creoles now united with the rebels and fought for independence. In 1821, Spain accepted Mexico's independence. In 1823, the region of Central America separated itself from Mexico. In 1841, the United Provinces of Central America split into five republics.

In Brazil, independence took a different turn. When Napoleon's armies entered Portugal in 1807, the royal family escaped to Brazil, its largest colony. For the next 14 years, it was the center of the Portuguese empire. By the time Napoleon was defeated, the people of Brazil wanted their independence. In 1822, 8,000 creoles signed a paper asking the son of Portugal's king to rule an independent Brazil. He agreed, and Brazil became free that year through a bloodless revolt.

❷ Europe Faces Revolutions

KEY IDEA *Liberal and nationalist uprisings challenged the old conservative order of Europe.*

In the first half of the 1800s, three forces struggled for power within the countries of Europe. Conservatives supported the kings who had ruled these lands for many centuries. These were nobles and other people who owned large amounts of property. Liberals wanted to give more power to elected legislatures. They were typically middle-class merchants and business people. They wanted to limit voting rights to people who were educated and owned property. Radicals wanted the end of rule by kings and full voting rights for all people, even the poor.

At the same time, another movement arose in Europe—nationalism. This was the belief that a person's loyalty should go not to the country's ruler but to the nation itself. Nationalists thought that many factors linked people to one another. First was nationality, or a common ethnic ancestry. Shared language, culture, history, and religion were also seen as ties that connected people. People sharing these traits were thought to have a right to a land they could call their own. Groups with their own government were called nation-states. Leaders began to see that this feeling could be a powerful force for uniting a people. The French Revolution was a prime example of this.

The first people to win self-rule during this period were the Greeks. For centuries, Greece had been part of the Ottoman Empire. In 1821, Greeks revolted against this Turkish rule. Rulers in Europe did not like the idea of revolts, but the Greek cause was popular. Other nations gave aid to the Greeks, helping to defeat the Ottomans' forces in 1827. The Greeks won their independence by 1830.

Other revolts broke out. In 1830, the Belgians declared their independence from rule by the Dutch. Nationalists began a long struggle to unify all of Italy, which had been broken into many different states. Poles revolted against Russian rule. Conservatives managed to put down these rebellions. However, new ones broke out again in 1848 among Hungarians and Czechs. Once again, they were put down forcefully.

Events differed in France. Riots in 1830 forced the king to flee and put a new king in his place. A new revolt broke out in 1848 that overthrew the king and established a republic. However, the radicals who had won this victory began arguing over how much France should be changed. Some wanted only political changes. Others wanted social and economic changes that would help the poor. When these forces fought in the streets, the French gave up on the radical program. They introduced a new government, with a legislature and a strong president. The new president was Louis-Napoleon, Napoleon Bonaparte's nephew. He later named

himself emperor of France. He built railroads and promoted the growth of France's industry. The economy revived and more people had jobs.

Russia in the early 1800s had yet to build an industrial economy. The biggest problem was that serfdom still existed there. Peasants were bound to the nobles whose land they worked. Russia's rulers did not wish to free the serfs, though. They feared they would lose the support of the nobles. In the 1850s, the Russian army lost a war to take over part of the Ottoman Empire. The new ruler of Russia, Alexander II, decided that Russia's lack of a modern economy caused the defeat. He decided to begin many reforms.

The first, in 1861, was to free the serfs. Though it seemed bold, Alexander's move went only part way. Nobles kept half their land and were paid for the half that went to the peasants. The former serfs were not given the land. They had to pay for it, and this debt kept them still tied to the land. The czar's efforts to make changes ended short when he was assassinated in 1881. Alexander III, his successor, brought back tight control over the country and moved to make the economy more industrial.

❸ Nationalism Case Study: Italy and Germany

KEY IDEA *The force of nationalism contributed to the formation of two new nations and a new political order in Europe.*

Nationalism can be a force uniting people who are divided from others like themselves. The case studies on Germany and Italy will show this. However, nationalism can also cause the break-up of a state. This may occur when a group resists being part of a state. The Greeks in the Ottoman empire are an example. Finally, nationalism can pull different groups together to build a nation-state. The United States is a good example of this.

In the late 1800s, feelings of nationalism threatened to break apart three aging empires. The Austrian Empire was forced to split in two parts, Austria and Hungary. However, nationalist feeling continued to plague these rulers for 40 years and the kingdoms later broke up into several smaller states. In Russia, harsh rule and a policy of forcing other peoples to adopt Russian ways helped produce a revolution in 1917 that overthrew the czar. The Ottoman Empire, like the other two, broke apart around the time of World War I.

Italians used national feeling to build a nation, not destroy an empire. Large parts of Italy were ruled by the kings of Austria and Spain. Nationalists tried to unite the nation in 1848, but the revolt was beaten down. Hopes rested with the Italian king of the state of Piedmont-Sardinia. His chief minister, Count Cavour, worked to expand the king's control over other areas of the north. Meanwhile, Giuseppi Garibaldi led an army of patriots that won control of southern areas. He put those areas under control of the king. In 1866, the area around Venice was added to the king's control. Four years later, the king completed the uniting of Italy.

Germany had also been divided into many different states for many centuries. Since 1815, 39 states had joined in a league called the German Confederation. Prussia and Austria-Hungary controlled this group. Over time, Prussia rose to become more powerful. Leading this move was prime minister Otto von Bismarck. He joined with Austria to gain control of new lands. He then quickly turned against Austria, defeating it in war to gain even more territory. Other German states formed a new confederation that Prussia alone controlled. Bismarck's next step was to win the loyalty of the remaining German areas in the south. He purposefully angered a weak France so that it would declare war on Prussia. When the Prussian army won, Bismarck reached his goal. The war with France had given the southern German states a nationalistic feeling. They joined the other states in naming the king of Prussia as head of united Germany.

As a result of these events, the balance of power in Europe had changed. Germany and Britain were the strongest powers, followed by France. Austria, Russia, and Italy were all even weaker.

❹ Revolutions in the Arts

KEY IDEA *Artistic and intellectual movements both reflected and fueled changes in Europe in the 1800s.*

In the early 1800s, the Enlightenment was replaced by another movement, called romanticism. This movement in art and ideas showed great interest in nature and in the thoughts and feelings of the individual person. Gone was the idea that reason and order were good things. Romantic thinkers valued feeling, not reason, and nature, not society. Romantic thinkers held idealized views of the past as simpler, better times. They valued the common people. As a result, they enjoyed folk sto-

ries, songs, and traditions. They also supported calls for democracy. However, not all romantic artists and thinkers supported these ideas.

Romantic writers had different themes. French writer Victor Hugo—who wrote *The Hunchback of Notre Dame*—told stories of the poor individual who fights against an unfair society. English poet William Wordsworth celebrated the beauty of nature. Novels such as Mary Shelley's *Frankenstein* were horror tales about good and evil.

Romanticism was important in music as well. Composers wrote music that tried to appeal to the hearts and souls of listeners. The German Ludwig van Beethoven was the foremost of these composers.

In the middle 1800s, however, the grim realities of industrial life made the dreams of romanticism seem silly. A new movement arose—realism. Artists and writers tried to show life as it really was. They used their art to protest social conditions that they thought were unfair. French writer Emile Zola's books revealed harsh working conditions for the poor, which led to new laws aimed at helping those people. In England, Charles Dickens wrote many novels that showed how poor people suffered in the new industrial economy.

A new device, the camera, was developed in this period. Photographers could use it to capture a real moment on film. In the 1860s, Parisian painters reacted against the realistic style. This new art style—impressionism—used light and shimmering colors to produce an "impression" of a subject or moment. Composers created moods with their music. They used combinations of musical instruments and tone patterns to create mental pictures. Things like the sight of the sea or a warm day were favorites of the composers.

Review

1. ***Making Inferences*** How did the divisions of Mexican society affect the movement to independence?
Drawing Conclusions
2. Explain how the freeing of Russia's serfs in 1861 was an example of both liberal and conservative thought.
3. Give one example each of how nationalism was a unifying and a destructive force.
4. ***Determining Main Ideas*** How did artistic ideas change in the 1800s?

Answer Key
Chapter 24
SUMMARY

Nationalist Revolutions Sweep the West,
1789–1900

Responses will vary but should include points similar to the following:

1. The divisions in society may have prevented Mexican independence from happening earlier. Creoles did not at first join the revolt because they were afraid of the lower classes.

2. Freeing serfs from being bound to the nobles for whom they worked was a liberal thought. However, making serfs pay for the land was a conservative thought. It created a debt that kept them tied to the land.

3. Nationalism was a destructive force in Austria, where it forced the empire to divide into the kingdoms of Austria and Hungary and later resulted in the complete breakup of those kingdoms. Nationalism was a unifying force in Italy.

4. In the early 1800s, the main artistic movement was romanticism, which valued feeling, nature, and the past. In the middle 1800s, the main movement was realism, which showed the world as it really was. Finally, impressionism caught an "impression" of a subject or a moment.

CHAPTERS IN BRIEF *The Industrial Revolution, 1700–1900*

CHAPTER OVERVIEW *Britain fueled an Industrial Revolution, which changed society. Workers benefited eventually, but at first they suffered bad working and living conditions. Other nations followed Britain's example and industrialized. Thinkers reacted to these changes by developing new views of society. Reformers pushed for changes to make society better.*

❶ The Beginnings of Industrialization

KEY IDEA *The Industrial Revolution started in Great Britain and soon spread elsewhere.*

In the early 1700s, large landowners in Britain bought much of the land that had been owned by poorer farmers. They introduced new ways of farming. One technique was to use a seed drill. This machine planted seeds in well-spaced rows. Before this, seeds were scattered by hand over the ground. As a result, more seeds sprouted. Another technique was to rotate crops annually. Those who raised livestock used new methods to increase the size of their animals. As a result of these improvements, farm output increased. More food was available, and people enjoyed healthier diets. The population of Britain grew. The agricultural revolution helped produce the Industrial Revolution.

The Industrial Revolution refers to the greatly increased output of machine-made goods that began in Great Britain in the mid–1700s.

For several reasons, Britain was the first country to have an economy based on industry. It had 1) coal and water to power machines, 2) iron ore to make machines and tools, 3) rivers to move people and goods, and 4) good harbors for shipping goods to other lands. Britain also had a system of banks that could fund new businesses. Finally, the British government was stable, which gave the country a positive attitude.

The Industrial Revolution began in the textile industry. Several new inventions helped businesses produce cloth and clothing more quickly. Business owners built huge buildings—factories—that housed large machines powered by water.

The invention of the steam engine in 1705 brought in a new source of power. The steam engine used fire to heat water and produce steam, which was used to drive the engine. Eventually steam-driven machines were used to run factories.

At the same time, improvements were being made in transportation. An American invented the first steam-driven boat. This allowed people to send goods more quickly over rivers and canals. The British also built better roads that included layers of stone and rock to prevent wagons from being stuck in the mud.

Starting in the 1820s, steam fueled a new burst of industrial growth. At that time, a British engineer set up the world's first railroad line. It used a steam-driven locomotive. Soon, railroads were being built all over Britain. The railroad boom helped business owners move their goods to market more quickly. The boom in railroad building created thousands of new jobs in several different industries. The railroad had a deep effect on British society. For instance, people who lived in the country moved to cities.

❷ Industrialization Case Study: Manchester

KEY IDEA *The factory system changed the way people lived and worked, ibringing both benefits and problems.*

The change to an industrial economy brought many benefits to British people. They used coal to heat their homes, ate better food, and wore better clothing. Many people also suffered, however. Industrialization caused many changes.

One change was a rise in the proportion of people who lived in cities. For centuries, most people in Europe had lived in the country. Now more and more lived in cities. The number of cities with more than 100,000 people doubled between 1800 and 1850. Because they grew quickly, cities were not ideal places to live. People could not find good housing, schools, or police protection. The cities were filthy with garbage, and sickness swept through slum areas. The average life span of a person living in a city was 17 years—compared to 38 years in the countryside.

Working conditions were harsh as well. The average worker spent 14 hours a day on the job, 6 days a week. Factories were dark, and the powerful machines were dangerous. Many workers were killed or seriously injured in accidents. Some rioted against the poor living and working conditions.

Some people improved their lives in the new economy. The middle class—made up of skilled workers, professionals, business people, and wealthy farmers—did well. They enjoyed comfortable lives in pleasant homes. This class began to grow in size, and some people in it grew wealthier than the nobles who had dominated society for many centuries. Still, nobles looked down on the people who gained their wealth from business. They, in turn, looked down on the poor workers.

Overall, the Industrial Revolution had many good effects. It increased the amount of goods and services a nation could produce and added to its wealth. It created jobs for workers and over time helped them live better lives. It produced better diets, better housing, and cheaper, better clothing. Many of these benefits were far in the future, however.

The English city of Manchester showed how industrialization changed society. Rapid growth made the city crowded and filthy. The factory owners risked their money and worked long hours to make their businesses grow. In return, they enjoyed huge profits and built huge houses. The workers also worked long hours, but had few benefits.

Many workers were children, some only six years old. Not until 1819 did the British government put limits on using children as workers. With so much industry in one place, Manchester suffered in another way. Coal smoke and cloth dyes polluted the air and water. Yet, Manchester also created many jobs, a variety of consumer goods, and great wealth.

❸ Industrialization Spreads

KEY IDEA *The industrialization that began in Great Britain spread to other parts of the world.*

Other countries followed the example of Britain and began to change their economies to an industrial base. The United States was one of the first. Like Britain, it had water power, sources of coal and iron, and a ready supply of workers. The United States also benefited from conflict with Britain. During the War of 1812, Britain stopped shipping goods to the United States. As a result, American industries had a chance to supply the goods that Americans wanted.

The switch to an industrial economy began in the United States in the textile industry. In 1789, based on memory and a partial design, a British worker brought the secret of Britain's textile machines to North America. He built a machine to spin thread. In 1813, a group of Massachusetts investors built a complex of factories that made cloth. Just a few years later they built an even larger complex in the town of Lowell. Thousands of workers, mostly young girls, came to these towns to work in the factories.

In the United States, industry grew first in the Northeast. In the last decades of the 1800s, a rapid burst of industrial growth took place that was more widespread. This boom was fueled by large supplies of coal, oil, and iron. Helping, too, was the appearance of a number of new inventions, including the electric light. As in Britain, railroad building was also a big part of this industrial growth.

Businesses needed huge sums of money to take on big projects. To raise money, companies sold shares of ownership, called stock. All those who held stock were part owners of the company. This form of organizing a business is called a corporation.

Industrial growth spread to Europe as well. Belgium was the first to adopt British ways. It was rich in iron and coal and had good waterways. It had the resources needed.

Germany was politically divided until the late 1800s. As a result, it could not develop a wide industrial economy. However, west-central Germany was rich in coal and did become a leading industrial site.

Across Europe, small areas began to change to the new industries. Industrial growth did not occur in France until after 1830. It was helped by the government's construction of a large network of railroads. Some countries—such as Austria-Hungary and Spain—had problems that stopped them from building new industries.

The Industrial Revolution changed the world. Countries that had adopted an industrial economy enjoyed more wealth and power than those that had not. The countries of Europe soon began to take advantage of lands in Africa and Asia. They used these lands as sources of raw materials needed for their factories. They saw the people only as markets for the goods they made. They took control of these lands, a practice called imperialism.

The Industrial Revolution changed life forever in the countries that industrialized. Problems caused by industrialization led to movements for social reform.

❹ Reforming the Industrial World

KEY IDEA *The Industrial Revolution led to economic, social, and political reforms.*

The new industrial economy led to new ways of thinking about society. Some economists thought that the government should leave business owners alone. Their view was called laissez-faire, from a French phrase meaning "let people do as they please." Adam Smith argued that putting no limits on business or on trade would help a nation's economy grow the most. He and other economists supported a system called capitalism. In a capitalist economy, people invest their money in businesses to make a profit. Over time, society as a whole would benefit, said Smith and the others. These people warned the government not to make laws trying to protect workers. Such laws would upset the workings of the economy, they said.

Other thinkers challenged these ideas. One group was called the Utilitarians. They thought that an idea or practice was good only as it proved useful. They thought it was unfair that workers should work so hard for such little pay and live in such poor conditions. They thought the government should do away with great differences in wealth among people.

Some thinkers went farther and urged that businesses should be owned by society as a whole, not by individuals. Then a few people would not grow wealthy at the expense of many. Instead, all would enjoy the benefits of increased production. This view—called socialism—grew out of a belief in progress and a concern for justice and fairness.

A German thinker named Karl Marx wrote about a radical form of socialism called Marxism. He said that factory owners and workers were bound to oppose one another in the struggle for power. Over time, he said, the capitalist system would destroy itself. The great mass of workers would rebel against the wealthy few. Marx wrote *The Communist Manifesto* in which he described communism, a form of complete socialism in which all production is owned by the people. Private property would not exist. In the early 1900s, these ideas would inspire revolution.

While thinkers discussed these different ideas, workers took action to try to improve their lives. Many formed into unions that tried to bargain with business owners for better pay and better working conditions. When business owners resisted these efforts, the workers went on strike, or refused to work. The struggle to win the right to form unions was long and hard for workers in Britain and the United States. Still, by the late 1800s, workers in both countries had made some progress.

The British Parliament and reformers in the United States also took steps to try to fix some of the worst features of industrialism. Britain passed laws that put limits on how much women and children could work. Groups in the United States pushed for similar laws.

Another major reform movement of the 1800s was the drive to abolish slavery. The British Parliament took the first step by ending the slave trade in 1807. It abolished slavery completely in 1833. Slavery was finally ended in the United States in 1865, after the Civil War. Spain ended slavery in Puerto Rico in 1873 and in Cuba in 1886. Brazil became the last country to ban slavery, which it did in 1888.

Women were active in these and other reform movements. As they fought for the end of slavery, many women launched an effort to win equal rights for women. The movement for equality began in the United States in 1848. In 1888, women from around the world formed a group dedicated to this cause.

Reformers took on other projects as well. Some pushed for—and won—improved education. Others hoped to improve conditions in prisons.

Review

1. *Analyzing Causes and Recognizing Effects* Why did the Industrial Revolution begin in Britain?

Determining Main Ideas

2. What was the impact of the railroad?

3. What reforms were popular in the 1800s?

4. *Analyzing Causes and Recognizing Effects* What effects did industrialization have on society?

5. *Developing Historical Perspective* How did industrialization spread in the United States?

Answer Key
Chapter 25
SUMMARY

The Industrial Revolution, 1700–1900

Responses will vary but should include points similar to the following:

1. Britain had some advantages: it had resources such as coal and water to power machines, iron ore to make tools and machines, rivers to move people and goods, and good harbors for shipping goods to other lands. Britain also had a system of banks that could fund new businesses. Finally, the British government was stable, and people were optimistic.

2. The railroad boom helped business owners move their goods to market more quickly. The boom in railroad building created thousands of new jobs in several different industries. People who lived in the country moved to cities.

3. Reformers pushed for limits on how much women and children could work, the end of slavery, equal rights for women, and improved education and prisons.

4. The population of cities grew, although cities were crowded, dirty, and unhealthy places. Economies grew, and people could enjoy a better standard of living. Diet and education improved. Many of these changes took a long time to reach the masses of workers, however.

5. After industrialization came to the United States, it was limited mostly to the Northeast. However, toward the end of the 1800s, it spread across the country. That spread was promoted by several inventions, the building of railroads, and the growth of cities.

Summary

CHAPTERS IN BRIEF *An Age of Democracy and Progress, 1815–1914*

CHAPTER OVERVIEW *In Britain, reforms gave all men the right to vote. A republic was proclaimed in France, but political conflict continued. Some British colonies won the right to govern themselves, but the struggle for that right was not easy in Ireland. The United States fought a civil war that finally put an end to slavery. New inventions and scientific advances made life more healthful and enjoyable.*

❶ Democratic Reform and Activism

KEY IDEA *Spurred by the demands of ordinary people, Great Britain and France underwent democratic reforms.*

Since the 1600s, Britain's government had been a constitutional monarchy. A king or queen ruled the country, but the elected legislature—Parliament—held the real power. Still, very few people could vote for members of Parliament. Only men who owned property—about six percent of the population—had the right. That changed in the 1800s.

The Reform Bill of 1832 was the first step. Middle-class people across England protested the fact that they could not vote. Worried by revolutions sweeping Europe, Parliament passed the Reform Bill. This law gave the right to vote to many in the middle class. It also gave seats in Parliament to the new industrial cities, which had not had any representatives before. Over time, Parliament made more changes. By 1884, almost all adult males in Britain could vote. Parliament also made votes take place by secret ballot. Another law gave pay to members of Parliament, which in effect opened that body to people who were not wealthy.

By 1890, a number of countries with industrial economies had given all men the right to vote. None, however, gave women that right. During the 1800s, women in the United States and Britain peacefully campaigned for the vote. Beginning in 1903, a group called the Women's Social and Political Union began a stronger campaign for women's suffrage in Britain. They held rallies and parades. They also broke up the speeches of government officials and sometimes set fire to buildings. When the leaders were arrested, they went on hunger strikes to gain publicity for their cause. It was not until after World War I, however, that women won the right to vote in both Great Britain and the United States.

The road to democracy in France was more rocky. After France's defeat at the hands of Prussia in 1870, France went through a series of crises. Finally a new government—the Third Republic—was formed. It lasted over 60 years, but France remained divided.

In the 1890s, French society was divided over the case of an army officer, Alfred Dreyfus, who was accused of being a traitor. The charge was false and was made largely because Dreyfus was a Jew. However, many believed the charge, and he was found guilty. A few years later, new evidence showed that he had been framed. Dreyfus was later declared innocent.

The affair revealed that many in Europe hated Jews. In Eastern Europe, the situation was very bad. The Russian government even allowed organized attacks on Jewish villages. From the 1880s on, many Jews fled to the United States.

❷ Self-Rule for British Colonies

KEY IDEA *Britain allowed self-rule in Canada, Australia, and New Zealand but delayed independence for Ireland.*

Britain had colonies all around the world. Three of them were settled by colonists from Europe who built societies strongly shaped by British culture. Canada, Australia, and New Zealand developed industrial economies. They reached a point where they hoped to have their own governments.

The white settlers of Canada were split into two groups. Britain had won Canada from France back in 1763. However, some French-speaking Catholics still lived in the colony. The other group was English-speaking and mostly Protestant. The two groups did not get along. In 1791, Britain split the colony into two provinces, each with its own government. The French-speaking people grew angry at British rule.

After a series of rebellions, the British Parliament put the two sections back together under one government. Other, smaller colonies were added to create the Dominion of Canada. Canadians had the right to make all laws concerning their own affairs. Parliament kept the right to make decisions about relations with other countries. By 1871, Canada stretched all the way to the Pacific Ocean.

New Zealand and Australia first became part of the British Empire around 1770. The first settlers sent to Australia were convicted criminals. Once they had spent the required amount of time, they won their freedom and had the right to buy land. In the 1800s, other settlers arrived, many to join in the growing sheep industry. The settlement of New Zealand went more slowly because the British government recognized that the native people—the Maori—had rights to the land. By the 1840s, though, the number of settlers was growing.

During the 1850s, these two countries became self-governing. However, they stayed in the British Empire and in the early 1900s became dominions. Australia was the first country to use secret ballots in voting for representatives. New Zealand—in 1893—was the first country to give women the right to vote. The native peoples of Australia and New Zealand enjoyed few of these rights, though. Like Native Americans, they suffered the spread of European settlement.

Irish self-rule took longer to achieve. Ireland bitterly opposed English rule from its start in the 1100s. Conflict also separated the Catholic Irish and the small group of English Protestants. When Ireland was made part of Britain in 1801, the Irish won representation in Parliament. A leader used that position to win back some rights for Irish Catholics.

In the 1840s, the Irish suffered a terrible famine. A disease destroyed the potatoes on which the Irish depended, causing many to starve. About 1 million died and another 1.5 million left for the United States and other countries. Meanwhile, the British forced the Irish to pay their rents. Many lost their land, and resentment against England grew even stronger.

In the late 1800s, some Irish pushed for complete independence. Most argued for home rule—the right to govern internal affairs. The British government opposed this move. They were afraid that the Catholic majority would harshly treat the

Protestants in the north. In 1914, Parliament finally gave home rule to the southern part of Ireland. When World War I delayed its enactment, Irish nationalists rebelled. Finally, Britain split Ireland in two. Northern Ireland remained part of Britain. The southern part became independent. Many people still seek independence for all of Ireland.

❸ War and Expansion in the United States

KEY IDEA *The United States expanded across North America and fought a bloody civil war.*

The United States had troubles of its own. In the early 1800s, the nation grew in size. It bought a huge piece of land from France in the Louisiana Purchase. Many said it was "manifest destiny"—the right of the United States to rule the land from the Atlantic Ocean to the Pacific. As white settlers moved farther and farther west, Native Americans suffered. In the 1830s, many thousands were forced to move from their homes in the eastern states to the present state of Oklahoma. The United States won a war with Mexico in the 1840s and thus gained even more land.

This growth raised serious questions. The southern states used slave labor to grow crops such as cotton. People in the South hoped to extend slavery to the new western lands. Many in the North, however, believed that slavery was wrong and should be ended.

Conflict over slavery eventually led to the Civil War. The southern states seceded, or pulled out of, the Union. When southern forces fired on a Union fort in 1861, war broke out. The fighting lasted four long and bloody years. The North won the war. During the fighting, President Abraham Lincoln declared that slavery was ended in the United States. Later, the Constitution was changed to make this the law of the land and to say that African Americans were citizens.

In the first few years after the war, newly freed African Americans enjoyed equal rights. Later, whites regained control of the governments of the southern states. They passed laws that took away the rights of blacks and treated them unfairly. It would be many years before African Americans could enjoy equality.

The economy of the South was destroyed by the Civil War. Elsewhere, though, the nation saw a surge of industrial growth. Helping achieve this great growth was a sharp rise in immigration from Europe and Asia. By 1914, more than 20 million people had come to the United States.

❹ Nineteenth-Century Progress

KEY IDEA Breakthroughs in science and technology transformed daily life and entertainment.

In the late 1800s, new inventions made major changes in how people lived. Thomas Edison got patents on more than 1,000 inventions. Among them were the electric light bulb and the phonograph. Alexander Graham Bell invented the telephone, and Guglielmo Marconi created the first radio.

There were big changes in transportation too. Though someone else invented the car, Henry Ford made it affordable to ordinary people. He had a factory with an assembly line that allowed him to quickly build cheap cars that cost as little as $300. In 1903, the Wright brothers flew the first motor-powered airplane flight. Soon there was an aircraft industry.

Medicine made advances. Until the mid-1800s, no one knew about germs. French scientist Louis Pasteur discovered that microscopic animals that he called bacteria could live in food. Soon he and others realized that bacteria could cause disease. British surgeon Joseph Lister took steps to kill bacteria, which helped more patients survive. Soon his practices became widespread. Public officials began to clean up plumbing and sewage systems. All these steps helped people lead longer and healthier lives.

English scientist Charles Darwin developed a new theory that was hotly debated. He said that all life on earth, even humans, had developed from simpler forms over millions of years. Many did not accept this idea, which they said went against the Bible.

In the mid-1800s, an Austrian monk named Gregor Mendel did some experiments that showed that parents passed on their traits to offspring. His work formed the basis of the science of genetics. Other scientists made new discoveries in chemistry and physics. They found that all matter is made of tiny particles called atoms. They also were able to identify the differences between different elements.

In the late 1800s, some thinkers began the new social science of psychology, which is the study of the mind. A series of experiments led Russian Ivan Pavlov to argue that people responded to certain situations because of how they were trained. By changing the training, he said, one could change the response. Austrian Sigmund Freud argued that powerful forces in the subconscious mind of a person shaped behavior. These views shocked many. They seemed to overturn the idea that people could use their reason to build better lives.

In earlier times, art, music, and the theater had been of interest only to the wealthy. With the rise of the middle class, culture became available to more people. One reason was that more people could read, which led to more newspapers, magazines, and books.

Another reason was that working people had more time to enjoy art, music, and recreation. People went to music halls to enjoy singing and dancing. In the early 1900s, they began to watch the first silent movies. People also began to enjoy sporting events, both as participants and as spectators.

Review

Comparing and Contrasting

1. Contrast the spread of democracy in Britain with that in France.
2. Compare the development of self-rule in the different colonies of Britain.
3. ***Determining Main Ideas*** How did the United States change during the 1800s?
4. ***Drawing Conclusions*** What important inventions were made in the late 1800s and early 1900s? Which one do you think was most important?
5. ***Analyzing Causes and Recognizing Effects*** How did new medical and scientific discoveries and ideas from the late 1800s change life?

Answer Key
Chapter 26
SUMMARY

An Age of Democracy and Progress, 1815–1914

Responses will vary but should include points similar to the following:

1. In Britain, Parliament extended the right to vote to more people through a peaceful series of changes. In France, the growth of democracy grew out of more conflict.

2. In Canada, self-rule was put in place to try to end the conflict between French-speaking and English-speaking settlers. In Australia and New Zealand, self-rule was granted with little conflict. In Ireland, however, self-rule was only given to part of the island, and that came only after many decades of rebellion.

3. During the 1800s, the United States expanded to the Pacific Ocean, ended slavery, changed to an industrial economy, and saw the arrival of millions of immigrants.

4. In the late 1800s and early 1900s, new inventions included the electric light, the telephone, the radio, the car, and the airplane. Of these, the light was the most important, because it allowed people to live and work at night and helped make streets safer.

5. New medical discoveries revealed that germs can cause disease and allowed doctors and public health officials to take steps to make hospitals and cities healthier. New scientific discoveries revealed new information about genes and atoms. Social scientists developed the new study of psychology, which tried to understand how hidden forces shaped people's behavior.

CHAPTERS IN BRIEF *The Age of Imperialism, 1850–1914*

Summary

CHAPTER OVERVIEW *Several factors led Europeans to claim control of almost all of Africa. Some Africans resisted, but most efforts failed. The Ottoman Empire broke apart, and European powers took some of its lands. The British took control of India, where they modernized the economy to benefit themselves. Europeans gained lands in Southeast Asia, and the United States sought colonies.*

❶ The Scramble for Africa

KEY IDEA *Ignoring the claims of African ethnic groups, kingdoms, and city-states, Europeans established colonial claims.*

In the early 1800s, European nations had just a toehold in Africa, holding only areas along the coast. In the mid-1800s, though, Europeans had renewed interest in Africa. This rose, in part, from a desire to create overseas empires, a movement called imperialism. European nations wanted to control lands that had raw materials they needed for their industrial economies. They also wanted to open up markets for the goods they made. Nationalism fed the drive for empires as well. A nation often felt that gaining colonies was a measure of its greatness. Racism was another reason. Europeans thought that they were better than Africans. Finally, Christian missionaries supported imperialism. They thought that European rule would end the slave trade and help them convert native peoples.

As a result of these factors, the nations of Europe began to seize lands in Africa. Technology helped them succeed. Steamships, railroads, and telegraphs made them able to penetrate deep into Africa and still have contact with the home country. Machine guns gave them a weapon of far greater power than any African peoples possessed. Finally, the drug quinine gave doctors a weapon against malaria, which struck Europeans. They were also helped by the lack of unity among African peoples.

The competition for African land, called the "scramble for Africa" began in the 1880s. The discovery of gold and diamonds in Africa increased European interest in the continent. So that they would not fight over the land, European powers met in Berlin in 1884–85. They agreed that any nation could claim any part of Africa simply by telling the others and by showing that it had control of the area. They then moved quickly to grab land.

By 1914, only Liberia and Ethiopia were independent of European control.

The Europeans began to build plantations where they grew peanuts, palm oil, cocoa, and rubber. They also mined Africa's important minerals. The Congo produced copper and tin. South Africa had gold and diamonds.

In South Africa, three groups struggled over the land. In the early 1800s, the Zulu chief Shaka created a large kingdom. The British seized control of this land in 1887. Meanwhile, the British won control of the Dutch colony on the southern coast. Many thousands of Dutch settlers, called Boers, moved north to escape the British. At the end of the century, the Boers fought a vicious war with the British. The Boers lost, and they joined the British-run Union of South Africa.

❷ Imperialism Case Study: Nigeria

KEY IDEA *Europeans embarked on a new phase of empire-building that affected both Africa and the rest of the world.*

European nations wanted to control more of the life of their conquered peoples. As a result, each colonized region operated under one of these forms:

- colony—governed by a foreign power
- protectorate—allowed its own government but was under the control of a foreign power
- sphere of influence—claimed as the exclusive investment or trading realm of a foreign power
- economic imperialism—controlled by private businesses rather than by a foreign government

The imperialist powers had two main methods of running their colonies. Britain and the United States used indirect control. In this system, local rulers had power over day-to-day matters. There were also councils of native peoples and government officials. These councils were a first step for native peoples to someday govern themselves.

Britain tried to rule Nigeria through indirect control. Because the area was huge and peopled by many different groups, it was difficult for the British to rule directly. They let local chiefs maintain order over their areas and collect taxes. The system did not always work. Chiefs had ruled before in the southeast and southwest of Nigeria. The chiefs resented having their power limited.

France and other European nations used the other method—direct control. Feeling that native peoples could not handle the complex business of running a country, the European power governed. The French also had a policy of assimilation. All institutions were patterned after their counterparts in France. They hoped that the native peoples would learn and adopt French ways.

Some Africans tried to resist imperialism. People in Algeria fought against the French for almost 50 years. In German East Africa, thousands died when they tried to use spiritual power to fight German machine guns. Only in Ethiopia did resistance succeed. There, Emperor Menelik II cleverly played one European country against another. In 1896, he used European weapons to defeat an invading Italian army. With this victory, Ethiopia stayed independent.

Africans did enjoy some benefits from colonial rule. European governments put an end to ethnic conflict. Colonial powers brought African economies fully into the world market and built railroads, dams, and telephone and telegraph lines.

For the most part, though, imperialism caused damage. Traditional African society was destroyed. People were forced out of their homes and made to work under horrible conditions. Finally, the political boundaries that Europeans drew had no relation to ethnic divisions in Africa. These boundaries created problems many decades later when the colonies became independent nations.

❸ Europeans Claim Muslim Lands

KEY IDEA *European nations expand their empires by seizing territories from Muslim states.*

The Ottoman Empire, based in modern Turkey, had lasted for hundreds of years. By the 1800s, it was weak. In 1830, Greece won its independence and Serbia won the right to govern itself. European

nations eyed what remained of the empire hungrily.

Russia hoped to win control of the Black Sea so it could ship grain across the Mediterranean Sea. It fought a war with the Ottomans in the 1850s but lost when Britain and France joined against it. Still, the Ottomans later lost almost all of their land in Europe and parts of Africa. By 1914, the empire was much smaller than it had ever been. Muslim leaders, seeing this decline, decided to modernize their countries.

In Egypt, Muhammad Ali broke away from Ottoman control. He put in place reforms to change the army and the economy. He pushed Egypt's farmers to grow cotton, a cash crop in demand in Europe. However, peasants suffered when they were turned away from growing food. His grandson continued to modernize. He joined with the French in building the Suez Canal, which connected the Mediterranean to the Red Sea. When Egypt had money troubles, Britain took control of the canal— and the country.

In Persia, the Russians and the British competed for control with local powers. Russia wanted to win Persia to have access to the Indian Ocean. Britain wanted some land there as a barrier between Russia and its colony in India. In the early 1900s, oil was discovered in Persia. A British company signed an agreement with Persia's ruler to develop these oil fields. Persians rebelled against their ruler—who was corrupt—and the growing influence of Europeans. Then Russia and Britain stepped in and took control of the land.

❹ British Imperialism in India

KEY IDEA *As the Mughal Empire declined, Britain seized almost the whole subcontinent of India.*

In the early 1700s, the Mughal Empire of India fell into decline. By the middle of the century, the British East India Company was becoming the most important power in India. It held huge amounts of land—almost the entire subcontinent.

British law forced India to supply raw materials such as tea, indigo (a dye), coffee, and cotton. The law also forced Indian manufacturing out of business. India became even more important when the East India Company built rail lines that linked growing regions in the interior with ports on the coast.

India enjoyed some gains from British rule. Its rail system was the third largest in the world and helped make the economy more modern. The

British made other improvements, too. They built telephone and telegraph lines, dams, bridges, and canals. They also improved sanitation and public health and built schools. More and more Indians learned to read.

British rule caused problems as well. Many economic benefits flowed out of India to Britain. Indian industry died out because of British trade laws. Many farmers and villages lost their ability to feed themselves because they were made to grow cash crops. Many peoples died when famines struck. British racist attitudes damaged Indian culture.

By the mid-1800s, many Indians felt growing resentment. When Indian soldiers heard rumors that offended their religious feelings, many rebelled. The East India Company needed a year— and British troops—to put it down. The Indians lost because of their own divisions. Muslims and Hindus did not trust each other. After the revolt, the British government took direct control of British India.

Indians tried other ways of resisting British control. Leaders such as Ram Mohun Roy urged changes in traditional Indian practices to make Indian society more modern. He hoped to free India of foreign control with these changes. Indians resented the fact that they were treated unfairly. They formed two groups—the Indian National Congress and the Muslim League. Both began to push the British to make changes. In the early 1900s, they called for self-government.

❺ Imperialism in Southeast Asia

KEY IDEA *Demand for Asian products drove Western imperialists to seek possession of Southeast Asian lands.*

European nations also grabbed land in Southeast Asia and the islands on the edge of the Pacific Ocean. They wanted the area for its resources and because it was close to China. The United States joined this quest for colonies.

European powers found that these lands were good for growing such cash crops as sugar, coffee, cocoa, rubber, and fruit. As trade in these items grew, Europeans moved to take more land. The Dutch ran Indonesia, where their settlers remained at the top of society. The British took the port of Singapore plus Malaysia and Burma (modern Myanmar). Needing workers, the British brought many Chinese to Malaysia. France grabbed

Indochina (modern Laos, Cambodia, and Vietnam). They made farmers grow rice for export. Because most of the rice was shipped away, the farmers had less to eat even though they were growing more rice than before. One land—Siam (modern Thailand)—stayed independent. King Mongkut and his son modernized Siam without giving up power.

Colonialism brought some features of modern life to these regions. However, economic changes benefited European-run businesses, not local people. The native peoples did benefit from better schooling, health, and cleanliness. Plantation farming brought millions of people from other areas to Southeast Asia. The mix of cultures and religions did not always go smoothly. Even today, some conflict between groups results from this period.

In the late 1800s, the United States also began to seek colonies. In 1898, as a result of the Spanish-American War, the United States won possession of Puerto Rico, Guam, and the Philippine Islands. Filipino nationalists fought Americans for their freedom, just as they had fought the Spaniards before. The United States defeated the rebels and promised to give the Philippines self-rule later. In the meantime, American businesses took advantage of Filipino workers.

Some American businessmen grew wealthy from sugar plantations in Hawaii. In the 1890s, when Queen Liliuokalani tried to regain control of her country, they overthrew her. They declared a republic and asked the United States to annex— take possession of—Hawaii. In 1898, it became a territory of the United States.

Review

1. ***Summarizing*** What led to European imperialism, and why did it succeed?
2. ***Analyzing Causes and Recognizing Effects*** What happened when Africans tried to resist imperialism?
3. ***Comparing and Contrasting*** Contrast how the British and French ruled their colonies.
4. ***Drawing Conclusions*** How were the effects of imperialism in Southeast Asia typical of those for other regions?

Answer Key
Chapter 27
SUMMARY

The Age of Imperialism, 1850–1914

Responses will vary but should include points similar to the following:

1. Imperialism arose because Europeans wanted to control lands that had raw materials and provided markets for the goods they made; to promote nationalism; to prove racial superiority; and to make it easier for Christian missionaries to convert native peoples. Imperialism succeeded because of technology (steamships, railroads, telegraphs, and machine guns) and because of the lack of unity among African peoples.

2. When Africans tried to resist imperialism, they were generally defeated, except in the case of the Ethiopian Emperor Menelik II, who had weapons equal to those of the European power he opposed.

3. The British tried to rule their colonies indirectly and hoped that eventually the native peoples could govern themselves. The French ruled their colonies directly and wanted native peoples to adopt French culture.

4. In Southeast Asia as in other regions, steps to modernize the economies generally benefited the European businesses and not the local people. Still, locals did enjoy better schooling, health, and sanitation.

CHAPTER

28

Summary

CHAPTERS IN BRIEF *Transformations Around the Globe, 1800–1914*

CHAPTER OVERVIEW *In China, a weak government could not resist European power. In Japan, a reforming emperor modernized the country and launched imperialist expansion. The Latin American economies fell prey to European businesses, and the United States became the dominant power in the region. A revolution freed Mexico from France, but civil war raged for decades.*

❶ China Resists Outside Influence

KEY IDEA *Western economic pressure forced China to open to foreign trade and influence.*

In the late 1700s, China was self-sufficient. It had a strong farming economy based on growing rice. Other crops, introduced from the Americas, helped to feed its large population. Industry made silk, cotton, and ceramics. Mines produced salt, tin, silver, and iron. China needed nothing from the outside world.

China allowed only limited trade with European powers, and it all had to come through one port. Also, the trade at this port was in China's favor. In other words, the Chinese sold more than they bought. Europeans, especially the British, were eager to find something that the Chinese would want in large quantities. In the early 1800s, they found it—the drug opium, shipped mostly from India. Soon millions of Chinese were addicted to opium, and the Chinese government complained. When the British refused to stop the trade, war broke out. Because British ships had more powerful guns, China lost the war. As a result, in 1842 the British took possession of Hong Kong. Later, the United States and European nations won the right to trade in five ports. The Chinese resented these treaties but could not stop them.

China had internal problems as well. The population had grown quickly. Yet food production had barely increased, so millions starved. The Chinese began to rebel against their government. A leader arose in southern China who hoped to save China. He launched a rebellion that won control of large parts of the south, including the city of Nanjing. The government needed 14 years to put down the Taiping Rebellion. The fighting resulted in the death of millions.

In the late 1800s, European powers and Japan each won a foothold in China—a "sphere of influence." This is a region in which a foreign nation controls trade and investment. The United States opposed these steps. It urged an Open Door Policy, in which all powers had equal access to Chinese markets. While the Europeans agreed, the result had little benefit for China. Though it was not formally carved into colonies, it was clearly dominated by foreign powers.

The Empress Cixi ruled China in fact, even though younger emperors ruled in name. She supported some reforms. She backed the self-strengthening movement, which produced new ships for China. The program was not a complete success, though. In 1898, the young Emperor Guangxu tried to put in place broader reforms. Conservatives didn't like this. The retired Cixi had him arrested and took back control of the government. China had lost a chance to change.

Many Chinese grew increasingly resentful of foreign influence. They formed the Society of Harmonious Fists, known as the Boxers. They wanted to get rid of all Western influence—including any Chinese who had accepted Western culture or the Christian religion. In early 1900, an army of Boxers surrounded Beijing's European section. After many weeks, they were finally driven out by a multinational army of soldiers.

Finally Cixi began to allow major reforms. Change came slowly, though. In 1908, the court said that China would become a constitutional monarchy by 1917. However, unrest would soon return.

❷ Modernization in Japan

KEY IDEA *Japan followed the model of Western powers by expanding its foreign influence.*

From the early 1600s to the mid-1800s, Japan was virtually isolated. It did have relations with China and Korea and had limited contact with Dutch traders. That changed in 1853 when American steamships, with cannons, entered Japanese waters.

The next year, Japan agreed to open up trade to the United States. Soon after, it made similar deals with European nations.

Many Japanese were upset with the shogun, the military dictator, who had agreed to these new treaties. The Emperor Mutsuhito rallied their support and managed to overthrow the shogun. For the first time in centuries, the emperor ruled Japan directly. He reigned for 45 years, from 1867 to 1912, in what is called the Meiji era. The name Meiji, which he chose for his reign, means "enlightened rule."

The emperor was determined to modernize his country. He sent government officials to Europe and the United States. From what they saw, they shaped a new Japan. They modeled the government after the strong central government of Germany. They patterned the army after Germany's and a new navy after Britain's. They adapted the American system of schooling for all children. The emperor also supported changes to Japan's economy. The country built railroads, mined coal, and constructed factories.

These steps had results. In just a few years, Japan's industrial economy equaled almost any in the world. By 1890, it was the strongest military power in Asia. It asked foreigners to give up their special rights in Japan. The countries agreed, and a proud Japan felt equal to them. Now, it wanted to demonstrate its power.

Japan began to expand its influence like the European powers. When China broke an agreement not to send armies into Korea, Japan went to war. It drove China out of Korea and gained Taiwan and some other islands as new colonies. In 1904, Japan and Russia fought a war over China's Manchurian territory. Japan surprised the world by defeating a larger power that was supposed to be stronger.

The next year, Japan attacked Korea, and by 1910 it had won complete control. The Japanese proved to be harsh rulers. They shut down Korean newspapers and changed schools so that only Japanese language and history were taught. They took away land from Korean farmers and gave it to Japanese settlers. They built factories to be run by Japanese only. Koreans were not allowed to start new businesses. Koreans bitterly resented these actions. They began a nationalist movement and protested against Japanese rule.

❸ U.S. Economic Imperialism

KEY IDEA *The United States put increasing economic and political pressure on Latin America in the 1800s.*

In the early 1800s, the new nations of Latin America had serious problems. Most people were poor. They worked on farms for large landowners who took advantage of them. Another problem was political unrest. Local leaders rivaled one another for power. Military dictators, or caudillos, generally held power with the backing of the landowners, because the dictators refused to give power to the mass of poor people. Only people with property could vote. Sometimes reformers did take office and lead their countries. They never lasted long, though. When their reforms upset the power of the wealthy too much, a caudillo would rise and remove them from office.

With Spain no longer ruling the lands, old trade laws were gone. The new countries could now trade with any nation. Britain and the United States became the chief trading partners. Soon businesses in these nations dominated Latin American economies.

The economies of Latin America depended on exporting goods. They shipped goods such as coffee, beef, fruits, and vegetables. Each country focused on producing and exporting one or two goods. The volume of exports rose rapidly during the 1800s. The coming of railroads and steamships helped. The invention of refrigerated cars helped also, allowing producers to increase food exports.

This trade mainly went to benefit other countries, though. Latin America did not develop industries of its own. It had to import manufactured goods, which cost more than what was earned from exports. Also, Latin American countries often borrowed money to expand the facilities used to increase those exports. They had to borrow the money from foreign banks. When they could not repay the loans, lenders took control of the businesses. In this way, much of Latin American business fell into foreign hands.

In the 1890s, the United States began to take a more active role in Latin American affairs. The people of Cuba were fighting for their independence from Spain. American businesses had important interests on the island. Also, Spain had placed Cuban citizens in concentration camps, which outraged many Americans. For these reasons, the United States joined the war. The Spanish quickly gave up, and the United States gained several new territories. After the war, though, the United States put a military government in place in Cuba. This step and others helped promote anger among many Cubans against the United States.

The United States next set its sights on Panama. Ships traveling from the east to the west coast had to go around the southern tip of South America, which took many weeks. Americans hoped to build a canal across Panama. President Roosevelt offered $10 million to Colombia—to which Panama belonged—for the right to build this canal. When Colombia asked for more money, the United States helped the people of Panama revolt for independence. In return, the United States won a ten-mile-wide zone in Panama in which to build a canal. The canal opened in 1914.

In 1904, Roosevelt said that the United States had the right to act as "an international police power" in the western hemisphere. Over the next decades, it acted on that belief many times. When trouble arose in various countries, the United States sent its troops. Sometimes they stayed for many years.

❹ Turmoil and Change in Mexico

KEY IDEA *Political, economic, and social inequalities in Mexico triggered a period of revolution and reform.*

Antonio López de Santa Anna was a leading figure in the early history of independent Mexico. He fought to win independence from Spain and led in another war when Spain tried to recapture Mexico. He served as president four times; shrewdly changing his positions in order to retain power.

In the 1830s, though, he was unable to prevent people in Texas from winning their freedom from Mexico. In the 1840s, the United States annexed Texas, which angered many Mexicans. When a border dispute broke out, the United States invaded Mexico. Santa Anna led his nation's army and was defeated. Mexico had to surrender huge amounts of land.

Another important leader of the middle 1800s was Benito Juárez. A Zapotec Indian, Juárez wanted to improve conditions for the poor in

Mexico. He led a movement called *La Reforma*—the reform—that aimed at breaking the power of the large landowners and giving more schooling to the poor. He and his liberal supporters won control of the government in the late 1850s. The conservatives who opposed them did not give up, however. They plotted with France to retake Mexico. In 1862, Napoleon III of France sent an army that captured the country in 18 months. He named a European noble as emperor. But, Juárez and his followers kept fighting. In 1867, they drove the French from Mexican soil and killed the emperor.

Juárez once again pressed for his reforms. He made some progress but died in office in 1872. Soon after, a new leader emerged. Porfirio Díaz dominated Mexican politics for more than 30 years. Díaz brought order to the country and encouraged economic growth. However, he sharply limited political freedom.

In the early 1900s, calls for reform got louder. Leaders "Pancho" Villa and Emiliano Zapata gathered support with their demand for better lives for the poor. They raised small armies and forced Díaz to step down. Fighting continued, however, for many years as several leaders struggled for power. In the midst of this turmoil, Mexico adopted a new constitution in 1917. It called for breaking up large landholdings and for limits on foreign ownership of business. It promoted the right to strike for workers and promised some rights for women. Conflict continued until a new political party gained control of Mexico in 1929. The Institutional Revolutionary Party (PRI) brought peace and political stability to a troubled land.

Review

1. ***Summarizing*** Describe China's two major attempts to remain isolated from the outside world.
2. ***Recognizing Effects*** What was the result of Japan's feelings of pride and strength in the late 1800s?
3. ***Evaluating Courses of Action*** Through what method did the Japanese modernize during the Meiji era?
4. ***Drawing Conclusions*** Why did the Latin American nations not benefit from growing trade?
5. ***Comparing*** What did Juárez, Villa, and Zapata have in common?

Transformations Around the Globe, 1800–1914

Responses will vary but should include points similar to the following:

1. In the late 1700s, China allowed only limited trade with Europeans. As a result, China had to fight a war with the British. It lost and was forced to open up the country to foreign trade. In early 1900, a group called the Boxers tried to rid China of Western influences by fighting Europeans in Beijing.

2. A proud Japan wanted the world to see its strength. It turned imperialistic in its own right and attacked China and then warred successfully with Russia.

3. The Japanese borrowed ideas and techniques from Western powers. They selectively took what they wanted from Germany, Britain, and the United States.

4. Latin American nations did not benefit from growing trade because they lacked industry to make manufactured goods. They thus had to buy these goods, but the value of those purchases was more than the value of their exports. Also, they borrowed large amounts of money to finance improvements in facilities. When they could not pay these loans back, foreign investors took control of their industries.

5. They all wanted to improve conditions for the poor in Mexico.

CHAPTER 29 Summary

CHAPTERS IN BRIEF *The Great War, 1914–1918*

CHAPTER OVERVIEW *Strong national feelings and strong armies produced competition between European nations and led to war. The system of alliances turned a local conflict into a general European war and then a world war. Horribly brutal, it changed the lives of millions and transformed Russia when it helped cause a revolution.*

❶ Marching Toward War

KEY IDEA *In Europe, military buildup, nationalistic feelings, and rival alliances led to a continental war.*

In the later 1800s, many people in Europe joined groups to promote peace. They met several times between 1843 and 1907 to urge their cause. While this movement for peace was building, so were other developments. These other factors would soon plunge Europe into war.

One of those factors was nationalism—the deep feeling of attachment to one's own nation. This force helped unify the people of a country. It also helped promote competition between countries. By 1900, six nations were rivals for power in Europe. These nations, called the Great Powers, were Germany, Austria-Hungary, Great Britain, Russia, Italy, and France. They competed economically, and they competed for neighboring land.

Imperialism was another force that helped lead to war. France and Germany, each seeking control of parts of Africa, almost came to war twice in the early 1900s. Such competition bred mistrust.

The third factor leading to war was a growing arms race. Each country in Europe—except Great Britain—built a large army. Generals in each country made complex plans to be able to mobilize their armies or rush troops to battle as quickly as possible.

Growing rivalry led the nations to make alliances with one another. Fearing that France would want revenge for its defeat in the Franco-Prussian War, Otto von Bismarck set out to isolate France. In 1879, he formed a Triple Alliance with Austria-Hungary and Italy, and a treaty with Russia. However, when Wilhelm II became kaiser, or emperor, of Germany, he did not want to share power. He forced Bismarck out and followed his own policy. He let the agreement with Russia expire, and Russia quickly allied itself with France. This alliance meant that Germany would have to fight enemies on east and west borders if there were a war with either country. Wilhelm II then moved to make the German navy larger. Britain grew alarmed

and began to build more ships of its own. It made a Triple Entente alliance with France and Russia. The six Great Powers had now formed two camps: Germany, Austria-Hungary, and Italy against Britain, France, and Russia.

Meanwhile, trouble was brewing in the Balkans, in southeastern Europe. The Ottoman Empire, which controlled this area, was breaking apart. Both Austria-Hungary and Russia wanted some of this land. The kingdom of Serbia, which was in this region, wanted to bring other Slavic peoples who lived in the Balkans under its control. In 1908, Austria-Hungary seized Bosnia and Herzegovina. These lands had Slavic peoples, and the Serbs were angered. However, their Russian allies were unwilling to support them, and they backed down.

By 1914, the situation was different. Serbia had gained land in other parts of the region and felt strong. Austria worried that Serbia might interfere with its control of Bosnia and Herzegovina. Amid these tensions, a shot rang out. In June 1914, a Serbian shot and killed the heir to the throne of Austria-Hungary. Austria-Hungary declared war on Serbia, Russia came to Serbia's defense, and soon most of Europe was at war.

❷ Europe Plunges into War

KEY IDEA *One European nation after another was drawn into a large and industrialized war that resulted in many casualties.*

The system of alliances turned the war between Austria-Hungary and Serbia into a wider war. Russia moved against Austria-Hungary. Figuring that Germany would support Austria-Hungary, Russia moved troops against Germany as well. Germany declared war on Russia. Soon after, it also declared war on France, Russia's ally.

Germany had a plan for winning the war on two fronts. It called for a rapid push through France, a quick defeat of that nation, and a turn to face Russia in the east. To capture France quickly, Germany moved through Belgium, which was a neutral country. Britain was outraged by this and declared war on Germany. France, Britain, and Russia were later joined by Italy, which broke from Germany and Austria-Hungary. They were called the Allies. Bulgaria and the Ottoman Empire joined Germany and Austria-Hungary. They were called the Central Powers.

After the German army moved almost to Paris, French defenses strengthened and stopped them in September 1914. Both sides became bogged down in a bloody conflict. Soldiers dug deep trenches into the ground, protecting themselves with barbed wire and machine guns. Inside the trenches, they lived in mud, suffered the lack of food, and were killed or wounded by exploding bombs. Attacks were even worse. Generals still hoped to win ground with massed attacks of huge armies. But, when soldiers left the trenches to storm enemy lines, they faced powerful weapons. Machine guns, tanks, poison gas, and larger pieces of artillery killed hundreds of thousands of soldiers. This was the war in France, which was called the Western Front.

The war on the Eastern Front showed more movement at first—but it was equally destructive. Russian armies attacked both Germany and Austria-Hungary. After some early success, they were driven back in both places. One reason was that Russia did not have a fully industrial economy. It could not keep troops supplied. Still, Russia had a huge population and could send millions to war. The large Russian army provided a constant threat to Germany, preventing it from putting its full resources against the allies in the west.

❸ A Global Conflict

KEY IDEA *World War I spread to several continents and used the full resources of many governments.*

The war moved into Southwest Asia when the Allies hoped to take a part of the Ottoman Empire called the Dardanelles. That would allow them to capture Constantinople—the Ottoman capital—and send supplies to Russia through the Black Sea. The attack failed with great loss of life. In another thrust at that empire, a British officer named T. E. Lawrence helped lead an Arab revolt against Ottoman rule. As a result, the Allies were able to capture several important cities in Southwest Asia.

Japan took German colonies in China and the Pacific Ocean. The Allies also captured three of the four German colonies in Africa. People in the Allies' colonies joined in the war effort. Some worked for the Allied cause. Others fought in the armies.

The British had used their strong navy to block all supplies from reaching Germany. In response, the Germans increased their submarine attacks on ships that brought food and supplies to the Allies. U.S. President Woodrow Wilson had protested this policy before, and did so again. When American ships were sunk, the American people grew angry. Then the British intercepted a secret message from Germany to Mexico. It offered to help Mexico regain land lost to the United States in the 1840s if Mexico allied itself with Germany. This and the submarine attacks turned many Americans against Germany. In April 1917, Congress declared war on Germany.

By that year, the war had had a terrible impact, killing millions and radically changing the lives of millions more—people at home as well as soldiers. This "Great War," as it was called, was a total war. It demanded all the resources of the countries that fought it. Governments took control of factories, telling them what to produce and how much of it to make. Governments rationed food and other goods, limiting how much people could buy and hold. That way they were sure to provide needed supplies to the armies in the field. They used propaganda to generate support for the war. They also took steps to put down any dissent against the war.

With so many men in the field, women played a growing role in the economies of the countries at war. They worked in factories, offices, and shops. They built planes and tanks, grew food and made clothing. These changes had an impact on people's attitudes toward what kind of work women could do.

In 1917, the United States entered the war, and Russia left it. Suffering during the war chipped away at the Russian people's support for the czar. In March, he stepped down. The new government hoped to continue fighting the war, but the Russian armies refused. Just months later, a new revolution struck. Communists seized Russia's government. They quickly made a treaty with Germany, giving up huge amounts of land in return for peace. In March 1918, Germany tried one final attack. Once again, the German army nearly reached Paris. The soldiers were tired, and supplies were short, though.

The Allies—now with fresh American troops—drove the Germans back.

Bulgaria and the Ottoman Empire surrendered. In October, a revolution toppled the emperor of Austria-Hungary. In November, Kaiser Wilhelm II was forced to step down in Germany. The new government agreed to stop fighting, and on November 11, 1918, Europe was finally at peace.

The war had made a great and terrible mark on the world. About 8.5 million soldiers had died and another 21 million had been wounded. Countless civilians had suffered as well. The economies of the warring nations had suffered serious damage, too. Farms were destroyed and factories ruined. One estimate said the war had caused $338 billion in damage.

Along with this death and destruction, the war had an emotional cost. People felt disillusioned since all the suffering did not seem to have a purpose. The art and literature of the years after the war reflected a new sense of hopelessness in people.

❹ A Flawed Peace

KEY IDEA After winning the war, the Allies dictated a harsh peace that left many nations feeling betrayed.

Many nations sent delegates to peace talks in Paris. The main leaders were Woodrow Wilson of the United States, Georges Clemenceau of France, and David Lloyd George of Britain. Germany and its allies and Russia were not present.

Wilson pushed for his peace plan called the Fourteen Points. He wanted to end secret treaties and alliances and give people the right to form their own nation. He also hoped to set up a world organization that could police the actions of nations and prevent future wars.

Britain and especially France had different views. They had suffered greatly in the war and wanted to punish Germany. After long debates, the leaders finally agreed on a peace settlement called the Treaty of Versailles.

The treaty called for a League of Nations—the world organization that Wilson wanted. It would include 32 nations, with the United States, Britain, France, Japan, and Italy making up the leadership. Germany and Russia were left out of the League. The treaty took away German land in Europe and took away its colonies. Limits were placed on the size of Germany's armed forces. Finally, Germany

was given complete blame for the war, which meant it would have to make payments to the Allies for the damage caused.

Germany's former colonies were given to the Allies to govern until they decided which were ready for independence. Poland, Czechoslovakia, and Yugoslavia were all declared independent. Finland, Estonia, Latvia, and Lithuania—once part of Russia—were made independent nations as well. The Ottoman Empire was broken up. The Ottomans kept control only of Turkey.

The treaty never made a lasting peace. This was in part because the United States Senate never approved either the treaty or joining the League of Nations. Also, Germans bitterly resented the treaty, which placed all the blame for the war on them. Colonial peoples in Africa and Asia had hoped that they could win their independence. They were angry when the treaty did not allow for that. Japan and Italy were also upset with the treaty. They had both joined the war in hopes of winning more land and were disappointed by getting few territorial gains.

Review

Analyzing Causes and Recognizing Effects

1. What factors led to World War I?
2. Why did a revolution occur in Russia?
3. *Summarizing* What was the war like on the Western Front?
4. *Analyzing Issues* How did the war change the countries that fought it?
5. *Forming and Supporting Opinions* Discuss the weaknesses of the Treaty of Versailles.

The Great War, 1914–1918

Responses will vary but should include points similar to the following:

1. The factors leading to World War I included nationalism, which caused competition among nations; imperialism; the growing arms race and mobilization plans; and the system of alliances that pushed Europe into two armed camps.

2. The war on the Western Front was characterized by the suffering of trench warfare—with mud, starvation, disease, and constant bombardment—interrupted by occasional attacks that produced great death and destruction because of new war technologies.

3. World War I was a total war, and the people at home had to contribute to the war effort. It demanded all the resources of the countries that fought it. Governments took control of factories, rationed food and other goods, and used propaganda to generate support for the war. Women played a larger role in the economies of the countries at war, which changed people's ideas of what kind of work women could do.

4. A revolution took place in Russia because the czar did not respond to increasing calls for democracy, because the economy was in poor condition, because soldiers were tired of fighting, and because dedicated revolutionaries worked to bring about this revolution.

5. The Treaty of Versailles was imperfect because Germans resented it for being harsh, the League lost authority when the United States did not agree to join it, and people who did not win the right to self-determination were angry and disappointed by it.

CHAPTER 30
Summary

CHAPTERS IN BRIEF *Revolution and Nationalism, 1900–1939*

CHAPTER OVERVIEW *Old problems in Russia produced a revolution that resulted in the first Communist government. Joseph Stalin took control of the Soviet Union and became a dictator. Nationalists tried to gain control of China, but the country was plunged into decades of fighting. Nationalists pushed for self-government in India and won that right in Turkey, Iran, and Saudi Arabia.*

❶ Revolutions in Russia

KEY IDEA Unrest in Russia erupted in revolution to produce the first Communist government.

In 1881, reforms in Russia stopped when the czar was killed by radical students. The new czar, Alexander III, took back control of the Russian government. He cracked down on anyone who seemed to threaten his government. He also oppressed all non-Russian peoples who lived within the Russian empire, especially Jews.

In 1894, his son Nicholas II became czar and continued the strong rule. He launched a program aimed at building up Russia's industry. Russia quickly became a leading producer of steel in the world. However, this rapid industrial growth brought problems. Working conditions were poor, wages were low, and children were forced to work. Workers grew angry and often went on strike. Revolutionary groups wanted to topple the government. Some followed the teachings of Karl Marx. In 1903, they argued about how to carry out their revolution, and they split into two groups. One group—the Bolsheviks—was led by Vladimir Lenin. He fled Russia a few years later to await a better time to push his ideas.

Russia suffered a huge defeat at the hands of Japan in a war that started in 1904. In early 1905, the Russian army killed hundreds of hungry workers who had peacefully gathered to ask for relief. Strikes spread in protest, and Nicholas was forced to allow some reforms to take place.

The suffering caused by World War I was the final blow against the czar's rule. In just the first few months of war, Russia had four million soldiers killed, wounded, or captured. As the war worsened, the czar lost control of Russia. Soldiers refused to fight, prices shot sky high, and people starved. In March 1917, almost 200,000 workers took to the streets of one city to protest high prices. Soldiers shot into the crowd. Later they fired at their officers and joined the protest. The czar was forced to step down. A year later, he and his family were executed. A government led by Alexander Kerensky was formed.

Kerensky hoped to keep Russia in the war. The decision cost him the support of soldiers who wanted to fight no longer and workers and peasants who wanted an end to food shortages. Across the country these forces formed local councils called soviets. In some cities, the soviets actually had more real power than the government.

In the midst of this unrest, Lenin returned to Russia determined to bring about his revolution. His slogan "Peace, Land, and Bread" was soon taken up by many people. In November 1917, armed workers took control of government offices. The Kerensky reign was ended.

To win the peasants' support, Lenin ordered all farmland be given to them. Workers were given control of the factories. Soon Lenin agreed to a peace treaty with Germany. It gave away large amounts of Russian land, but it ended the war. Then, forces opposed to Lenin's revolution—supported by the Allies who fought Germany—tried to defeat Lenin's army in battle. The civil war lasted three years. The fighting and the famine that followed it killed 15 million Russians. In the end, though, Lenin's Red Army won.

In 1921, Lenin launched a new plan to rebuild the Russian economy. It allowed for some private ownership of property, relaxing Lenin's desire for complete state control. He also changed the government to form a new nation—the Soviet Union. It would be run by the leaders of the Communist Party. By the late 1920s, the Soviet economy had come back. Farms and factories were producing as much as they had before World War I.

❷ Totalitarianism
Case Study: Stalinist Russia

KEY IDEA *After Lenin died, Stalin seized power and transformed the Soviet Union into a totalitarian state.*

The term *totalitarian* describes a government that takes complete control over all parts of life in a country. This includes both public and private life. To keep everything under control totalitarian governments use several tactics. These include: police terror, propaganda, and persecution. The case study uses Joseph Stalin and Russia to show how a totalitarian state operates.

Joseph Stalin joined Lenin's revolutionary movement. Over time, he slowly built up his power. When Lenin died in 1924, Stalin took control of the Communist Party. He was less interested than Lenin in promoting revolution around the world. He wanted to increase the power of the Soviet Union. To achieve that, he built a totalitarian state. Government had total control over its people's lives.

Stalin kept tight control by creating a powerful secret police. In the mid-1930s, he turned against enemies—both real and imagined—within the Communist Party. Thousands were arrested and sent to exile or killed. Stalin also used propaganda to keep control. Official literature praised the government and its success. Any writings that expressed a different view were seized and their authors punished. Stalin's government also moved against religion. Churches were destroyed, and church leaders killed or sent into exile.

Stalin built a command economy—one in which the government makes all decisions of economic life. He pushed to complete the work of making the economy fully industrial. All resources were devoted to this effort. As a result, the Soviet people lacked food, housing, and clothing for many years. The plan did not meet Stalin's goals, but the industrial part of the economy did grow.

Stalin also launched a farming revolution. The government took control of the farms that people owned. It put them together in large, government-owned farms called collective farms. When peasants resisted, millions were killed, and millions more were sent to Siberia. With these brutal methods, Stalin got farm output to rise.

Stalin completely changed Soviet society. Women enjoyed equal rights—though rights were few. They filled all kinds of jobs on the farms and in factories.

They studied for careers that had been closed to them before. People in general were more educated.

❸ Imperial China Collapses

KEY IDEA *After the fall of the Qing Dynasty, nationalists and communists struggled for power.*

Unrest also plagued China. Many Chinese resented the great control that foreign nations had over their economy. Some wanted to modernize China so it could regain power. One of the leaders of this push was Sun Yixian. His group was called the Kuomintang, or Nationalist Party. In 1912, he led a revolt that toppled the Qing Dynasty and was made the president of the new republic.

Sun had three main principles. He wanted political and economic rights for all Chinese people and an end to foreign control of China. Sun turned over his presidency six weeks later to Yuan Shikai, who became a military dictator. After Yuan died in 1916, civil war broke out. The people suffered terribly from famine and brutal attacks. Sun could not reorganize his Kuomintang.

China's leaders hoped to win the support of the Allies during World War I. They declared war on Germany. When the war ended, though, they were disappointed. Instead of giving China freedom from foreign influence, the Treaty of Versailles merely changed masters. The parts of China that had been controlled by Germany were handed over to Japan. Angry Chinese protested.

In the 1920s, rebels began to look to Marxism and the Russian Revolution for a solution to China's problems. The Communist Party in China was organized. One of the leaders was Mao Zedong. The Communists joined with the Kuomintang. Sun died in 1925, and Jiang Jieshi became leader of the Kuomintang. Many in the party were business people. They now feared Communist ideas about government control of economic life. Jiang agreed with them.

Jiang did not move against the Communists at first. In 1927, though, his forces struck against them. Only a few Communists survived, and they were forced into hiding. In 1928, Jiang became president of China. Soon China was torn by a civil war between the remaining Communists and Jiang's forces.

The Communists, under Mao Zedong, moved to south-central China. They built an army of peasants that struck quickly against Jiang's forces. In 1933, Jiang's army completely surrounded them. But the Communists sneaked away on a famous Long March of 6,000 miles to the north. Thousands died, but the Communists survived, hiding in caves.

At the same time, China had other problems. In 1931, Japan invaded the part of China called Manchuria. They took control there and six years later began a new invasion of other areas. They were able to quickly seize large parts of the country. With this new threat, Jiang and the Communists agreed to join together to fight the Japanese.

❹ Nationalism in India and Southwest Asia

KEY IDEA *Nationalism triggered independence movements to overthrow colonial power.*

Many Indians of the upper classes were educated in British schools. They learned the Western ideals of nationalism and democracy. They also grew angry at British domination of Indian life. Some formed into two groups, the Congress Party and the Muslim League.

More than a million Indians served in the British army in World War I. The British promised to make changes to the government of India that would give the Indian people greater control of their own nation. After the war, though, returning Indian soldiers were once again treated as second-class citizens. Reforms were not made. When Indians protested, the British Parliament passed a law that allowed protesters to be jailed without a trial. Indians were further enraged. About 10,000 Indians gathered to protest this act. The British had also banned such public meetings, but the crowd was mostly unaware of that fact. British troops fired on the crowd, killing several hundred. The massacre at Amritsar sparked further protests.

Mohandas K. Gandhi became the leader of India's protest movement. He organized a widespread campaign of noncooperation with the British and passive resistance to unjust laws. He asked Indians to stop buying British goods, attending British schools, paying British taxes, or voting in British-run elections. He also convinced his followers to take these actions without using violence.

British jails filled with thousands of Indians who broke British laws in order to protest them.

Indians resented a British law that forced them to buy salt only from the government. Gandhi organized a huge march to the sea to make salt by evaporating sea water. At a related march, police beat many people protesting the salt tax. In 1935, the British finally gave in. They passed a law that allowed local Indian limited self-government. Though they had met some success, Indians had other problems. Tensions between Hindus and Muslims were high.

Other changes took place in Southwest Asia. Mustafa Kemal, a military commander, became the leader of a new republic in Turkey. He took many steps to modernize society and the economy in Turkey. He loosened Islam's hold on Turkish law. Another commander led a revolt in Persia that won independence from Britain in that land. He also modernized his country, and he changed its name to Iran. In both Turkey and Iran, women gained new rights. A new leader also emerged in Arabia. He united different groups into one kingdom, which he called Saudi Arabia. While he took steps to modernize life in his land, he kept the traditional practices of Islam strong.

Starting in the 1920s, Southwest Asia saw a major new economic change. Western companies discovered large reserves of oil in several countries in this part of the world. Oil brought huge sums of money to these countries. The desire to tap into this wealth also persuaded Western countries to try to gain power in the area.

Review

1. ***Drawing Conclusions*** How did the problems of the early 1900s lead to the Russian Revolution?
2. ***Comparing and Contrasting*** Compare Kerensky's and Lenin's plans.
3. ***Summarizing*** In what ways was Stalin's government an example of totalitarian rule?
4. ***Analyzing Causes and Recognizing Effects*** How did the Treaty of Versailles add to China's problems?
5. ***Determining Main Ideas*** Explain Gandhi's ideas of noncooperation and nonviolent protest.

Answer Key
Chapter 30
SUMMARY

Revolution and Nationalism, 1900–1939

Responses will vary but should include points similar to the following:

1. Rapid industrial growth in Russia in the early 1900s resulted in poor working conditions, low wages, and angry workers who often went on strike. Rebels formed revolutionary groups that wanted to topple the government. The war against Japan led to a demonstration that resulted in soldiers firing into the crowd. Strikes and violence spread in protest.

2. Kerensky wanted to continue the war, which cost him the support of soldiers and of workers and peasants who wanted an end to food shortages. Lenin urged "Peace, Land, and Bread"—an end to the war to win the favor of the soldiers, and food and land to win the masses.

3. Stalin controlled all aspects of people's lives. He devoted all economic resources to making the economy fully industrial, even though it meant shortages of consumer goods for people. He forced farmers to organize farms and killed those who resisted. He used secret police to remove rebels or enemies in the party. He censored ideas that he did not like.

4. Chinese leaders had hoped to win their freedom from European control by declaring war on Germany. Instead of getting freedom, though, China suffered. Parts of China that Germany had controlled were simply handed over to Japan. This led to widespread discontent.

5. With noncooperation, Gandhi wanted Indians to stop buying British goods, attending British schools, paying British taxes, or voting in British-run elections. By nonviolence, he wanted Indians to protest British laws on purpose in order to protest them but not to resort to destruction of property or injuring of people.

CHAPTERS IN BRIEF *Years of Crisis, 1919–1939*

CHAPTER
31
Summary

CHAPTER OVERVIEW After World War I, new ideas and technologies changed old ways of thinking and living. The economic collapse called the Great Depression tested weak democratic governments in Europe. This crisis helped bring dictators to power in eastern Europe in the 1930s. Meanwhile, Japan, Germany, and Italy took actions that would soon plunge the world into another war.

❶ Postwar Uncertainty

KEY IDEA The postwar period was one of loss and uncertainty but also one of invention and creativity.

Two thinkers developed radical new ideas that challenged old ways of thinking. Albert Einstein revolutionized physics with his ideas about space, time, matter, and energy. He said that as moving objects neared the speed of light, space and time become relative. That means they change. His idea is the theory of relativity. Sigmund Freud's work changed the way people thought about the human mind. He said that much of human behavior was irrational—due to urges and desires buried in the unconscious mind of each person. Though resisted at first, Freud's ideas gained wide influence.

Looking at the destruction of World War I, many philosophers lost faith in reason and progress. One group of them was called existentialists. They argued that there is no universal meaning to the world. Each person must give it his or her own meaning through actions taken. They were influenced by Friedrich Nietzsche, a German philosopher of the late 1800s. He said that reason, democracy, and progress were empty ideas. He urged people to adopt the values of pride and strength.

Some writers, like Franz Kafka, showed the horrors of modern life. His novels put people in threatening situations that they could not understand or escape.

Artists rebelled against traditional painting. They did not merely re-create realistic objects. Paul Klee used bold colors and distorted lines. Pablo Picasso founded a style called Cubism that broke objects into geometric shapes. Painters called surrealists showed a dreamlike existence outside of reality.

Composers created a new style of music. Some, like Igor Stravinsky, used unusual rhythms or harsh, rather than pleasing, sounds. African-American musicians in the United States developed a lively, loose form of popular music called jazz.

Society changed after World War I as well. Young people experimented with modern values. Women set aside earlier forms of dress, wearing new styles that were looser and shorter. Many women also began to work in new careers.

Technology brought about changes to society as well. Improvements to the automobile helped make cars more desirable and affordable. As a result, more and more people bought cars. They began to move to suburbs outside cities, using their cars to travel to work. The auto boom also gave a boost to some industries. Another change was the growth in air travel. American pilot Charles Lindbergh caught the world's attention when he flew alone across the Atlantic Ocean in 1927. In 1932, Amelia Earhart became the first woman to make the flight alone.

The radio developed during World War I. In the 1920s, large radio networks were built. They offered programs such as news, plays, comedies, and sports. Soon millions of people were entertained by radios in their homes. Millions more went to movie theaters to watch motion pictures. Movies were produced all over the world, especially in southern California.

❷ A Worldwide Depression

KEY IDEA An economic depression in the United States spread to the world and lasted a decade.

After the war, European countries were in bad shape. European influence in world affairs was declining. The new republics that had formed out of the old empires of Europe often had shaky governments. Even nations that had had democracy for many years experienced problems. They had so many political parties that no one party could rule alone. There were so many governments formed that it was difficult to develop policies.

The situation was worst in Germany. The people felt little loyalty to the government, and the economy was weak. Prices rose sharply, and money lost its value. An American drew up a plan that used American bank loans to help the German economy recover. By 1929, German factories produced as much as they had before the war.

World nations also took steps to try to ensure peace. France and Germany promised never to attack one another. Most countries of the world signed a treaty in which they pledged not to use war to gain their goals. There was no way to enforce the treaty, however, which made it weak.

The economy of the United States enjoyed a boom in the 1920s. But this growth hid problems. Workers were unable to buy all the goods produced, and when their purchases slowed, factories slowed production. Farmers faced falling food prices and slow sales. They were unable to repay loans and lost their farms. In 1929, stock prices in the United States plunged. The Great Depression was on.

The American Depression hit other countries. Nations raised tariffs—taxes on goods imported from other countries—to keep import prices high. They wanted to increase sales by local companies. But it all backfired. Trade between nations dropped, and unemployment shot up in many countries. The world suffered, including Latin America. As world trade went down, few countries bought the sugar, beef, and copper they produced.

Each country met the economic crisis in its own way. In Britain, a new multiparty government took over. It took steps that slowly improved the economy and cut unemployment. By 1937, production was up again. In France, after several governments lost support, moderates and Socialists combined to form a government. It passed laws to help workers, but companies raised prices to cover their costs. As a result, unemployment was still high.

In Sweden, Norway, and Denmark, the governments played active roles in the economy. They taxed people with jobs to have money to pay benefits to people without jobs. The governments also created jobs by hiring out-of-work people to build roads and buildings.

In the United States, Franklin D. Roosevelt became president in 1932. He began a program that he called the New Deal. The government began large public works projects. This effort created jobs for millions. Businesses and farmers also got help from the government. The American economy got better but the recovery was slow.

❸ Fascism Rises in Europe

KEY IDEA *Because of political and economic problems, Italy and Germany turned to dictators.*

In other countries, the economic crisis of the Great Depression led to the loss of democracy. There, millions of people turned to strong rulers to try to solve their economic problems. These tough leaders followed a set of beliefs called fascism. Fascist leaders were strongly nationalist. They believed in strength and power and built strong military forces. Fascist governments were controlled by one party, and that party was dominated by one leader. The leader was the nation's dictator. Fascist governments did not give any rights to their people.

Fascism arose in Italy because people there were angry that the treaty that came after World War I did not give them more gains in territory. Also, people with more money feared that unrest in Italy would result in a Communist government, as had happened in Russia. Benito Mussolini rose to power promising to revive the economy and armed forces of Italy. He used armed thugs who made threats to political opponents. The king of Italy was forced to let Mussolini lead the government.

Another Fascist arose in Germany. Adolf Hitler was the leader of the Nazi Party. He tried to take control of the government of Germany in 1923, but the attempt failed. He was sent to prison, where he wrote a book that summarized his ideas. Hitler believed that Germans were superior to all other people. He said that the Treaty of Versailles treated Germany unfairly, and that a crowded Germany needed the lands of eastern Europe and Russia. When the Depression hit Germany, the country was in terrible shape. Hitler was named leader of the German government but soon took the powers of a dictator. All those who opposed him were arrested. His economic program gave work to millions but took away their rights to organize into unions or to strike. He took control of all areas of life. He burned books that went against Nazi ideas and forced children to join Nazi groups. Hitler also launched attacks on Germany's Jews. Laws took away their rights. In November 1938, mobs destroyed thousands of Jewish-owned buildings and attacked Jewish people.

Dictators took control in other countries as well. Hungary, Poland, Yugoslavia, Albania, Bulgaria, and Romania all had dictators—or kings who ruled like dictators. Only Czechoslovakia remained as a democracy in eastern Europe.

❹ Aggressors Invade Nations

KEY IDEA *As Germany, Italy, and Japan conquered other countries, the rest of the world did nothing.*

In the 1930s, the major democracies—Britain, France, and the United States—still faced serious problems at home. Dictators in Germany and Italy took advantage of this and began moving to gain territory. So, too, did Japan, now ruled by generals. These military leaders had taken power when the Depression struck. They planned to capture China as a part of a Pacific empire.

In 1931, the Japanese army captured Manchuria, a part of China. It was rich in coal and iron and as a result provided valuable resources for the Japanese economy. Other countries protested in the League of Nations but did nothing else. Japan ignored the protests and in 1933 pulled out of the League. It stayed in Manchuria, though. Four years later, Japan invaded China. The strong Japanese army swept Chinese fighters aside. It killed tens of thousands of Chinese in the city of Nanjing. Chinese forces—both the Nationalists of the government and Communist rebels—continued to fight Japan.

Italy's Mussolini wanted an Italian empire in Africa, and in 1935 he invaded Ethiopia. His troops won easy victory. Haile Selassie, the emperor of Ethiopia, pleaded to the League of Nations for help. The League did nothing.

Hitler made moves also. He broke the Versailles Treaty by rebuilding Germany's army. In 1936, he sent troops into an area of Germany that the treaty had forbidden them to enter. France and Britain again refused to stand up to Germany. This move won Hitler more support in Germany. That year, he signed an agreement with Mussolini and also with Japan. The three nations were called the Axis Powers.

In 1936, Spain erupted in civil war as the army revolted against a leftist government. Hitler and Mussolini sent aid to the army, which was backed by Spanish Fascists. The Soviet Union sent aid to the government. In 1939, the army won and Francisco Franco became Spain's Fascist dictator.

In March 1938, Hitler moved his troops into Austria. He made it part of Germany, breaking the Versailles Treaty again. France and Britain once more did nothing. The next year, Hitler demanded that Czechoslovakia give up part of its land to Germany. The country refused, but Britain and France agreed to allow Germany to take the land. Hitler promised to respect the new borders of Czechoslovakia, but a few months later he took the entire country.

In the summer of 1939, Hitler made a similar demand of Poland. That nation also refused to give up land. Britain and France now said that they would protect Poland. But Hitler guessed they would not back this up. Meanwhile, he made an agreement with Soviet dictator Joseph Stalin in which the two countries promised never to attack each other.

Review

Clarifying

1. What ideas of Einstein and Freud challenged old ways of thinking?
2. How did technology change society after the war?
3. ***Comparing and Contrasting*** Compare the French approach to the Depression with the New Deal.
4. ***Analyzing Causes and Recognizing Effects*** What European nations came to be ruled by dictators, and why?
5. ***Following Chronological Order*** Describe the sequence of events in the 1930s that led to war.

Answer Key
Chapter 31
SUMMARY

Years of Crisis, 1919–1939

Responses will vary but should include points similar to the following:

1. Einstein's new physics made people see the world differently. Freud's theories about the unconscious mind undercut people's faith in reason, which was reflected in philosophy and art. Artists, writers, and musicians all broke with traditional forms and styles of expression.

2. The automobile boom changed society by making people more mobile and sending more of them to live in the suburbs and to travel by car. New technologies such as the radio and movies created mass entertainment media.

3. In France, the government tried to pass laws that would benefit workers, but the companies simply raised prices to cover their higher costs. As a result, unemployment did not go down. In the United States, the New Deal created new jobs in public works programs, but not enough to make the economy recover completely.

4. Dictators took control of Italy, Germany, and all the nations of eastern Europe except Czechoslovakia. They took advantage of people's resentment over the terms of the Treaty of Versailles, fears of communism, economic troubles of the Depression, and their own strong-arm tactics that suppressed opposition.

5. 1931: Japan invades Manchuria. 1933: Japan pulls out of the League of Nations. 1935: Mussolini invades Ethiopia. 1936: Hitler sends troops into areas where Germany was forbidden to put them. 1936: Germany, Italy, and Japan sign agreement. 1936–1939: Spanish Civil War; Fascists are supported by Germany and Italy. 1937: Japan invades China. 1938: Hitler moves troops into Austria. 1939: Hitler takes Czechoslovakia. 1939: Hitler threatens Poland; 1939: Hitler and Stalin sign treaty in which each promises not to attack the other.

CHAPTER 32 Summary

CHAPTERS IN BRIEF *World War II, 1939–1945*

CHAPTER OVERVIEW *Germany's Adolf Hitler began World War II, which the United States entered after a Japanese attack on a U.S. naval base. Hitler's racial hatred resulted in the deaths of millions of people, many of them Jews. After years of struggle, the Allies won the war, but millions had died and large parts of Europe and Japan were destroyed.*

❶ Hitler's Lightning War

KEY IDEA *Using sudden, mass attacks, Germany over-ran much of Europe and North Africa.*

In 1939, having conquered Austria and Czechoslovakia, Adolf Hitler decided to move on Poland. He had signed an agreement with Stalin of the Soviet Union. In it, they agreed to split Poland between them. This deal removed the threat of the Soviets attacking Germany from the east.

So, on September 1, the German army invaded Poland. Using planes, tanks, and troops, it moved suddenly in a technique called blitzkrieg—"lightning war." Britain and France declared war, but Poland fell before they could help. On September 17, Stalin invaded Finland and eastern Poland.

In April 1940, Hitler's armies conquered Denmark and Norway. Within two months, they also captured Belgium, the Netherlands, Luxembourg, and France. Some French, led by Charles de Gaulle, escaped to Britain to continue fighting. By then, Italy's Benito Mussolini had joined Hitler's side.

Great Britain—now led by Winston Churchill—stood alone. To prepare for an invasion of Britain, the German air force launched bombing attacks to weaken the country. The British air force fought back. It was helped by the newly developed radar that warned of coming attacks. Also, the British had broken the German army's secret code. The air war over Britain lasted many months. Unable to break British defenses, Hitler called off the attacks.

He next turned to the Mediterranean and the east. Germany sent troops to North Africa, where its ally, Italy, was losing to British forces. German troops joined the battle and fought a seesaw struggle with the British. Hitler forced Bulgaria, Romania, and Hungary to join Germany in the war. In April 1941, German armies quickly took control of Yugoslavia and Greece. In June, Hitler turned on his one-time ally and launched a surprise invasion of the Soviet Union. The Red Army, though the largest in the world, was not well-equipped or well-trained. The Germans quickly pushed deep into Soviet land. As the Red Army was forced to retreat, it destroyed everything left behind to keep supplies out of German hands. Stopped from taking Leningrad in the north, the Germans turned on Moscow, the Soviet capital. A strong Soviet counterattack, combined with fierce Russian winter weather, forced the Germans back.

The United States watched these events. Many Americans did not want to join in the war. President Roosevelt wanted to help the Allies, however. He persuaded Congress to allow Britain and France to buy American weapons. Soon American ships were escorting British cargo ships carrying guns. By the fall of 1941, U.S. ships had orders to fire on German submarines. The United States and Germany had an undeclared naval war.

Roosevelt met with Churchill in August of 1941. Although the United States was not officially in the war, the two leaders issued a statement called the Atlantic Charter. It supported free trade and the right of people to form their own national government.

❷ Japan's Pacific Campaign

KEY IDEA *Japan attacked Pearl Harbor in Hawaii and brought the United States into World War II.*

The military leaders who ran the Japanese government also had plans to build an empire. They captured part of China in 1931. In 1937, they invaded the center of China but met strong resistance. Needing resources for this war, they decided to move into Southeast Asia. The United States feared that Japanese control of this area would threaten U.S. holdings in the Pacific. Roosevelt gave military aid to China and cut off oil shipments to Japan. The Japanese decided to attack the United States.

On December 7, 1941, the Japanese navy began a surprise attack on the U.S. Navy base at Pearl Harbor in Hawaii. In just two hours, Japanese planes sank a major part of the U.S. Pacific Fleet. The next day, Congress declared war on Japan. The attack on Pearl Harbor was just one of many sudden strikes. Japan also captured Guam and Wake Islands, and the Philippines. It took Indonesia from the Dutch and Hong Kong, Malaya, and Singapore from the British.

In April 1942, the United States sent planes to drop bombs on Tokyo. The attack raised the morale of Americans. In May 1942, at the Battle of the Coral Sea, the Allies suffered heavy losses but were able to stop the Japanese advance and save Australia. The next month, the U.S. Navy scored an important victory near Midway Island in the central Pacific. In this battle, Japan lost four aircraft carriers, the most important naval weapon in the war. The victory turned the tide of war against Japan.

The United States now went on the attack. General Douglas MacArthur proposed hopping past the strongly defended Japanese-held islands. He wanted to attack weaker ones. The first attack came at Guadalcanal, in the Solomon Islands, where the Japanese were building an air base. However, it took six months for U.S. and Australian troops to clear Japanese soldiers off the island.

❸ The Holocaust

KEY IDEA *During the Holocaust, Hitler's Nazis killed six million Jews and millions of other "non-Aryans."*

Part of Hitler's new order for Europe included getting rid of "inferior" people. Hitler believed in a German "master race." He had a deep-seated hatred of people who were not German and especially of Jews. He and his Nazis made persecution of Jews government policy.

During the 1930s, Hitler passed laws that took away the rights of German Jews. One night in November 1938, Nazi mobs attacked Jews throughout Germany. They destroyed homes and businesses and killed or beat many people. Thousands of Jews tried to leave Germany. Other countries accepted a large number but were unwilling to take all those who wished to leave. Hitler ordered all Jews in Germany and his conquered lands to live in certain parts of cities called ghettos.

Hitler took steps to kill as many Jews as possible. The plan was the "Final Solution" to what the Nazis called the "Jewish problem." Germans also turned on many other people—Roma (gypsies), Poles, Russians, and those who were mentally or physically disabled. The Germans put the most attention on Jews, however.

Thousands of Jews were shot to death by "killing squads." Millions were gathered and placed in concentration camps. These prisons used the inmates as slave workers. Many in the camps died of starvation or disease. Starting in 1942, the Nazis built "death camps." At these camps, thousands of Jews were gassed to death in huge gas chambers. In the end, six million Jews were killed by the Nazis. Fewer than four million European Jews survived.

❹ The Allied Victory

KEY IDEA *The United States, Great Britain, and the Soviet Union scored key victories and won the war.*

In 1942, Roosevelt, Churchill, and Stalin planned the Allies' strategy. Stalin wanted Britain and the United States to attack Germany to relieve the pressure on his armies. They agreed but chose to attack in North Africa. In late 1942, the British army drove the Germans out of Egypt and back to the west. Meanwhile, American troops landed behind the Germans and began moving east. The Germans were finally forced to abandon Africa in May 1943.

At the same time, the Soviets enjoyed a major victory. German troops had invaded the Soviet city of Stalingrad in 1942. The Red Army forced the Germans to surrender in February 1943.

American and British soldiers next invaded Italy and captured Sicily. Mussolini was forced from power and the new Italian government surrendered. Hitler was unwilling to give up Italy. His army fought fiercely there until 1945.

While the Allied armies fought, people at home suffered. Some British and Soviet citizens died. In the United States, citizens faced shortages. Goods such as food, tires, gasoline, and clothing were in short supply. The government rationed these items—limiting how much a person could have—to make sure that there were enough for the armies.

Some Americans were even imprisoned. Since bitter feelings against the Japanese became widespread, mistrust of Americans of Japanese heritage grew. The U.S. government gathered thousands of Japanese Americans who lived on the West Coast and forced them to move to concentration camps in the western United States. Two-thirds of them were American citizens.

In early 1944, the Allies built a massive force to retake France. In June, an invasion of thousands of ships, planes, and soldiers was launched. The Allies suffered heavy losses but gained control of northern France. A month later, Allied forces broke out and began to pour through German lines. By September, the Allies had forced the Germans out of France, Belgium, Luxembourg, and much of the Netherlands.

At the same time, the Soviets were pushing the Germans back in eastern Europe. In late 1944, Hitler ordered his army to make one final, large-scale attack in the west. In the Battle of the Bulge, it punched through Allied lines until an Allied counterattack forced it back to Germany. By late April 1945, Soviet troops surrounded Berlin, Hitler's headquarters. Hitler killed himself, and a week later, the Germans surrendered. Roosevelt had not lived to see this victory, however. He had died in early April. Harry Truman was now president.

In the Pacific, the Allies advanced on Japanese territory starting in 1943. By the fall of 1944, they had landed troops in the Philippines. The Japanese sent their remaining ships to try to destroy the U.S. Navy near the Philippines. In the Battle of Leyte Gulf, in October 1944, the Japanese lost badly, and their navy was crushed. American troops began to move closer to Japan. In March 1945, they captured an island called Iwo Jima. By June, they had won control of Okinawa, an island just 350 miles from Japan.

Japan was the next stop. But the U.S. military feared that an invasion of Japan would cost half a million Allied lives. In August, President Truman ordered an experimental atomic bomb dropped on the city of Hiroshima to try to quickly end the war. Three days later, a second bomb was dropped on Nagasaki. Tens of thousands of Japanese died. In September, Japan surrendered.

❺ Europe and Japan in Ruins

KEY IDEA *World War II cost millions of lives and billions of dollars in damage. It left Europe and Japan in ruins.*

The war had left Europe in ruins, with about 60 million dead and hundreds of cities destroyed. Suffering continued for many years in Europe.

The old Fascist governments had disappeared. At first, the Communist parties grew strong in France and Italy. People who opposed communism grew alarmed. They voted leaders from other parties into power. When the economies of these lands improved, communism lost appeal. During efforts

to rebuild Europe, the Allies held trials in the city of Nuremberg, Germany. There, captured Nazi leaders were charged with crimes against humanity. They were found guilty, and some were executed.

The U.S. Army occupied Japan under the command of General MacArthur. He disbanded the Japanese army and took steps to give farmers and workers more power in the economy. He led the effort to write a new constitution for Japan, which changed how the Japanese viewed the world. The emperor was forced to declare that he was not a god. The new constitution gave all power to the Japanese people, who voted for members of a parliament that would rule the land. All Japanese over age 20—including women—were given the right to vote. In 1951, other nations finally signed a formal peace with Japan. A few months later, U.S. military occupation ended.

Review

1. **Summarizing** What was the first stop to Hitler? How did it affect later events?
2. **Analyzing Causes** What led to tensions between the United States and Japan before war broke out?
3. **Recognizing Effects** How did the American occupation change Japan?
4. **Following Chronological Order** Outline the fate of European Jews from the early 1930s to the Holocaust.
5. **Forming and Supporting Opinions** Do you think it was justified to drop the atomic bomb on Japanese cities? Explain your answer.

Answer Key
Chapter 32
SUMMARY

World War II, 1939–1945

Responses will vary but should include points similar to the following:

1. The first stop to Hitler's advances was the Battle of Britain, in which he was unable to weaken Great Britain enough for an invasion. His failure there led to an attack on the Soviet Union, which he was unable to conquer.

2. Japan hoped to expand its holdings in Southeast Asia, which the United States feared would threaten its own colonies in the Pacific. The United States imposed an oil embargo on Japan, which angered the Japanese.

3. At first, German Jews lost their rights. Then they were attacked by mobs. Next Jews in Germany and conquered lands were ordered to live in ghettos. Many were shot to death by killing squads. Finally, they were systematically put into camps as slave workers and then put into "death camps" and killed.

4. Was justified: American military leaders believed that an invasion of Japan would cost half a million American lives. They had a responsibility to protect their soldiers' lives. Was not justified: The atomic bomb was a terrible weapon, and an attack that led to the deaths of tens of thousands of civilians is not justified.

5. The American occupation resulted in the Japanese emperor acknowledging that he was not a god, in a major change to the government of Japan, and in economic changes that gave farmers and workers more power in Japanese society.

CHAPTER

33

Summary

CHAPTERS IN BRIEF *Restructuring the Postwar World, 1945–Present*

CHAPTER OVERVIEW *The United States and Soviet Union opposed each other as they tried to achieve different goals. Communists won a civil war in China, making it the world's second Communist nation. The United States fought two wars in Asia trying to contain communism. The Cold War also spread to Latin America and elsewhere. The superpowers later began to enjoy better relations.*

❶ Cold War: Superpowers Face Off

KEY IDEA *The conflicting aims of the United States and the Soviet Union led to global competition.*

The United States and the Soviet Union were allies during World War II. In February 1945, they agreed that Germany would be divided into separate zones. Each zone would be occupied by the soldiers of one of the main Allied powers. They also agreed that Germany would have to repay the Soviet Union for damage and loss of life. Soviet leader Joseph Stalin, in turn, promised free elections in Eastern Europe and to declare war on Japan. These allies also were among 50 countries that formed the United Nations in 1945. This new world body was pledged to save the world from war.

Still, the two superpowers had sharp political and economic differences. They also had different goals after the war. The United States wanted to encourage democracy and trade. It wanted to put the different zones of Germany back together to make one nation. The Soviet Union had these goals: to promote communism, to take advantage of raw materials in Eastern Europe and rebuild its own economy, and to keep Germany divided and weak.

After the war, Stalin made sure Communist governments were in place in Eastern Europe. This divided Europe between the Communist East and the democratic West. This division was called the "iron curtain." U.S. President Harry Truman then began a policy of containment to block further Soviet expansion. As part of this policy, the United States adopted the Marshall Plan in 1947. The plan donated food and materials such as machines to European countries, helping them rebuild from war.

In 1948, the Soviets and Americans clashed over Germany. France, Britain, and the United States agreed to pull their troops out of Germany and let the three zones that they occupied unite. The Soviets refused to leave their zone, however. Then they cut off all highway and train traffic into Berlin, which was deep within the Soviet zone. The United States and British responded with the Berlin Airlift. They flew food and supplies into the city for 11 months. Finally, the Soviets lifted the blockade.

The growing struggle between Americans and Soviets came to be called the Cold War. Many other countries allied with one superpower or another. The United States, Canada, and several countries in Western Europe formed the North Atlantic Treaty Organization (NATO). In this military alliance, each nation promised to defend any other member that was attacked. The Soviets and the countries of Eastern Europe made a similar agreement. It was called the Warsaw Pact.

In 1949, the Soviet Union announced that it, like the United States, had developed an atomic bomb. Three years later, both superpowers had a newer, even more deadly weapon—the hydrogen bomb. Soon both nations were involved in an arms race, as they produced growing numbers of nuclear weapons and developed new ways to deliver them.

In 1957, Soviet scientists shocked the world by launching *Sputnik,* the world's first human-made satellite. Many Americans felt that the Soviets were far ahead in science and technology. The United States then began spending huge amounts of money to improve science education.

❷ Communists Take Power in China

KEY IDEA *Chinese Communists defeated Nationalist forces, and two separate Chinas emerged.*

Nationalists and Communists fought for control of China in the 1930s. When Japan invaded China, the two sides joined to fight the common enemy. After World War II, they began fighting each other again. Their renewed war lasted from 1946 to 1949. The Communists won because their troops were well-trained in guerrilla war. They also enjoyed the backing of the peasants to whom they had promised land. In 1949, Jiang Jieshi and other Nationalist leaders fled to the island of Taiwan. The United States helped Jiang set up a new government there. The Nationalists called their land the Republic of China. The Soviets helped Mao Zedong and his government, the People's Republic of China.

Mao began to rebuild China. He seized land and gave it to the peasants. But he also forced the peasants—in groups of 200 to 300 households—to join collective farms. The people on each of these farms were given the land as a group. He also took control of China's industries. Under Mao's plan, production of industrial products went up.

With this success, Mao launched the "Great Leap Forward." He wanted to make the collective farms larger and more productive. The plan failed. People did not like strong government control. Planning by the government was not good. Poor weather produced a famine that killed millions.

After this failure, Mao played a smaller role in the government. He grew unhappy with the direction the country was taking, however. In 1966, he launched the Cultural Revolution. Using young students formed into groups called Red Guards, Mao tried to revive the revolutionary spirit in China. The Red Guards struck at teachers, scientists, and artists. They shut down schools and sent intellectuals to the country to work on farms. They killed thousands of people who resisted. China was in chaos, with factories shut down and farm production dropping. Eventually, Mao finally put an end to the Cultural Revolution.

❸ Wars in Korea and Vietnam

KEY IDEA *In Asia, the Cold War flared into actual wars supported mainly by the superpowers.*

After World War II, Korea was divided into a Soviet-backed north and an American-supported south. On June 25, 1950, North Korea invaded the South. President Truman fought this move with United Nations help. The United States and other countries sent troops to assist South Korea. At first, the North Korean army captured almost all of South Korea. Then the UN army began a bold counterattack. In just two months, it had pushed the North Koreans far back, nearly to

China. The Chinese then entered the war and drove the UN forces back. Bitter fighting continued until 1953. That year, the two Koreas agreed to a cease-fire. The earlier boundary splitting North and South Korea at the 38th parallel remained the same.

North Korea developed as a Communist country following the war. It had a strong army and tight government control, but it also had many economic problems. South Korea's economy grew, in part because it received U.S. aid. However, for more than 30 years, dictators ruled the country. Free elections were held only after a new constitution was accepted in 1987.

The United States faced another war against Communists, this time in Vietnam. That area had been a French colony until Japan invaded it early in World War II. When Japan lost, the French returned. A Vietnamese nationalist named Ho Chi Minh wanted to win independence. First, he drove the French out of Vietnam. A peace conference split Vietnam in two, with Ho taking charge in North Vietnam. He made it a Communist state. Communist rebels—the Vietcong—stayed active in the South.

Seeing that the government of South Vietnam was threatened by Communists, the United States began to send large numbers of soldiers. First it sent advisers, later combat troops. By 1968, more than 500,000 U.S. troops were there. They could not win the war on the ground. The United States also tried bombing or burning forests in the South to drive the Vietcong from their hiding places. These actions made peasants in the South more likely to support the North. Many in the United States came to oppose the war.

In the late 1960s, President Richard Nixon began to cut the number of U.S. troops in Vietnam in order to turn the fighting over to the South Vietnamese. The last American troops left in 1973. Two years later, North Vietnam overran the South and made Vietnam one country again. About 1.5 million people fled Vietnam. Today, Vietnam remains Communist but is looking for other nations to invest in its economy.

Fighting in Vietnam spilled over into its neighbor Cambodia. Rebels there set up a brutal Communist government. It killed 2 million people and imposed its will. In 1978, the Vietnamese invaded the country, overthrowing the rebels. Vietnam withdrew in 1989. In 1993, Cambodia held free elections.

❹ The Cold War Divides the World

KEY IDEA *The superpowers supported opposing sides in Latin American and Middle Eastern conflicts.*

After World War II, many nations in Africa, Asia, and Latin America had serious problems. They were plagued by ethnic conflict, lack of education and technology, poverty, and political unrest. Some of these countries tried to stay neutral in the Cold War. Others actively sought American or Soviet aid.

In Cuba, the United States supported a dictator in the 1950s. In 1959, a young lawyer, Fidel Castro, led a successful revolt. Castro then turned to the Soviets for aid. In 1962, the Soviets and Americans almost went to war over Soviet nuclear missiles placed in Cuba. The Soviets finally pulled the missiles out. Over time, the Cuban economy became more dependent on Soviet aid. When the Soviet Union dropped communism in 1991, this aid stopped. It was a serious blow to Cuba's economy.

The United States had also backed a dictator in Nicaragua. He fell in 1979 to Communist rebels. When the new government began helping leftist rebels in nearby El Salvador, the United States struck back. It began to support forces in Nicaragua that wanted to overthrow the Communists. The civil war lasted more than a decade. Finally, the different sides agreed to hold free elections.

The Middle East often saw conflict between those who wanted a modern, more Western-style society and those who wanted to follow traditional Islam. Such a struggle took place in Iran. In the 1950s, a group tried to take control of the government from the shah, or ruler, who was pro-West. The United States helped the Shah defeat them.

Over time, the Shah tried to weaken the influence of the Islamic religion in Iran. A Muslim leader, the Ayatollah Ruholla Khomeini, led a successful revolt. In 1979, the Shah was forced to leave the country. Khomeini made Islamic law the law of the land and followed a foreign policy that was strongly against the United States. He also led his country to a long war with Iraq, its neighbor.

The Soviets gained influence in Afghanistan after 1950. In the 1970s, Islamic rebels threatened the country's Communist government. The Soviets sent in support troops. The United States felt its Middle East oil supplies were in danger and supported the rebels. In 1989, after a costly occupation, Soviet troops left Afghanistan.

❺ The Cold War Thaws

KEY IDEA *The Cold War began to thaw as the superpowers entered an era of uneasy diplomacy.*

When Stalin died in 1953, Nikita Khrushchev became the Soviet leader. Soon protest movements in Eastern Europe challenged the Soviets' hold there. In 1956, protesters and the army toppled the Communist government of Hungary. Khrushchev sent Soviet tanks to put the Communists back in power. Similar events took place in Czechoslovakia in 1968. That time it was new Soviet leader Leonid Brezhnev who sent the tanks.

The Soviets did not have the same control over their larger neighbor, China. Although the Soviet Union and China enjoyed friendly relations at first, they gradually grew apart.

In the early 1970s, President Richard Nixon began following a policy called détente. This was a lessening of tensions between the superpowers. He became the U.S. first president to visit Communist China and the Soviet Union. In 1972, Nixon and Brezhnev signed a treaty to limit the number of nuclear missiles each country could have.

The U.S. retreated from détente after the Soviet Union invaded Afghanistan in 1979. In 1981, Ronald Reagan, a fierce anti-Communist, became president. Then the Soviets grew angry over U.S. support for the rebels fighting Communists in Nicaragua. Tensions increased until 1985 when the Soviet Union got a new leader.

Review

Determining Main Ideas

1. What factors divided the United States and the Soviet Union?

2. How did the two superpowers tangle in the Americas?

3. **Summarizing** Describe the Great Leap Forward and the Cultural Revolution.

4. **Analyzing Causes and Recognizing Effects** Why did the United States fight in Korea and Vietnam? What were the outcomes of these wars?

5. **Making Inferences** How did the Soviet Union act toward Eastern Europe?

Answer Key
Chapter 33
SUMMARY

Restructuring the Postwar World, 1945–Present

Responses will vary but should include points similar to the following:

1. The United States and Soviet Union had deep economic and political differences and had come out of the war with different goals. The United States wanted to encourage democracy and trade and wanted to reunify Germany. The Soviet Union wanted to promote Communism and to take advantage of raw materials in Eastern Europe to rebuild its own economy. It also wanted Eastern Europe as a zone of defense. The Soviets wanted to keep Germany divided so it could not start another war.

2. The two superpowers first tangled over Cuba. When the Soviet Union placed missiles on the island, the United States protested. The Soviets finally withdrew the missiles. Later, when communists took control of Nicaragua, the Americans gave aid to rebels against the new government.

3. The Great Leap Forward was Mao's effort to improve the Chinese economy. It failed due to people's resentment of government control, poor planning, and bad weather, which destroyed crops. The Cultural Revolution was Mao's attempt to revive the spirit of revolution in China. Red Guards—an army of students—attacked and harassed intellectuals, scientists, and artists. The movement threw Chinese society into a shambles.

4. The United States—along with other UN nations—fought the Korean War because North Korea had invaded South Korea. After a bitter war, the two sides settled into an uneasy peace. The United States sent troops to South Vietnam to try to combat Communist rebels there. When the war became unpopular, the American government pulled out its troops. Two years later, North Vietnam conquered South Vietnam and unified the country.

5. In both the 1950s and 1960s, the Soviet Union used force to put down movements that threatened Communist control in Hungary and Czechoslovakia.

CHAPTER
34
Summary

CHAPTERS IN BRIEF *The Colonies Become New Nations, 1945–Present*

CHAPTER OVERVIEW *India and its neighbors won independence from Great Britain, but their histories have been spoiled by conflict. Many new nations arose in Southeast Asia and in Africa after World War II as colonial empires collapsed. In the late 1940s, Jewish people were given their own country in the Middle East, where fighting between Jews and Arabs has erupted many times.*

❶ The Indian Subcontinent Achieves Freedom

KEY IDEA *A number of new nations emerged from the British colony of India.*

Many Asians served in the armies of the colonial powers during World War II. The fight for freedom from Nazi tyranny deepened their desire for independence from colonial control. Also, the Japanese victories over European powers made Asian nationalists realize that the colonial rulers could be defeated. At the same time, people in Europe began to wonder if it was right for one nation to have another as a colony.

After World War II, Britain was prepared to grant independence to India—home to a large Hindu and smaller Muslim population. The British Parliament passed a law granting independence in July 1947. It created the separate Hindu and Muslim nations of India and Pakistan. The law gave people only one month to decide which country they wanted to live in and to move there. As millions of people began to move, violence broke out. Muslims, Hindus, and Sikhs—another religious group—killed each other. Leader Mohandas Gandhi pleaded to end all violence. A Hindu extremist assassinated him for protecting Muslims.

Jawaharlal Nehru became the first prime minister of India, and he led the country for 17 years. His new nation and Pakistan, however, quickly fell to war over the state of Kashmir. It bordered both countries, with a Hindu ruler and large Muslim population. Conflict over this state continues today.

Nehru tried to reform Indian society. He hoped to improve the status of the lower castes and of women. Shortly after he died in 1964, his daughter, Indira Gandhi, became prime minister. She took steps to increase food production. In 1984, she ordered an attack on Sikh rebels. A few months later, she was killed by Sikhs. She was followed by her son Rajiv Gandhi, but he, too, was assassinated

as a political protest. Separatist movements continue to disrupt Indian society.

Pakistan, too, has been marked by violence. When first formed, the nation had east and west parts that were separated by India. In a bloody fight in 1971, the eastern part won independence as the new nation of Bangladesh. Power struggles have caused turmoil in the western part since then.

Ceylon, an island on the southeastern coast of India, won its independence in 1947 as well. In 1972 it was renamed Sri Lanka. Since 1983, a Hindu minority on the island—the Tamils—have led a bloody fight to form a separate nation.

❷ Southeast Asian Nations Gain Independence

KEY IDEA *The European colonies in Southeast Asia became independent countries in the postwar period.*

In 1946, the United States gave the Philippines independence. From 1966 to 1986, Ferdinand Marcos led the country. He was elected president but after a few years ruled as a dictator. He then harshly put down dissent and stole millions of dollars from the country. When he lost an election in 1986, he refused to leave office. A large public outcry forced him to step down.

Burma was the first British colony in Southeast Asia to become independent. It changed its name to Myanmar in 1989. Since 1962, generals have ruled the country, which has often been torn by conflict.

After World War II, the British moved back into the Malay peninsula. They tried to form a country, but ethnic conflict between Malays and Chinese who lived in the area doomed the effort. In 1957, independence was given to Malaya, Singapore, and parts of two distant islands. Some years later, Singapore declared independence as a city-state.

After World War II, Indonesia became independent. The nation is spread out. It has 13,600 islands and includes people from 300 different groups speaking 250 different languages. Bringing these different people into one unified country has been difficult. In 1967, a general named Suharto took control. Many criticized him for taking over the island of East Timor and for corruption in his government. He resigned in 1998 under intense public pressure.

❸ New Nations in Africa

KEY IDEA *After World War II, African leaders threw off colonial rule and created independent countries.*

During World War II, Africans fought as soldiers along with Europeans. As a result, Africans were unwilling to suffer further domination by colonial European powers after the war.

Soon the British began letting Africans take a greater part in the colonial government of its Gold Coast colony. Kwame Nkrumah headed a movement to push for Britain to act more quickly. The effort succeeded, and in 1957 the colony became independent—the first former colony in sub-Saharan Africa. The new nation took the name Ghana.

Nkrumah had ambitious plans for building the economy of Ghana. These plans were very expensive, though, and opposition grew. Some people in Ghana criticized him, too, for the time he spent trying to form a group of African leaders. Though the Organization of African Unity was formed in 1963, Nkrumah remained in trouble at home. Finally, the army seized power in 1966 and ruled for many years.

The strong leadership of nationalist Jomo Kenyatta helped Kenya achieve independence in 1963. So, too, did an uprising of Africans called Mau Mau. This protest aimed at frightening the British settlers to leave. Kenyatta became president of the new nation. He tried to unite the many different peoples in his country. His successor, Daniel Arap Moi, had little success in governing the country. He stepped down in 2002, and a new party gained power through free elections.

Belgium granted independence to the Congo in 1960. In 1965, Mobutu Sese Seko took control. He renamed the country Zaire and ruled until 1997. Though Zaire had rich mineral resources, Mobutu's harsh and corrupt rule made it a poor country. He was overthrown in a coup in 1997, when the country's name was changed to the Democratic Republic of the Congo.

A bloody conflict for independence took place in Algeria. About 1 million French settlers lived there. They were unwilling to give up their control of the colonial government. Violence broke out in 1945 and continued for many years. In 1962, the French finally granted independence to Algeria. From 1965 until 1988, Algerians tried to modernize their country and give it an industrial economy. These efforts failed, and an Islamic party won elections in 1991. However, the government rejected the vote. Today, a deadly civil war between Islamic militants and the government rages on.

The colonies of Portugal were the last to gain their independence. In the 1970s, Portuguese troops left Angola—without putting any group in charge. Rebel groups fought a long civil war. The war stopped in 1989, but soon started again. A peace agreement in 2002 finally ended the conflict.

❹ Conflicts in the Middle East

KEY IDEA *Postwar division of Palestine made the Middle East a hotbed of nationalist movements.*

The movement to settle Jews in Palestine began in the late 1800s. These Jews believed that Palestine belonged to them because it was their home 5,000 years ago. Muslims had lived there for 1,300 years, however.

At the end of World War II, the United Nations divided Palestine in two. It left part for the Palestinian people and set aside part for Jews. Islamic countries voted against the plan, and the Palestinians opposed it. Many countries, seeing the suffering Jews had experienced in World War II, backed the idea of a separate Jewish state. On May 14, 1948, Jews declared the existence of the Jewish nation of Israel.

The next day, six Islamic neighbors invaded Israel. With strong support from the United States, Israel won the war in a few months. It also won three later wars and seized much Palestinian land.

In 1977, Egyptian leader Anwar Sadat signed a peace agreement with Israeli prime minister Menachem Begin. Egypt thus became the first Islamic country to recognize Israel. This enraged many Arabs, and Sadat was assassinated in 1981. His successor, though, kept peace with Israel.

Despite many efforts, though, Israel and the Palestinian people have not made peace. Palestinians living in Israel dislike Israeli rule. They want a nation of their own. The Palestinian Liberation

Organization (PLO), led by Yasir Arafat, became a leading group in the struggle for self-rule. During the 1970s and 1980s, the military arm of the PLO made many attacks on Israel. That nation responded by invading Lebanon to attack bases of the PLO. In the late 1980s, many Palestinian people in Israel began a revolt called the intifada, or "uprising." It lasted for years.

In the early 1990s, the two sides made some progress toward peace. Israel agreed to give Palestinians control of an area called the Gaza Strip and of the town of Jericho. The Israeli leader who signed this agreement, Yitzhak Rabin, was assassinated by a Jewish extremist who opposed giving in to Palestinians. In 2003, the two sides renewed their peace efforts with a commitment to a U.S. sponsored plan known as the "road map."

❺ Central Asia Struggles

KEY IDEA *The former lands of the Soviet Union in Central Asia struggled to become thriving nations.*

In 1991 the Soviet Union broke apart. As a result, the republics that it had conquered became fifteen independent states. These states include nine countries in Central Asia. Geographers often group these nations into two geographic areas. Armenia, Azerbaijan, and Georgia make up the Transcaucasian Republics. Uzbekistan, Turkmenistan, Tajikistan, Kazakhstan, and Kyrgyzstan comprise the Central Asian Republics.

Since independence, the countries of Central Asia have faced a number of challenges. Many of these countries were economically dependent on the Soviet Union. Thus, they have had a hard time standing on their own. In addition, hostility has arisen among some of the different ethnic groups that inhabit the area. This in turn has led to the outbreak of several regional wars.

Located just below the countries that comprise Central Asia is Afghanistan. This nation endured a long history of struggle for independence. However, it is the nation's more recent battles that have brought it much international attention.

During the 1970s, a Communist group supported by the Soviet Union sought to take control of Afghanistan. A rebel group known as the mujahideen fought the communists. The Soviets soon invaded and attempted to make Afghanistan part of their empire. Despite their superior military might,

Soviet forces could not defeat the determined Afghan guerrilla fighters. After nearly 10 years of bloody fighting, the Soviet Union withdrew.

After the Soviets left, various Afghan rebel troops fought each other for control of the country. By 1998, an Islamic group known as the Taliban controlled most of Afghanistan. The Taliban practiced an extreme version of the Islamic religion— one that many other Muslims opposed. Taliban leaders forbade women to attend school or hold jobs. They also prohibited citizens from watching television and movies or listening to modern music. Punishment for disobeying their rules included beatings and even execution.

What's more, the Taliban allowed terrorist groups to train in Afghanistan. One such group was al-Qaeda, whose leader was Osama bin Laden. Many believe this group to be responsible for the attacks on New York and Washington, D.C. on September 11, 2001.

In the wake of those attacks, the U.S. government demanded that the Taliban turn over bin Laden. The Taliban refused. Beginning in October 2001, the United States took military action against Afghanistan. By December, the United States had driven the Taliban from power. In the months that followed, Afghanis created a new government and began working to rebuild their country after decades of war.

Review

Analyzing Issues
1. What difficulties face anyone trying to make a unified country out of Indonesia?
2. Which change to self-rule do you think went the smoothest in Africa? Why?
3. ***Determining Main Ideas*** What type of struggle dominates the history of independence in Southeast Asia?
4. ***Analyzing Causes and Recognizing Effects*** Why were Sadat and Rabin assassinated?

The Colonies Become New Nations, 1945–Present

Responses will vary but should include points similar to the following:

1. Indonesia is a land of many different peoples and languages. It would be very difficult for any leader to try to unite them.

2. Several of the new nations of Southeast Asia have been caught in a struggle between democracy and the rule of a dictator or military leadership.

3. The change to independence for Ghana was the smoothest—even though the first government of Ghana was overthrown in a coup. The reason is that the British took some steps to first bring Africans into colonial government.

4. Sadat and Rabin were both assassinated by fanatics of their own ethnic groups because they dared to make peace with or compromise with their rival group.

CHAPTERS IN BRIEF *Struggles for Democracy, 1945–Present*

CHAPTER OVERVIEW The history of Latin America revealed how difficult it is to set up a democracy. In Africa, ethnic conflicts worked against democracy. In the early 1990s, communism fell in Eastern Europe and the Soviet Union. But long-hidden ethnic tensions broke the regions into smaller countries. In China, communist leaders made economic changes but kept tight political control.

❶ Democracy–Case Study: Latin American Democracies

KEY IDEA *In Latin America, economic problems and authoritarian rule delayed democracy.*

For democracy to work, there must be free and fair elections. There must be more than one political party. The people of the country should have a good education so that they can make informed choices. They should share a common culture. All must accept the idea that everyone has equal rights. Finally, there must be rule by law, not by power. Many nations in Latin America have had difficulty achieving democracy because all these factors are not present.

In 1822, newly independent Brazil began life as a monarchy. After 1930, a dictator ruled. But, in 1956, an elected leader tried to make the economy better. He broke up large estates and gave land to the peasants. Landowners opposed the plan. They backed a group of army leaders who took power in 1964. The military ruled Brazil for 20 years. The country's economy grew, but the people had few rights. When the economy soured in the 1980s, the army gave up power to an elected president. In 2002, Luiz Inacio Lula da Silva, a leftist candidate, was elected president.

Mexico has had stable government for almost all of the 1900s. Since the 1920s, one political party—now called the Institutional Revolutionary Party (PRI)—has been in power. The PRI has controlled the local, state, and national governments. At times, the party acted harshly to stop any dissent. In recent years, though, the party has opened up the political system to candidates from other parties. In 1997, two opposition parties won enough seats to the national legislature to deny the PRI control of that congress. In 2002, Mexican voters ended PRI rule by electing Vicente Fox as president.

Argentina has struggled toward democracy, too. In the 1940s and 1950s, Juan Perón was a popular dictator. He put in place many programs to benefit the masses. In 1952, though, the army overthrew him and kept control of the government for the next 30 years. Army leaders ruled harshly, killing many who opposed them. In 1982, the army suffered a stinging defeat in a war with Britain. The generals agreed to step down. Since 1983, Argentina has been led by freely elected leaders. However, it faces severe economic problems. In 2003, Nestor Kirchner became president.

❷ The Challenge of Democracy in Africa

KEY IDEA *Recent histories of Nigeria and South Africa show ethnic and racial conflict hindering democracy.*

Nations have had a hard time setting up democracy in Africa because of colonial rule. European powers drew up borders in Africa that paid no attention to ethnic groupings. They put people who disliked each other in the same area, causing conflict. Also, they never developed the economies of their colonies. Most of the colonies lacked a middle class or skilled workers. Both are needed for a strong democracy. When Britain and France gave their African colonies independence, they gave them democratic governments. Soon, though, problems arose between rival groups.

Nigeria is an example of this. In 1960, it became independent from Britain. But conflict broke out in just a few years. The people of one ethnic group tried to break away from Nigeria but lost in a three-year civil war. After a period of military rule, Nigeria finally got an elected government. Army officers said the government was corrupt, though, and overthrew it. Once in power, they treated the people from other ethnic groups harshly. They allowed elections in 1993 but did not accept the results. In 1999, Nigerians elected their first civilian president in 20 years, Olusegun Obasanjo. He was re-elected in 2003.

In South Africa, the conflict was between races. A white minority ruled a black majority. In 1948, they put in place a policy called apartheid—the strict separation of blacks and whites. Black South Africans were denied many basic rights. Some joined together in a group called the African National Congress (ANC) to fight for their rights. The government cracked down, putting many ANC leaders in prison.

By the late 1980s, several riots had taken place, as blacks angrily struck back at the system. Also, many nations would not buy goods produced in South Africa. They hoped to persuade the government to end apartheid. In 1990, new President F. W. de Klerk took that step. He made the ANC legal and released ANC leader Nelson Mandela from prison. Parliament passed a law ending apartheid. In April 1994, all South Africans—even blacks—were able to vote in an election for a new leader. The ANC and Mandela won easily. In 1996, the new government approved a new constitution. It gave equal rights to all South Africans. In 1999, ANC official Thabo Mbeki won election as president.

❸ The Collapse of the Soviet Union

KEY IDEA *Soviet leaders Mikhail Gorbachev, Boris Yeltsin, and Vladimir Putin promoted democratic reforms and economic restructuring.*

During the 1960s and 1970s, the leaders of the Soviet Union kept tight control on society. In 1985, Communist Party leaders named Mikhail Gorbachev as the leader of the Soviet Union. He was the youngest Soviet leader since Joseph Stalin. He was expected to make minor reforms. Instead, he launched a revolution.

Gorbachev felt that Soviet society could not improve without the free flow of ideas and information. He started a policy called glasnost, or openness. He opened churches and released dissenters from prison. He allowed books to be published that in the past had been banned. Then he began a new policy called perestroika, or restructuring. It aimed at making the Soviet economy perform better by lifting the tight control on all managers and workers. In 1987, he opened up the political system by allowing the Soviet people to elect representatives to a legislature. Finally, Gorbachev changed Soviet foreign policy. He moved to end the arms race.

People from many different ethnic groups in the Soviet Union began calling for the right to have

their own nation. In 1990, Lithuania declared itself independent. Gorbachev sent troops, and they fired on a civilian crowd, killing a few people. This action and lack of reform cost Gorbachev support among the Soviet people.

Many people began to support Boris Yeltsin. Old-time communists, at the same time, were becoming angrier at Gorbachev's changes. They thought the changes made the Soviet Union weaker. In August 1991, they tried to take control of the government. Thousands rallied in the streets. When the army refused to back the coup leaders, they gave up.

To strike back the parliament voted to ban the party from any political activity. Meanwhile, more and more republics in the Soviet Union declared their independence. By the end of 1991, Gorbachev announced that the Soviet Union would no longer exist. Russia and the other 14 republics were each becoming independent states.

Gorbachev lost all power, and Yeltsin became president of Russia. He faced many problems. Efforts to move the Russian economy toward capitalism caused suffering. In addition, rebels in the small republic of Chechnya declared their independence from Russia. Yeltsin refused to allow it. He sent thousands of troops, who were caught in a bloody war for two years. In 2000, Vladimir Putin was elected president of Russia and dealt forcefully with the rebellion in Chechnya, but the fighting dragged on. Putin also dealt with economic, political, and social problems in Russia.

❹ Changes in Central and Eastern Europe

Key Idea *Soviet Reforms of the late 1980s brought big changes to Central and Eastern Europe.*

Gorbachev urged leaders in Central and Eastern Europe to change their policies. They resisted, but the people of their countries wanted reform. Protest movements began to build. In Poland, many years of economic problems led the government to lift a ban on a workers' movement called Solidarity. Facing growing unrest, the government was forced to allow elections. The Polish people voted overwhelmingly against the communists and for Solidarity. However, the Polish people became frustrated with how long and painful the process was to achieve democracy and capitalism. In elections in 1995, they voted the former leader of

Solidarity out as president of Poland and elected Aleksander Kwasniewski in his place. In Hungary, reformers took over the communist party. Then it voted itself out of existence.

Change soon came to East Germany. Its leaders resisted at first. Then thousands of people across the country demanded free elections. Soon the Berlin Wall, which divided East and West Berlin, was down. By the end of 1989, the communist party was out of power. The next year the two parts of Germany, East and West, were united once again. The new nation had many problems, though. It had to fix the problems in the old East German economy.

In Czechoslovakia, similar calls for reform took place. When the government cracked down on protesters, thousands of Czechs poured into the streets. One day hundreds of thousands of people gathered to protest in the nation's capital. The communists agreed to give up power. Democracy led to a breakup. In 1993, the country split into two separate nations: the Czech Republic and Slovakia.

In Romania, a tough dictator used the army to shoot at protestors. The incident enraged Romanians. Massive protests forced him out. He was captured and executed in 1989. General elections followed.

Yugoslavia was made up of many different ethnic groups, and in the early 1990s they began fighting. When Serbia tried to control the government, two other areas declared independence. Slovenia beat back a Serbian invasion, but Serbia and Croatia fought a bloody civil war. In 1992, Bosnia-Herzegovina also declared independence. Serbs who lived in that region opposed the move. Using aid from Serbia, they fought a brutal civil war with Muslims, the largest group in Bosnia. The United Nations was able to stop the fighting, but peace remained uncertain. The change to democracy and capitalism in Central and Eastern Europe was not smooth.

❺ China: Reform and Reaction

KEY IDEA *China's government has experimented with capitalism but has rejected calls for democracy.*

Mao Zedong had tried to build a China on the ideas of equality, revolutionary spirit, and hard work. But his policies kept the economy from growing very quickly. Other leaders tried to modernize the economy. This caused Mao to launch the

Cultural Revolution of the 1960s. The result was chaos, and it was followed by a period of more moderate government action.

During this time, China had little role in world affairs. Zhou Enlai, another Chinese leader, worried about this. He worked with U.S. President Richard Nixon to improve U.S.–Chinese relations.

After Mao and Zhou died in 1976, moderates took control of the government. The chief leader was Deng Xiaoping. He tried to modernize the economy. He ended farming communes and allowed farmers more freedom. He made similar changes to industry. Suddenly, people had more income. They began to purchase appliances and other goods that had been scarce before.

Deng's new plan caused problems. The gap between rich and poor grew wider, which caused unrest. Western political ideas entered the country. In 1989, thousands of Chinese students gathered in a public square in the capital of Beijing. They called for democracy and freedom. Deng responded by sending army troops and tanks to put down the rally. Hundreds were killed and thousands wounded. China has continued to stamp out protest to this day. Deng died in 1997, and was replaced as president by Jiang Zemin. Eventually Jiang retired and was replaced by Hu Jintao.

Another major issue for China was the status of Hong Kong. The island became part of China again in 1997 when the British gave it back after 155 years of colonial rule. China promised to respect Hong Kong's freedom for 50 years, but many worried.

Review

1. ***Determining Main Ideas*** In what ways do Brazil, Mexico, and Argentina show how difficult it is to establish democracy?
Identifying Problems and Solutions
2. What problems in establishing democracy occurred in Nigeria and South Africa?
3. What reforms did Gorbachev put in place?
4. ***Analyzing Causes and Recognizing Effects*** Why did the Soviet Union break apart?
5. ***Drawing Conclusions*** What path did China take, and what difficulties did it meet?

Answer Key
Chapter 35
SUMMARY

Struggles for Democracy, 1945–Present

Responses will vary but should include points similar to the following:

1. Brazil, Mexico, and Argentina all have had periods of democratic rule that have alternated with times of dictatorship. In Brazil and Argentina, problems arose because those who hold economic power resisted the actions of democratic governments. In Mexico, the problem has been that one party controlled the political process for many years.

2. In Nigeria, democracy has been hampered by ethnic conflict. In South Africa, the problem was domination by one race over another.

3. Gorbachev tried to make Soviet society more open with his policy of glasnost and tried to reform the economy with perestroika. He opened the political system to limited free elections, and he changed Soviet foreign policy by taking steps to end the arms race.

4. The Soviet Union broke apart because restless groups within it wanted their own nation and because the Communist Party had become discredited. When army leaders tried to resist the move, the people and army troops did not support their actions.

5. China took steps to make the economy more capitalistic. This led to more economic freedom, higher wages, and more consumer goods. Finally, people began to desire political freedom as well—freedoms that the government was unwilling to give.

CHAPTER
36
Summary

CHAPTERS IN BRIEF *Global Interdependence,*
1960–Present

CHAPTER OVERVIEW New technologies have brought people around the world closer to one another and improved their lives. The world's economies have also grown closer to one another. Nations around the world have worked together to try to bring peace and end terrorism. Because of technology, the world's cultures have more influence on one another now.

❶ The Impact of Science and Technology

KEY IDEA *Advances in technology after 1945 led to increased global interaction and improved quality of life.*

From the 1950s to the 1970s, the United States and Soviet Union took their Cold War rivalry to space. This space race also led to more global cooperation. In 1975, U.S. and Soviet spacecraft docked, or joined together, in space. Later, American and Soviet space missions included scientists from other countries. In the late 1990s, the United States, Russia, and 14 other nations worked together to build the International Space Station (ISS).

Some space missions did not include human crew members. Unmanned flights sent back pictures and information about other planets. In 1990, the United States and European countries sent the Hubble Space Telescope into orbit around the earth. This satellite continues to send back stunning images of objects in space.

Another advance in technology has been the computer. Computers have shrunk in size and grown in power since they were first invented. Consumer goods such as microwave ovens, telephones, and cars often include computer chips to keep them running. Millions of people around the world use personal computers at work or at home. Many of these people are connected through the Internet, a worldwide network of computers. The Internet allows people to access information or communicate with one another.

New technology has changed medicine as well. Surgery using lasers allows doctors to fix problems in the eye or the brain. New methods for making images of the body help doctors locate problems. Research into genes has helped unlock the secrets of some diseases.

In the 1960s, agricultural scientists started the green revolution, an attempt to increase food production worldwide. This involved the use of fertilizers, pesticides, and high-yield, disease-resistant strains of crops. The green revolution did increase crop yields. However, it had its negative side, too. Fertilizers and pesticides can pollute the environment.

Advances in genetics research seem to be helping to fulfill some of the goals of the green revolution. Resistance to pests and tolerance to poor soil are bred into plant strains, reducing the need for pesticides and fertilizers. This holds great promise for increasing food production in a world with an expanding population.

❷ Global Economic Development

KEY IDEA *The economies of nations are so tightly linked that the actions of one nation affects others.*

Technology has also changed the world's economies. In the 1950s, scientists found a new way to make plastics, which came to be widely used. In recent years, industries have begun using robots to make products. These changes have required workers to have more and different skills than before. The industrialized nations changed the focus of their economies. They came to have more jobs in service and information industries. Manufacturing jobs were more often found in the emerging nations where labor costs less.

A global economy linking the economies of different nations developed in the 1980s. In recent years, this process of globalization has speeded up. Telephone and computer links connect banks and other financial companies around the world. Multinational corporations have offices and factories in many countries. Their decisions affect workers all over the world.

An important aspect of globalization is free trade—no barriers to block goods from one country from entering another country. Many steps have been taken to put free trade in practice. In 1951, some nations in Europe joined together to create free trade among their people. That group, now called the European Union (EU), has grown to become a powerful trading block. To compete, the United States, Canada, and Mexico agreed to the North American Free Trade Agreement (NAFTA) in 1994. Organizations in Asia, Africa, Latin America, and the South Pacific have also created regional trade policies.

In recent years, there has been considerable disagreement on the impact of economic globalization. Supporters suggest that open, competitive markets and the free flow of goods, services, technology, and investments benefit all nations. Opponents charge that globalization has been a disaster for the poorest countries. Many, they suggest, are worse off today than they were in the past.

The development of the global economy has had a major impact on the use of energy and other resources. Manufacturing and trade both use huge amounts of energy. Oil has been a major source of this energy. Whenever the flow of oil has been threatened, the world's economies have suffered severe shocks.

Growth has also caused problems for the environment. Burning coal and oil has polluted the air. It has caused acid rain and brought about a general rising of temperatures on Earth. Release of some chemicals into the air has weakened the earth's ozone layer. This layer of air blocks out dangerous rays from the sun.

Many scientists understand the need to continue to let economies grow. They urge, though, that this growth take place without using up the world's resources too quickly. This movement centers on an idea called "sustainable growth."

❸ Global Security Issues

KEY IDEA *Since 1945, nations have used collective security efforts to solve problems.*

After World War II, the Cold War created new tensions among the world's nations. This uneasy situation threatened world security. So, nations began to work together to find peaceful solutions.

The United Nations (UN) was formed at the end of World War II to promote world peace. The UN provides a place for countries—or groups within countries—to speak their views. When groups at war request it, the UN can send troops as a peacekeeping force. These soldiers—who come from member nations—help stop violence from breaking out. As of 2002, the UN had 40,000 soldiers and police in 13 peacekeeping forces around the world.

Another approach to greater peace and security has been the attempt to limit weapons of mass destruction. These include nuclear missiles, chemical weapons, and biological weapons. In 1968, many nations signed a treaty agreeing not to develop nuclear weapons. In the 1990s, the United States and Russia have made agreements to destroy many of their nuclear weapons. In another treaty, many nations promised not to develop chemical or biological weapons. Threats to safety remain, however. Some nations have tried to develop and use these weapons. As a result, weapons of mass destruction continue to be a global security problem.

Another source of world conflict has been the struggle between different ethnic and religious groups. Violence has killed thousands. One effort to solve this problem has been the movement for human rights. In 1948, the UN approved the Universal Declaration of Human Rights. This statement lists specific rights that all people should have. Later, the Helsinki Accords, signed by many nations in 1975, included such rights as the freedom to exchange information. Many groups throughout the world keep a close eye on how well nations do in providing these rights for their people.

Recently, the enjoyment of a decent standard of health has become recognized as a basic human right. However, for many people across the world, poor health is still the norm. Perhaps the greatest global challenge to the attainment of good health is AIDS, or acquired immune deficiency syndrome. AIDS is a worldwide problem. However, Sub-Saharan Africa has suffered most from the epidemic. The disease has had devastating impact on the populations and economies of many countries in this region.

In recent years, millions of people have moved from one country to another. Some seek better jobs. Others hope to escape harsh treatment at home. Immigrants can bring many benefits to their new home. While people have a right to leave, every country does not have to accept them. Sometimes these people have to live in crowded refugee camps. They suffer hunger and disease and can cause political problems for the country where they are held.

❹ Terrorism

KEY IDEA *Terrorism threatens the safety of people around the world.*

Terrorism is the use of violence against people or property to force changes in societies or governments. People resort to terrorism to gain independence, to rid their country of foreigners, or to change their society. Recently, another motive for terrorism has emerged. Some people, driven by radical religious and cultural ideals, have tried to destroy what they consider the forces of evil.

The most common weapons used by terrorists are bombs and bullets. Terrorist attacks involving these weapons usually target crowded places. Some terrorist groups have used biological and chemical weapons. Others have employed cyberterrorism—attacks on information systems such as computer networks. Governments take various actions to combat terrorism. These include conducting military operations against terrorist training camps, cutting off terrorists' sources of funds, and tightening security measures at vulnerable targets.

Few areas of the world have escaped incidents of terrorism. In the Middle East, Palestinians and Israelis have argued for decades about land ownership. This argument has resulted in many terrorist acts. In Northern Ireland, the Irish Republican Army (IRA) has done terrorist acts for many years. The IRA wants the British to give up control over Northern Ireland. Terrorist groups have also been active in Asia, Africa, and Latin America.

The United States also has been the target of international terrorism. On the morning of September 11, 2001, 19 Arab terrorists hijacked four airliners, crashing them into the World Trade Center in New York City and the Pentagon in Washington, D.C. The United States responded by launching a military attack on Afghanistan, where the hijackers were trained. In addition, the United States Congress passed the USA Patriot Act, which gave the government several powers to help chase and capture of terrorists. The Congress also created the Department of Homeland Security to organize the fight against terrorism in the United States.

❺ Cultures Blend in a Global Age

KEY IDEA *Technology has increased contact among the world's people, changing their cultures.*

Changes in technology have made it possible for people to share their cultures with one another. Television is one of the main forces in this trend. Movies and radio also have had an impact in bringing the world's people together.

As a result of these mass media, the world's popular culture now includes elements from many different cultures. Popular culture includes music,

sports, clothing styles, food, and hobbies. American television shows have become popular around the world. So, too, have athletes from many countries. Broadcasts of the sports events can reach millions of people in all corners of the globe.

When elements of different cultures are combined, it is called cultural blending. In recent times, ideas from the United States and Europe have been a major force in this blending. One reason is that Western nations dominate the mass media. This trend also results from the influence that the West has had in recent centuries. As a result, English is now a major world language. About 500 million people speak English as their first or second language. More people speak Mandarin Chinese. However, English speakers are more widely spread throughout the world. Western clothes can be seen throughout the world. Western foods—such as hamburgers and soft drinks—are enjoyed everywhere. Some ideas have also traveled from East to West.

Some see this growing international culture as a problem. They worry that their own culture will be drowned in a sea of influences from other lands. Some countries limit the amount of broadcast time given to foreign television programs. Others use censorship to keep unwanted ideas from entering the land. In some areas, people have revived old traditions in order to keep them alive.

Despite these difficulties, it is clear that the people of the world are more dependent on one another. All through human history, people have faced many challenges to their survival. In the 21st century, those challenges will be faced by different people around the world. They are people who are in increasing contact with others. They are people with a greater stake in living in harmony.

Review

1. ***Recognizing Effects*** How have computers affected the way people gather information and communicate with one another?
2. ***Drawing Conclusions*** How have economies changed since World War II?
3. ***Identifying Problems*** What problems come with economic growth?
4. ***Summarizing*** What efforts have countries made to increase peace and security in the world?
5. ***Clarifying*** Give two examples of cultural blending.

Answer Key
Chapter 36
SUMMARY

Global Interdependence, 1960–Present

Responses will vary but should include points similar to the following:

1. The system of computer networks known as the Internet allows people to gather information quickly from many different sources. The Internet also allows people to communicate with others around the world.

2. Since World War II, the world's economies have grown more tightly linked. Also, changes in technology have brought in new materials, such as plastics, or manufacturing processes, such as using robots. The nations that had industrialized first began to change their economies away from manufacturing. Those jobs went to nations that were still developing.

3. Economic growth has also led to the heavy use of world resources such as oil and to pollution, acid rain, global warming, and the shrinking of the ozone layer.

4. To increase peace, many nations have joined the United Nations, which has sent peacekeeping forces to try to end some conflicts. Many nations have also signed a treaty promising not to develop nuclear weapons, and the United States and Russia have agreed to reduce their arsenal of nuclear arms.

5. Student answers will vary but may include such phenomena as the adoption of Western clothes or fast food in Africa and Asia or the popularity of international entertainers in the United States.